CAVES, COPROL
AND CATASTRO

CAVES, COPROLITES, AND CATASTROPHES

The Story of Pioneering Geologist and Fossil-Hunter William Buckland

Allan Chapman

spck

First published in Great Britain in 2020

Society for Promoting Christian Knowledge
36 Causton Street
London SW1P 4ST
www.spck.org.uk

British Library Cataloguing-in-Publication Data
A catalogue record for this book is available from the British Library

ISBN 978-0-281-07950-6
eBook ISBN 978-0-281-07952-0

1 3 5 7 9 10 8 6 4 2

Typeset by Nord Compo
First printed in Great Britain by Jellyfish Print Solutions

eBook by Nord Compo

Produced on paper from sustainable forests

To Rachel:

Wife, Scholar, and Best Friend

Contents

Contents

Contents

Contents

Contents

List of Illustrations

1 William Buckland in Doctor of Divinity gown,
from a portrait by T. C. Thomson

2 Three sketches of geological jollifications in the field,
at Shotover, near Oxford

3 William Buckland delivering a geological lecture
in the Ashmolean Museum in 1822

4 Kirkdale Cave, north Yorkshire, c.1821,
showing the newly made opening

5 Cartoon of William Buckland entering Kirkdale Cave,
by Revd Dr William D. Conybeare, c.1823

6 Section through the Paviland Cave, south Wales

7 Section through the Dream Lead Mine cave, Derbyshire

8 Section through the Gailenreuth bone cave, Franconia, Germany

9 William and Mary Buckland and their son Frank,
surrounded by some of their fossil treasures,
from a silhouette by Auguste Edouart, 1829

10 'Awful Changes': Professor Ichthyosaurus giving a lecture on
the fossilized skull of a presumably extinct human being,
cartoon by Sir Henry De la Beche, 1830

11 *Duria Antiquior*, or prehistoric Dorset, reconstructed
by Sir Henry De la Beche, 1830

12 William Buckland carrying his famous 'Blue Bag',
from a painting by Richard Ansdell, c.1843

13 William Buckland in 'Ice Age' field costume,
cartoon by Thomas Sopwith

14 Ichthyosaurus skeletons, from William Buckland's
Geology and Mineralogy

Preface

Coprolites! What on earth are coprolites? We all know what caves are, and catastrophes, though we may not be familiar with the latter when used as an old geological term. A coprolite is a rounded lump of stone, generally between one and two inches in diameter, and three or four inches long. And some are spiral in shape, like a lump of barley sugar.

Millions of years ago, these rocky lumps now in museum cases were pieces of excrement, which had passed through the gut of a long-extinct giant marine reptile such as an ichthyosaurus, then fallen to the seabed and slowly petrified to hard stone. They were named 'coprolites' from the Greek *kopros* (faeces) and *lithos* (stone). Yet in 1829, William Buckland quickly recognized their great scientific significance on three grounds. First, they provided clues to the anatomical location of the intestinal tract of a long-dead beast. Second, when broken open they sometimes contained undigested fish bone fragments, suggesting the eater's diet. And third, when ground up, coprolites were discovered, from their chemical content, to make excellent fertilizers for agricultural land. We will return to coprolites, along with caves and catastrophes, in the following chapters.

But this book is not just about geology, for it attempts to set Buckland and his friends and colleagues, along with geology, natural history, and the other sciences, in their wider historical context. And this was a time when British and European society and culture were changing fast. The impact of French Revolutionary ideas, rapid economic and industrial development, acute social distress, and new forms of art, literature, painting and music were providing fresh challenges, for this was what historians now style the 'Romantic Age'. By the early years of Queen Victoria's reign, indeed, after 1837, new social currents were on the move, and if romanticism coloured the first part of William Buckland's life, so the focused, determined energy, pride and optimism of the early Victorian age influenced the latter part.

In this book, moreover, we will never lose sight of the fact that in addition to his scientific work, William Buckland was an active and committed priest of the Church of England; and as we shall see in the following pages, Buckland's Christian faith and work as a leading scientist were never in conflict. In Chapter 1, where we look at Buckland's roots in the Devon clergy and gentry from which he sprang, we will also examine the English clergyman-scientist as a social phenomenon.

Like many clergymen-scientists, Buckland was a Natural Theologian, who saw God's design and guiding hand in all aspects of the natural world, from the mathematical logic of the solar system to the beauty of a flower or a bird. I discuss Buckland's own theology and the wider world of Natural Theology in several chapters in this book, along with attitudes towards Holy Scripture and how it might be respectfully re-interpreted and understood in the light of new discoveries made through the exercise of humanity's God-given intelligence. Not all educated Georgians and Victorians were happy with scriptural interpretation, however, and in Chapter 11, I examine the ideas and publications of the scriptural geologists.

It is important to emphasize that between c.1810 and 1850 William Buckland was a figure of international fame and standing, his career culminating in his preferment to the Deanery of Westminster in 1845. He was a true pioneer of geological science, and a teacher of scientific geology to many generations of the University of Oxford students, to say nothing of his addresses to the crowds who packed the meetings of the British Association for the Advancement of Science after 1831 and other scientific and popular educational bodies. This reputation would be elegantly summed up in the final paragraph of Professor Sir William Boyd Dawkins's 'Preface' to Elizabeth Oke Gordon's *Life and Correspondence of William Buckland*, published in 1894.

Yet sadly, Buckland's towering contemporary reputation has come to be sidelined by later generations, who seem more concerned with concentrating upon him as a Victorian eccentric and general 'character'. And yes, William Buckland most certainly was a 'character', and a highly entertaining figure. But he was very much more besides, and it is a pity that one only seems to encounter him today either in academic publications on geological history or in popular anthologies of eccentrics. Indeed, one sometimes finds his eccentricities conflated with those of his eldest son,

Francis (Frank) Trevelyan Buckland, who, while a surgeon, naturalist and distinguished pioneer of fish-cultivation, was probably an even greater eccentric than his father.

Unfortunately, even William Buckland's major achievements in geology and other branches of science tend to get dismissed by many modern writers, who simply see him, incorrectly, as a stalwart advocate of Noah's Flood as the primary geological agent that shaped the globe. Just a colourful figure who got geological and natural history wrong, and who needed Charles Darwin to set things on the right track after his death.

In discussions of Buckland's life and activities, moreover, his wife, Mary, generally appears only as an incidental figure, a good Victorian housewife who operated behind the scenes. Yet what will become evident in this book is the fundamental role played by this remarkable woman in William's career following their marriage in 1825. For far from being a shadowy Victorian mamma, Mary, both as Miss Morland and then as Mrs Buckland, was an internationally recognized scientist in her own right. A highly skilled fossil geologist, who as a motherless child had grown up in the house and amid the collections of Sir Christopher Pegge, her father's friend and the Regius Professor of Medicine at Oxford. Mary was also an informed anatomist, scientific draughtswoman and accomplished microscopist, who, both during their marriage and following William's death in 1856, would advance the study of microscopic marine fauna in collaboration with a physician and Fellow of the Royal Society, Dr James Bowerbank.

In addition to the geological science, I attempt in the following pages to explore other concerns of both Bucklands which scarcely get a mention in the 'colourful eccentric' genre of popular Bucklandia. These include William Buckland's active involvement in social reform and what might be called 'making the world a better place', including a range of science- and technology-related activities ranging from improved gas lighting to drive out ancestral darkness to public health, water and sanitation measures. The Bucklands' lifelong involvement in helping the poor, not just with generous handouts but also with experiments to improve food production, will receive full coverage in this book. And let us not forget that in the decades following the Battle of Waterloo in 1815, when agricultural distress and high food prices prevailed across most of Britain, even

Buckland's experiments with eating squirrels, toasted mice and a host of other commonplace wild inhabitants of the countryside – creatures not covered by the punitive Game Laws – had an ulterior motive. For could not these animals help to fill the bellies of the distressed and starving with tasty, nutritious meat?

Indeed, when one reviews Buckland's writings and activities, one cannot help but be struck by the range and consistency of his and Mary's charitable commitments. The recipients included the bargee families who plied the boats on the Oxford canal, labourers, quarrymen's families, street children, the community of poor Jews who lived in Oxford's St Ebbe's parish only a couple of minutes' walk from Christ Church's Tom Tower gate and unemployed workmen in Westminster. Allotments, coffee clubs and lectures delivered by William and his son Frank to provide intellectual stimulus for the poor and outcast, were all part of their tireless 'social outreach' activities. Nor was William Buckland shy about using the Westminster Abbey pulpit to expose and condemn slum landlords and others who exploited the poor.

Of course, the pragmatic hands-on approach to the poverty crisis formed a natural adjunct to Buckland's own theology as a Christian priest. As will become clear in the following chapters, Buckland was not especially inspired by mystical or intense spiritual traditions, nor by the post-1833 Oxford Movement, but by the joy and abundance of the natural world. His geology and beneficent Natural Theology thus fused together. For God the Creator had provided a glorious creation, which the human mind could fathom and read alongside the revealed glory that one found in the pages of Scripture. And all pointed to joy, providence and Christ's gospel injunction that those who had must share with and help those who had not.

It is a pity that Buckland's 'eccentricities' have also been allowed to obscure his deeply held and genuine Christian theology: a theology, alas, which was becoming distinctly out of fashion in Tractarian, Oxford Movement England. Yet the power of its message remains, for many people are still brought to God – me included – by contemplating or studying the sheer glory, order and logic of the natural world.

Likewise, much of Buckland's geological work, and especially his geological interpretations, have also and inevitably slid out of fashion. But this is one of the penalties which any daring pioneer or original thinker must pay. For perhaps more than any other individual scientist between 1813 and 1840, William Buckland not only laid geology on a firm, empirical foundation, but propelled it ahead as a new and potent intellectual force. And needless to say, while he got much right – such as in his work on fossil anatomy – he got a great deal wrong, as new evidence dug up and new interpretations framed by his younger disciples, friends and rivals superseded his ideas on matters like the Flood of Noah.

Yet few things reveal Buckland's true character more than his response to those new discoveries, many made by his own pupils and protégés, which undermined in various ways his own original findings from the 1810s and 1820s. His old pupil Charles Lyell's uniformitarian geology after 1831 fundamentally challenged Buckland's catastrophism, yet their friendship stayed intact. Likewise, uniformitarian ideas and related geological discoveries seriously undermined Buckland's Noachian Deluge theory, yet friendships remained unbroken. Indeed, he not infrequently applauded the new theories that emerged from the new discoveries, for was this not how science advanced: by fresh discoveries leading to fresh interpretations? Indeed, William Buckland's love of friendship, his intellectual curiosity and his delight in learning shine through, and it is interesting how his *magnum opus*, *Geology and Mineralogy* (1836), reflects his response to these changes in his own ideas.

For example, while Flood geology had been fundamental to Buckland's whole interpretative schema in 1820, one looks in vain for anything more than passing references to the Deluge, as he has clearly come to an accommodation with the later uniformitarian interpretations. What is more, one looks in vain for rearguard defences of his earlier chosen interpretations, or for disparaging remarks against new geological ideas.

In the following pages, I hope to capture something of Buckland the man, the geologist and the priest, and to set him in his historical context, and I hope that you find him as captivating as I do. So, read on!

Acknowledgements

I first encountered William Buckland and his world of geology and theology as an undergraduate science historian at Lancaster University around 1971, and am indebted to Professors Robert Fox and John Hedley Brooke for their early inspiration and continuing friendship. For assistance with my later work, and the research lying behind this book, I would like to thank the staff of the Oxford University Natural History Museum, which now curates many of Buckland's specimens, and the Geological Society, London. For information about Buckland in his native Devon haunts, I must thank Sam Fletcher, a University of Oxford student of mine in 2012, who, as one familiar with the Lyme Regis and Axminster areas, kindly supplied me with some useful contacts regarding the local history of the Buckland and Oke families. Canon Ann Barwood, of Exeter Cathedral, kindly sent me material pertaining to the Devon parishes held by the Reverend Charles Buckland, William's father. My thanks also go to Renée Jackaman of the Devon Heritage Services, Devon Record Office, Exeter, and to Julian Reid, Archivist of Corpus Christi College, Oxford.

I owe an especial debt of gratitude to the staff of Christ Church Library, Oxford, and in particular to Dr Cristina Neagu, Alina Nachescu (who very kindly photographed all the illustrations for me), and Judith Curthoys, whose enthusiastic assistance and support have simply been invaluable. I am further indebted to the Dean and Chapter and Governing Body of Christ Church, not only for their generous permission to reproduce pictures held in their collections, but also for continuing academic sanctuary and friendship. My thanks go, too, to my friend Dr Martin Grossel, of Christ Church, Oxford, and to Professor Simon Conway Morris, of Cambridge University, who kindly read and made constructive comments on the manuscript.

At SPCK, I would like to thank Tony Collins, who took on this book, and Philip Law and the rest of the editorial, design and production team for all their help and encouragement. In particular, I thank Ali Hull, my editor, for all her advice and encouragement over the years we have worked together and for her sensitive efficiency in weeding out the inevitable errors and stylistic infelicities.

But my greatest thanks go to my classicist wife, Rachel, who has worked alongside me at every stage of this book (and many others), for her manifold skills, judgement, encouragement, efficiency, and endless patience with my administrative and digital ineptitude. Once again, she has typed this book from my original fountain-pen-written manuscript, checked and edited it, and has made the whole process of producing this work immeasurably easier than it would otherwise have been. That is why I dedicate the book to her.

Allan Chapman

Chapter 1
The British Parson-Scientist: William Buckland in Context

It may strike many people as strange today that in 1784, when William Buckland was born at Axminster, south Devon, science was an active clerical pursuit. Far from being perceived as in conflict, science and the Christian faith were seen to go hand in hand and to be in harmony. For could one not 'read' the divine mind by studying the logic, beauty and usefulness of the world and the universe, and did not revelation and reason complement one another? This, indeed, was 'Natural Theology', to which we will return shortly.

Father and son geologists

William Buckland belonged firmly to this tradition. His father, the Revd Charles Buckland, was Rector of Templeton and Trusham in south Devon, two parishes over 20 miles apart, and though tragically blinded in an accident, Charles remained a keen naturalist over the last 20 sightless years of a long life. William's paternal uncle, the Revd John Buckland, had been a Fellow of Corpus Christi College, Oxford, and would play a major role in young William's higher education. His mother, Elizabeth Oke Buckland, came from an established south Devon gentry family who owned considerable property around Axminster; it is likely that it was in one of the houses of his Oke relatives, perhaps at Combpyne near Axminster, that William was born.[1]

Charles Buckland, on their rambles together, taught his son the behaviour of animals, plants and natural phenomena, as well as how to find those curious figured stones in which south Devon abounds – the fossils of what is now called the 'Jurassic Coast'. What were they, where did they

1

come from, and how did they relate to the modern animals mentioned in the Bible? It was not for nothing that William later recalled that he was virtually a born geologist, and always said that growing up near the coast sharpened his curiosity about nature, for the area around Axminster in south-east Devon, and especially the valley of the river Axe, has some of the most fossil-rich rocks in Britain, containing amongst their treasures the remains of fossilized ancient forests, and even the bones of prehistoric elephants.

One can understand what he meant, growing up as he did in the lush, green countryside of south Devon, with its rolling landscapes, well-tilled farms, abundant animal life, precipitous cliffs punctuated by steep-sided smuggler-haunted coves and stream-eroded valleys plunging down into the English Channel. These coastlines, moreover, would have been alive with all sorts of maritime activity: fishing boats, local coastal vessels, traders out of Exeter and the King's frigates and great men o' war out at sea coming in and out of Portsmouth or Plymouth on a daily basis. For let us not forget that Buckland's formative years, from his early childhood to the age of 31, would have been overshadowed by the French Revolutionary and Napoleonic wars, and ships were equated with protection as well as prosperity.

His learned parson father, a Sidney Sussex College, Cambridge, graduate, was not only William's first mentor in natural history and mineralogy, but his first academic teacher as well, for much of his early education, no doubt in classics, history and religion, took place not in school but at home – a not uncommon circumstance 200 years ago. Study at home, then rambling the coasts and countryside – for Axminster and Trusham were only a few miles from the sea, and Templeton about 20 miles inland – formed his early education, and as a young gentleman he would have picked up those social skills that he would display throughout the rest of his life. One suspects that his genial personality, sometimes outrageous sense of humour, playfulness and gift for mimicry, so well attested in the adult Buckland, were shaped and honed during these years.

For Buckland instinctively knew how to have good relationships, not only with gentlefolks but also with quarry-workers, farm labourers, sailors and other people who knew the lore and life forms of the countryside and the sea. Indeed, he would later recall that when he walked along the beach to Lyme Regis, the local boys would bring him strange 'golden serpent' (pyritous ammonite) fossils from the overhanging cliffs. For in winter especially, after violent Channel storms had pounded the cliffs, the beach was often strewn with curious ammonite and other fossils washed out of the crumbling rock face, as still occurs today. Many years later, the Revd Dr William Daniel Conybeare, Dean of Llandaff and a friend of Buckland's since their undergraduate days at Oxford, would write to Frank Buckland (William's son) to discuss his father's early influence. Conybeare was at pains to point out how the south Devon landscape, with its wildlife and geology, had played a formative role in the early awakening of William Buckland's inspiration as a natural history and geological scientist.[2]

In 1797, at the age of 13, William Buckland was sent to what was then Blundell's Grammar School in Tiverton, Devon (where his own father had been educated), and the following year he won a scholarship place at the prestigious Winchester College public school. It is unfortunate that nowadays the great boarding schools are often popularly regarded as 'posh' or 'elite'. Yet this was not the case in the past, for most academic schools, including the grammar schools, were – for boys who lived more than a few miles away – boarding schools, for the simple reason that public transport was slow at best and non-existent in the countryside. And most of these schools, including Blundell's and Winchester, had (and still have) scholarships, which opened them up to a wide cross-section of the population. Indeed, William of Wykeham, who founded Winchester College back in 1387, had risen through education from a Hampshire farmyard to the Bishopric of Winchester and the Chancellorship of England.[3]

Indeed, giving back when you had done well and helping the next generation to rise, was an integral part of Christian culture, for 'charity' did not mean being condescending to the lower orders, but rather showing *caritas*, or practical love and assistance. And countless bright boys had risen up from the vicarage, the farm, the shop counter or the workbench to high office in Church, state and the learned professions over the centuries – William Buckland did, and many more would do after him.

At Winchester, William would have deepened his knowledge of Latin, Greek, Divinity and mathematics, which constituted a scholarly education 200 years ago, and his masters commended his assiduity. His passion for natural history deepened as well, as he ransacked St Catherine's Hill and the surrounding countryside for plants, animals and fossils, while working towards another scholarship: to the University of Oxford. However, we will return to his education shortly.

Where did the money come from to pay for these school and college scholarships, and indeed the stipends of the clergy and the incomes of the gentry? Some, it is true, came from mercantile wealth, such as that generated by the City of London and other great trading cities. But the greater part of it came from the buoyant and very efficient agriculture of Britain. An eighteenth-century clergyman, don or gentleman would have had an informed knowledge of farming, quarrying, fishing or arboriculture because this is where the rentals that supplied his livelihood came from. From God's abundance on land and sea, indeed: a natural abundance made even richer by the use of the providence-bestowed gifts of ingenuity and intelligence, which were what separated humans from brute beasts. It is hardly surprising, therefore, that intelligent men and women were driven to inquire into the inner mechanisms of nature, to obtain a scientific understanding of God's bounty. Buckland and his father were by no means unusual: they were part of a much wider movement. From this manner of thinking Natural Theology was born, and so intelligent people, including the clergy, saw it as perfectly natural to trace the doings of the divine hand in nature, from the complex astronomy that produced the seasons, to the rich harvests from the well-tilled fields.

British Natural Theology

Natural Theology as Buckland knew it really began in the seventeenth century, although elements of this rationally comprehended aspect of divine providence had gone back through the Middle Ages to the early Christian centuries. What triggered it in a big way, however, was fresh scientific discovery, as experimental scientists and explorers encountered all kinds of new and wonderful phenomena. Not only had God shown the early geographical discoverers like Columbus, Magellan and Drake new continents, seas and natural phenomena, but through the gift of ingenuity to mankind he had enabled us to devise and build great ocean-going ships; and then there was the wonderful regularity of the tides, the trade winds, the seasons and even the earth's magnetic field, which made the mariner's compass possible.

Then as the seventeenth century progressed, there was a flood of discoveries, in medicine, physics, chemistry, biology and astronomy, following from newly invented instruments such as the telescope, microscope and barometer. It is hardly surprising, therefore, that when a group of scientific friends approached His Majesty King Charles II, the Royal Society of London for Improving Natural Knowledge was founded in 1660, and received its royal charters in 1662 and 1663.[4] The Royal Society became a driving force not only for the new, rapidly advancing experimental science, but also for Natural Theology. Eminent scientifically minded clergy, such as Bishops John Wilkins, Thomas Sprat and Seth Ward, and Archbishops Gilbert Sheldon and John Tillotson, along with the Revd Dr Thomas Gales, Headmaster of St Paul's School, and later Dean of York Minster, joined the Fellowship. This is not to mention a host of ordained academics and devout Christian laymen such as the Hon. Robert Boyle (of 'Boyle's Law' of gases fame), Dr Thomas Willis (the neurologist discoverer of the brain's Circle of Willis), and Sir Christopher Wren (astronomy don and architect).

These men were coming to see the natural world as a great and complex machine, devised by God, and amenable to human exploration and understanding. And what a wonderful machine it was, as each new discovery, from the perfection of the celestial movements to the functioning of the human heart, suggested a Great Designer. Even the earth itself and its rocks and land masses were becoming increasingly amenable to such rational investigation. For it was Robert Hooke, FRS, and holder of a Lambeth Doctorate in Medicine from his friend Archbishop Tillotson, who seriously suggested that the fossils found in the rocks of his native Isle of Wight and adjacent Dorset coast – only 60 miles away from the young Buckland's Axminster and Lyme Regis – were the remains of long-extinct animals. Indeed, between 1664 and 1700, Hooke, and his younger contemporary the astronomer Edmond Halley, were even to suggest that the earth's surface appeared to have been modelled and remodelled many times, maybe in a pre-Noachian remote antiquity, and that our planet's surface, like its magnetic field and complex climate, was dynamic. Foundations of William Buckland's thinking, no less.

Yet far from being conducive to atheism, all of this new natural knowledge, from stars to stones, was seen as a display of God's providence and loving design, which became more awe-inspiring and wonderful with each new discovery. And while there were academic disagreements about how old the world and the universe might be, and whether Noah's Flood had only been the last of several cycles of prehistoric deluges, most of the fresh knowledge was accommodated within a Natural Theological interpretation.

But it was John Ray's *The Wisdom of God as Manifested in the Works of Creation* (1691) that really articulated the 'Argument from Design' and its ensuing Natural Theology in a big way, presenting it in a manner accessible to a wider readership. And what Ray had to say would have a major interpretative influence on British scientific and theological thinking throughout the eighteenth-century. On the other hand, what would define Natural Theology for Buckland's generation and thereafter was William Paley's *Natural Theology or Evidences of the Existence and Attributes of the Deity* (1802). Though most of Paley's arguments were not especially original, he articulated them in a way that would colour the thinking of the next 60-odd years of university undergraduates, scientists, clergy and laity.

Paley's style was accessible, powerful, and radiated a confident joy in creation. Old analogies were recast in a memorable way, such as his celebrated 'Watchmaker' analogy. Imagine that you found a ticking watch lying on the sandy beach of an uninhabited island. Would its presence not tell you that, far from its being a lucky freak of nature, an ingenious mind and skilful hand had once been at work? Otherwise, how could such a complex thing as a watch exist? And not only was the watch a symbol of past ingenuity, one could argue that it also signified a foreknowledge on the part of the watchmaker, namely, that at some stage in the future someone would want to know the time.

Of course, the 'Watchmaker' analogy was not without its philosophical flaws, for after all, the maker of the timepiece might now be dead or uninterested – as the deists argued, when they said that ingenious as the Designer-God undoubtedly had been, the presence of the watch was no guarantee that he still existed or cared. And by extension, the whole of nature and the cosmos, for which the watch was an analogy, might now have been abandoned by its creator. Yet while there were deists in Britain – proud as it was of its free speech and toleration – Natural Theological analogies were seen as proof of a benign Deity by the vast majority of British people. For it had been Robert Boyle, in the late seventeenth century, who argued that, clock-like in its complex perfection as the world was, God could be seen as the ever-present spring whose love drove the creation along. And did not the teachings of Jesus and the Old Testament prophets provide a different yet complementary substantiation for the presence of a loving God who was active in the world?

Central to Natural Theology, and in particular to the Revd William Paley's interpretation of it, were providence, meaning and joy. Integral to his thinking, indeed, was the very interconnectedness of both natural and spiritual knowledge, which enlivened the mind and brought us a realization of God's love, bounty and providence. And were not things such as affection, care and even morality part of God's wider providence? One could even see this providential joy suffusing the animal kingdom, as Paley describes shoals of simple shrimps seemingly frolicking in the sea and brilliant sunlight that God had provided. Even brutal death in the animal kingdom was not entirely bad: most wild animals had a quick despatch from the jaws of a predator, leaving few to grow old and infirm, which was just as well considering they lacked loved ones to care for them. God's cycle of providence continued, moreover, as the dead beast's flesh provided nourishment for the next generation. All this would come to colour and shape Buckland's own interpretive schema, as we shall see in the following chapters.

Providence, progress and joy

To Paley it all made sense, for design, providence and simple delight were fused together, displaying the hand of a loving God not only as a *Creator* but also as a *sustainer, friend* and *Saviour* moving through the world.

It is all too easy for us moderns to smile condescendingly, or even sneer, at such a felicitous view of providence. For what, a modern person might ask, about post-Freudian *angst*, unbelief, economic instability, terrorism and the 'age of uncertainty' in which we live today? The fashionably articulated 'living hell' of modern life, in fact? Yet let us be careful, for Paley's time was, in many ways, very much grimmer than our own. Death in childbirth and in infancy were commonplace, medicine was feeble, and surgery ghastly; and the 1790s and 1800s were decades of profound political instability, as revolutionary fanatics, military dictators and often violent evangelical atheists rampaged across Europe and were only kept out of Britain care of the policies of Prime Minister William Pitt, the evangelical Christian admiral and naval strategist Sir Charles Middleton, Lord Barham (who masterminded the Trafalgar Campaign), Lord Nelson and the Royal Navy. For a more recent comparison, to give a sense of the grimness of that age, just think of the haunting sense of menace experienced during the Cold War decades of the 1950s to 1980s – but worse – and you might glimpse the realities of the world of Buckland's childhood and youth.

What is more, taxation also reached unprecedented levels, and the early industrial revolution was beginning to spell disaster and ruin for the old-fashioned artisan and the farm labourer. And if you think that Paley himself lived in splendid isolation from all these troubles in his Carlisle Cathedral archdeaconry, just remember that while writing *Natural Theology* he was suffering the onset of a terminal intestinal disease which he lightly referred to as 'the Scorpion' because of the largely unrelieved pain it caused him, and against which contemporary medicine was impotent.

To appreciate the world in which Natural Theology held such compelling appeal, however, one must think of a country where belief in God and a familiarity with the Bible formed the bedrock of popular culture. Yes, there *were* atheists, conventional yet uncommitted 'believers' who snored in church on Sundays, and then got drunk, blasphemed and kicked the servants on Monday, along with freethinking republicans who were fans of Tom Paine, or wanted a French-style revolution in England. Likewise, there were absentee, idle and neglectful clergy who gave not a fig for their parishioners. Indeed, the long-absentee ecclesiastical incumbent was still around in the 1850s, as witnessed by the fictitious Dr Vesey Stanhope in Anthony Trollope's *Barchester Towers* (1857). But such people were by no means the norm, and disagreements and bickering apart, historical evidence suggests that a broad foundation of Protestant Christian values about God, right, wrong and duty was widely shared across much of society – a major reason, it has been suggested, why Methodism had a far greater impact upon the thinking of ordinary people than did French Revolutionary ideology.

To this society, its diversities and disagreements notwithstanding, a general belief in a providential tendency would have seemed normal and natural. Hence, Paley could be read without sneering, for rough-and-tumble, riotous, prizefighting and even murderous as the late Georgian and early Victorian society in which William Buckland lived could be, it was not cynical. Indeed, even *bon viveur* clergy such as the gourmandizing diarist parson, James Woodforde, and the rich, patronage-hunting Sydney Smith could be surprisingly generous and charitable towards their parishioners and were popular locally, for was it not the duty of a Christian priest and an English gentleman to help those whom God had placed in their care? Such a sense of duty would also shape Buckland's future conduct and ministry.

Had this society been cynical, indeed, or in doubt about its values, it would never have prospered the way it did, nor would it have found the resources – financial, social, technical and spiritual – to stand up to 23 years of threatened French invasion between 1792 and 1815 and then emerge victorious after Wellington's defeat of Bonaparte at Waterloo. Nor in the thick of this conflict would it have found the moral courage to abolish, and enforce the abolition of, the slave trade in 1807, then deal with serious post-war economic depression and political unrest, and, starting with the Reform Bill of 1832 and the abolition of the Corn Laws seen through Parliament by Buckland's future friend Sir Robert Peel, embark upon a sustained programme of root and branch social reform which would lead to the prosperity of high Victorian Britain. For Britain had been unique in Europe in moving from the late eighteenth to the late nineteenth century without bloody revolution, brutalizing foreign invasion, economic catastrophe and serious menace to traditional Christian institutions.

And what made much of this possible was not only a stable Parliamentary system of government and a 'balanced' constitution of king, commons, lords, judges and bishops, but a broadly consensual nation. A nation, moreover, in which the Christian faith played a major role, in which Dissenters, Catholics and Jews were legally 'tolerated' and had protected rights, and in which an Anglican state church provided a broad spiritual foundation across its length and breadth.

The clerical scientist and society

I go into all of this detail for three reasons. First, because it goes towards explaining why Natural Theology, the 'Argument from Design' and belief in a divinely ordained beneficent providence retained such a deep and enduring appeal, both intellectually and spiritually. Second, because it helps us to understand the social and intellectual role of clergymen, Anglican and other denominations, in that society, and by extension, why so many of them were active in the practice and advancement of science. And third, because this is the very world into which William Buckland was born, lived and died, and it shows us how a Devonshire parson's son could not only become a scientist of international standing, but could combine this achievement with being an ordained Oxford don, a cathedral canon, a leading Natural Theologian and a Dean of Westminster – a quintessential parson-scientist, in fact.

Ordained astronomers

Mention was made at the beginning of this chapter of how ordained clergymen were active across the sciences on a serious research level from at least the seventeenth until well into the nineteenth century. It is now time to back up this statement with specific examples, to give a measure of William Buckland's scientific and spiritual brethren.

Let us begin by looking at those men who held the office of Astronomer Royal and directed the Royal Observatory at Greenwich. Four of the five men who were Astronomers Royal between 1675 and 1811 were in Anglican Holy Orders. The only one not to have been a priest was Edmond Halley, a merchant's son and an ex-captain in the Royal Navy, who was at Greenwich between 1720 and 1742. The four ordained men – John Flamsteed, James Bradley, Nathaniel Bliss and Nevil Maskelyne – were all top-flight physical scientists who undertook major researches into celestial mechanics, optics, gravitation theory and the finding of the longitude at sea. Some of them held clerical benefices (often administered on a daily basis by curates) and also taught in the universities. The man who became Chief Assistant to the lay Astronomer Royal Sir George Airy between 1835 and 1860, the Revd Robert Main, was an Anglican priest who, while not permitted by that date to jointly hold a clerical benefice, nonetheless collected theological books and often deputized for absent clerical colleagues and guest-preached in local churches on Sundays while working as a full-time scientist at the Greenwich Observatory. (The Revd Robert Main has many parallels today: men and women who combine a non-stipendiary clerical vocation with earning their salaries as full-time professional scientists.)

And then there were the Professors of Astronomy in the universities. The University of Oxford and the University of Cambridge (England's only two universities before 1828) very often had astronomy dons in Anglican Holy Orders. The first two directors of Oxford's prestigious Radcliffe Observatory between 1771 and 1826, Thomas Hornsby and Abram Robertson (himself an ex-domestic servant and Christ Church scholarship beneficiary), were clergymen; while the third, Stephen Peter Rigaud, was a devout Anglican layman, and the fourth, Manuel Johnson, an ex-military-officer don and a layman. Johnson, indeed, was a devout High Church Christian and a good friend and supporter of John Henry Newman (Newman tells us that he spent his last night in Oxford, before leaving to become a Roman Catholic, in Johnson's Radcliffe Observatory house). Johnson, his Radcliffe Observatory predecessors, and Buckland must inevitably have often encountered each other around Oxford. And when Johnson died in 1859, the Revd Mr Main, ex of Greenwich, succeeded him as Radcliffe Observer. Ireland's Armagh Observatory operated under the patronage of the Archbishop of Armagh, and the Revd Dr Thomas Romney Robinson, a Fellow of Trinity College, Dublin, then director of Armagh Observatory for 59 years in the nineteenth century was one of Ireland's leading men of science. Clerical scientists were commonplace at the four Scottish universities, while the first government astronomer sent out to found and direct the new Cape of Good Hope Observatory in 1821 was the Revd Fearon Fallows.[5] The early Victorian Stonyhurst College Observatory, Lancashire, and Maynooth College, Ireland, both Roman Catholic foundations, had gifted Jesuit astronomy and physics teachers and researchers on their staffs.

All of these clerical scientists, moreover, held official or academic posts of some kind, although salaries were modest, and it was invariably taken for granted that a Protestant reverend professor had other sources of income on which to live, such as an ecclesiastical benefice, teaching fees or private means. The great majority were also Fellows of the Royal Society, and after its foundation in1820, of the Royal Astronomical Society as well.

But when one considers the non-official, self-funded private research astronomer (a breed that I have styled 'Grand Amateurs'), one finds clerical astronomers quite literally in shoals between the seventeenth and early twentieth centuries, working, in most cases, from well-equipped vicarage observatories – not to mention ordained schoolmaster astronomers. Let us simply cite one: the Revd John Michell FRS, of Thornhill, near Leeds. In 1784 this former Cambridge mathematics don, now a country vicar, postulated something resembling a black hole. For, as he told the Royal Society and published in its *Philosophical Transactions*, if a condensing star cluster became so dense that its enormous gravitational attraction would not even allow light to escape from it, it would cease to be visible.[6] In addition, Michell was an active mineralogist and geologist, who made significant contributions to our understanding of earthquakes, which he came to view as caused by subterranean rock slippages and shock waves. John Michell had also built an early torsion balance with which he hoped to be able to measure and quantify the density of the earth. Michell's balance would inspire the Hon. Henry Cavendish to build an improved balance, which in 1798 enabled him to obtain a figure for the terrestrial density that came remarkably close to the figure we accept today.

Buckland himself possessed a good knowledge of astronomy and would have known astronomers in Oxford, the Royal Society and after 1831 especially, the new British Association for the Advancement of Science. What particularly interested him about the heavens, however, was the sun's radiant heat, and solar and lunar gravitational influences upon the earth. For Buckland came to realize that the geological record revealed instances of extreme and often violent climatic, temperature and sea-level changes on earth that were most likely attributable to astronomical causes. What, for example, had caused the Ice Ages on the one hand and the hot steaming jungles of the Carboniferous period on the other?

The clerical chemists

Just as clergymen abounded in astronomy, so they flourished in chemistry, medicine and natural history. One of the most remarkable chemical researchers of the first half of the eighteenth century was the Revd Stephen Hales, FRS, Minister of Teddington, Middlesex. Hales's faith and his science were inextricably bound up with each other, as he traced the working of divine design through biological and chemical processes. His commitment to ministering to his parish flock and to his experimental researches was such that he even refused a prestigious canonry of Windsor, as it would have taken up too much of his time.

Since his Cambridge days, Hales had been fascinated by chemistry and medicine in particular. He was a pioneer gas chemist, studying the different 'airs' and building, in many ways, upon the earlier Oxford researches of Robert Hooke, Robert Boyle and John Mayow. At a time when there was no clear concept of a chemically-specific gas, it was generally assumed that the fiery 'air' given off when metals were immersed in sulphuric acid (hydrogen), the 'air' given off by toasted saltpetre or red lead, which could make a candle burn uncommonly bright (oxygen) and that which came off coal when it was heated in a closed vessel (largely methane and hydrogen) were normal air in different stages of compression. Hales developed a water trough apparatus for collecting these 'airs' for experimental purposes and identified the characteristics, without naming them, of several of what we call 'gases'. Hales's water trough would become the ancestor of the troughs and gas jars of school chemistry teaching.

Hales even explained will o' the wisp lights that flickered on swamps and in graveyards on moonless nights in terms not of wandering spirits, but of glowing combustive 'airs' emitted by decomposing organic matter. He was also to pioneer the chemistry of plant respiration and how plants are affected by light.

Hales's magisterial two-volume treatise, *Vegetable Staticks* ('Statistics', 1727), became a defining text of early chemistry and a precise model of how to generate, collect and experiment upon a variety of 'airs'. It certainly influenced Joseph Priestley, the Dissenting Minister and gas and electrical chemist who first prepared that gas, which would later be called oxygen in 1774.

Purges from the parson:
the medical clergyman

It may strike one as incongruous today to think of the local vicar (or his wife) as the person to whom you might go if you were feeling ill – and go, moreover, not only for spiritual comfort, but also for physical help. Indeed, medicine was another subject actively cultivated by numerous clergy. Yet before the Medical Registration Act of 1858, medicine was practised by a wide variety of people. I am not talking here of quacks and charlatans, for at a time when formally-trained medical men, be they physicians, surgeons or apothecaries, were scarce outside the main towns – expensive of access and incapable of curing many diseases anyway – your best option of finding relief was to seek a scientifically-minded clergyman. After all, an Oxbridge Master of Arts in good academic standing, widely read in ancient and modern medicine, an astute observer and good with his hands, was likely to provide comfort much more cheaply in rural England than purchasing the nostrums of the fairground mountebank. And especially so if his medical calling had led him to obtain an Archdeacon's or Bishop's licence to practise – invariably free of charge – in a diocese or archdeaconry.

Natural science, Natural Theology, cure of body and cure of soul came together in the priest-doctor, often wedding intellectual curiosity to wider Christian ministry and practical help, and it is likely that Buckland would have met and known such men in his extensive geological travels around Britain.

Stephen Hales not only 'physicked' his ailing parishioners when they were unwell, but also, along with his chemical and natural history research, made major discoveries in experimental physiology. His *Haemostaticks* ('Blood Measurements') of 1733 described meticulous experiments aimed at measuring and quantifying blood flow, and also reported his elegantly-conducted experiments on what we now call 'blood pressure', when he discovered that the cardiac pumping force was greater in the arteries than in the veins: the systolic and diastolic pressures, as a modern doctor would call them. But let us not forget that the Revd Mr Hales was an FRS, after all.

Many parts of eighteenth-and early-nineteenth-century Britain were less well-drained than they are today, and in consequence, mosquitos abounded, making a type of malaria common: the 'quakes', 'shakes' or 'agues' referred to in the literature of the period. Quinine, or Peruvian bark from South America, was an excellent 'fever-breaker', but was very expensive. And this is where another parson scientist came in. The Revd Edward Stone, an Oxfordshire vicar and Wadham College, Oxford, graduate, moved in scientific as well as clerical circles and knew the Earl of Macclesfield, then President of the Royal Society. In addition to his published works on astronomy, Stone had heard of willow bark as a folk cure for the 'ague' and began to perform quantitative tests on 50 of his sick parishioners, giving them carefully measured doses of dried and powdered willow bark and recording their effect. He published his clinical trial results – which were spectacularly successful – in the *Philosophical Transactions of the Royal Society* (1763). Stone also made the observation that willow trees liked damp ground, the very places that bred 'agues', as it was believed in that pre-bacterial age. So, was it not a mark of providence that God had placed the means of cure adjacent to the source of the disease?

What Stone had discovered was crude aspirin, the active ingredient of which is salicylic acid, from *salix*, the Latin for willow. Pure salicylic acid was isolated by nineteenth-century organic chemists and could also be extracted from the plant meadowsweet, known in Latin as *spiraea* – hence the name 'aspirin' (Latin *a* means 'from'). The drug itself came on to the market in our now familiar tablet form after being developed and tested by German scientists in 1900.

The Revd Dr Sydney Smith, whom we met briefly above, was a celebrated wit, writer, ecclesiastical politicker, careerist and place-seeker. Yet he was not only a popular priest in his Foston, north Yorkshire parish, but was also a skilled and courageous unofficial medical practitioner, who had previously attended lectures in anatomy and medicine at both the University of Oxford and Edinburgh University. When a deadly fever hit his parish in 1816, he dosed and tended his poor parishioners as well as any doctor. Throughout his rural ministry, indeed, Smith continued to dispense proper medicines (by the standards of the day) from the vicarage door to all and sundry – free of charge and out of his own pocket. To some preparations he gave amusing and non-frightening names, such as 'Rub-a-Dub'.

As well as battling with fevers and administering embrocations and purges, Smith became interested in what would later become the specialism of rheumatology. For in the chilly, damp climate of north Yorkshire, and especially among people who did heavy work in the fields, sprains and muscular and joint problems were common. Working on the premise that rheumatic conditions were helped by heat, Smith designed and had made by a tinsmith a set of specially shaped hot-water bottles, his 'rheumatic armour', contoured to fit different parts of the body, such as the shoulders, knees and feet. These would be loaned out gratis to the local folk, who could fill them with hot water, tie them on, and use them to gently ease their joints: the ancestors of modern-day heating pads, in fact.

In addition to medical clergymen, one must not forget clerical wives, who ran similar services. One of the greatest of all medical careers, that of Dr Thomas Willis in the seventeenth century, was inspired when, as an Arts student in Oxford, he lodged in the house of Canon Thomas Isles of Christ Church. It was through assisting Mrs Isles in dispensing her medicines to the poor that his fascination with medicine began. For Willis had intended to become a clergyman, until the Puritans temporarily abolished the Church of England. Instead, he became a doctor and a deeply devout layman and medical scientist. Mrs Isles was only one of a type, for clergy-wife healers often assisted with women's illnesses, childbirth and childcare in particular, especially among the poor, until well into the Victorian age.

The ordained 'mad doctor' or psychiatrist

But there was one branch of medicine at which parson doctors were often remarkably successful, well into Buckland's middle age, and that was what we call psychiatry, but they called 'mad doctoring'. Although organic neurological illness, such as epilepsy, had been attributed to problems in the brain cortex since Greek times, conditions such as depression, erratic behaviour and delusion had generally been seen as disturbances of the soul, and hence falling within the expertise of the priest. Many clergy, indeed, who felt that they possessed the right calming gifts, took on the management of the mentally ill, and some vicarages gave them a home for a modest fee. William Cowper, the probably bipolar poet and hymn-writer, for example, after receiving medical treatment from the humane and pious physician Dr Nathaniel Cotton, was given lodgings by the Revd Mr Morley Unwin and his wife, Mary, at Olney, Huntingdon, from where Cowper wrote his celebrated 'Olney hymns'. And William Tuke, the wealthy Quaker tea merchant and philanthropist of York, founded a model asylum, the York Retreat, in 1796. Prayer, treating the patient as a loved child of God rather than a freak, and creating an environment that was quiet, kind and yet firm, were found to work wonders, and many such 'mad doctors' claimed 'discharge cured' rates that may seem to us amazing. And while not a practising 'mad doctor' himself, when the Revd Dr Samuel Warneford, a very rich Christian philanthropist, founded the Warneford Hospital, Oxford, in the 1820s, it was this kindly mode of treatment that he ensured was adopted.

Without doubt, the most famous parson doctor of the eighteenth century was the Revd Dr Francis Willis, DM (no relation to Thomas Willis), whose successful treatment of the mentally ill encompassed a spectrum from Lincolnshire shepherds to crowned heads of Europe. His most famous patient of all was His Majesty King George III in 1788–1789. We now have reason to believe that the King's illness, probably porphyria, could have had a chemical cause. What cannot be denied, though, is Willis's astounding success over nearly 60 years of psychiatric practice. So much so, indeed, that he regularized his practice by returning to Oxford to take a medical doctorate (a DM degree, I may say, from the University of Oxford does not call its medical doctorate an MD). Yet true to his Christian vocation, the elderly Willis was described by the writer Hannah More as 'the very image of simplicity, quite a good, plain, old-fashioned country parson'.[7]

If the preceding pages give a sense of the sheer activity of parson scientists before, during, and after the so-called 'Age of Reason', let me remind the reader that I have said virtually nothing about the biggest single ordained scientist category: namely, Buckland's own category of parson natural history scientists. Men, indeed, who studied and often wrote and taught about plants, birds and animals, or who recorded the weather, or variations in the earth's magnetic field. Men who collected fossils and 'geologized' and 'naturalized' their parishes or counties, and nearby seashores. Men like the Revd Charles Buckland, in fact, who was so successful in transmitting his interests to his son William.

Perhaps the most famous of these parson naturalists, before Buckland himself, was the Revd Gilbert White, whose classic, *The Natural History of Selborne* (1789), is still in print today: a living testimony, indeed, to a quiet country life dedicated to serving God and his flock, and using his intellect to explore the rich abundance of nature in his local world. And he did not just look at nature, but made careful comparisons of seasonal and climatic changes, regularly monitoring his thermometer and barometer, and corresponding with his friends Thomas Pennant, the Hon. Daines Barrington and others.

The clerical men of science mentioned above, I must emphasize, are only a small sample of the breed: outstanding, perhaps, for the quality of their published research or public scientific achievements, but in no way unique. For when one reads the letters, diaries and published works of the period, one quickly becomes aware of a very large body of men across Great Britain who may never have written a scientific paper or attended a Royal Society or other high-level, learned society meeting, yet who, in their vicarages and manses, took an informed delight in the study of the heavens, the earth, living creatures and all manner of natural things. Men who would have been nonplussed at the idea of their science being fundamentally in conflict with their Christian faith, and would have read 'the book of nature' with the same understanding and delight with which they read their Bibles.

So science, one might say, was part of the Georgian landscape. To get an idea of the world in which it prospered, of country houses, vicarages, county towns and London, one might imagine the novels of Jane Austen, or a little later in the early Victorian age, those of Anthony Trollope, with the added ingredient of science. One only needed to give Mr Darcy a geologist's hammer, or Archdeacon Grantly one of the new high-powered microscopes of the 1850s, to see Buckland's world in context.

Curiously enough, had Trollope's fictional Archdeacon Grantly really been a microscopist, he might have anticipated a major biological discovery made by a Methodist minister in the 1880s. This was the Revd William Henry Dallinger FRS, who was ministering to a poor parish in

Liverpool at the same time that he was conducting cutting-edge biological research. Impressed by Darwin's *The Origin of Species* (1859), Dallinger the microscopist was investigating the reproductive cycles of newly discovered bacteria, and in particular, those of a 'monad' type, with only a four-minute reproductive cycle. Dallinger realized that with fast reproducing bacteria one might detect evolutionary responses, which in higher animals might take tens of thousands of years to arise. He went on to discover, through studying successive generations of monads' responses to temperature change, that they did indeed manifest behaviour that was congruent with Darwinian natural selection. So it would be a Methodist minister who would provide the first experimental evidences for Darwinian natural selection.[8]

All of these parson scientists belonged to a tradition that – even omitting the monk-scientists of the Middle Ages – is now a good half a millennium old. It dates from at least the early sixteenth century and extends right up to the present day, with an unbroken succession of men (and now women), from the Tudor priest-naturalist-physician William Turner to early twenty-first-century high-powered ordained scientists, and from working parish clergy who in their scarce free time took a serious interest in ornithology, botany and fossil collecting, or set up substantial astronomical telescopes in their vicarage gardens to their modern day equivalents. And one of the truly outstanding figures in that 500-year-old tradition was William Buckland.

William Buckland: from Winchester schoolboy to Oxford undergraduate

Buckland left Winchester College in 1801 after what was a clearly distinguished school career, having been told by Dr Goddard, his Head Master, 'Well, Buckland, it is as difficult to keep a good boy at the bottom of his class as it is to keep a cork under water.'[9] So as both an accomplished scholar and an already established naturalist, young Buckland followed his uncle John to Corpus Christi College, Oxford, at a time when the science of geology was passing from infancy to childhood. He would look back with pleasure on his years at Winchester, becoming a loyal

'Wykehamist' who regularly attended the old boys' dinners in London, while going on to send his own sons Frank and Edward to Winchester.

By the time of his death in 1856, geology was moving from vigorous late adolescence to a strong and confident early adulthood. And I believe that no single individual played a more formative role in that vigorous growth process than did William Buckland.

Chapter 2
A Geologist at Oxford

Having distinguished himself at Winchester, and no doubt often spending time with his family in south Devon, the 17-year-old William Buckland came up to Oxford in spring 1801.

Buckland would probably have travelled in the 'upstairs' or cheaper outside seat of the mail coach, along the smooth new turnpike roads, which had transformed and sped up travel across England over the previous 30 years. Even so, the journey of some 160 miles, even from a major staging post such as Exeter or Taunton, would have taken a good couple of days, with probably a change of coaches in Bristol. To speed up the Royal Mail, moreover, the new, fast coaches generally ran around the clock, with precisely orchestrated changes of drivers and horses at the 'stages' along the way. Trying to catch some sleep on the hard wooden seats, while hoping not to fall off as the coach rattled along at eight or so miles per hour, could not have been easy. On the other hand, Buckland would have already been something of a seasoned traveller, after several years of regular coaching between Devon and Winchester.[1]

To get a sense of such a long coach journey running round the clock, one should read the fictional yet very authentic-sounding journey of Tom Brown to Rugby School in Thomas Hughes's *Tom Brown's School Days* (1857), set in *c*.1830. William Buckland no doubt shared a similar sense of excitement, anticipation and discomfort with Tom Brown, as the vehicle rattled from the West towards Oxford. Buckland entered Corpus Christi College, Oxford, in April 1801, at the very dawn of the nineteenth century, and his joy was complete by 13 May when he wrote to his father to say that Corpus Christi had elected him to a scholarship. This would have given him a better set of college rooms, certain privileges and a small income, which Buckland, a thrifty as well as a clever young man, further augmented by giving extra tuition to less able fellow undergraduates.

21

Stagecoach riding would figure prominently in Buckland's early days as a geologist and a professor; when travelling on the top of the mail coach, it was not unknown for him to deliberately throw his hat overboard if his sharp eye spotted an interesting fossil or rock formation. Stopping the coach under the pretext of recovering his hat, he would take his geological hammer out of his overcoat pocket, adroitly break the fossil loose, and then, with his recovered hat in hand, climb back on board. (In his professorial years, Buckland also rode an elderly mare that instinctively stopped whenever she passed a quarry where fossils might be found.)

William Buckland
the Oxford undergraduate

When William Buckland 'matriculated', or became a formal member of the University of Oxford and an undergraduate at Corpus Christi College, Oxford, in 1801, no one embarked upon a degree in a specialist subject as one would do today. Instead, the young gentleman would go up to read for an 'Arts' degree, consisting of studies in the classical languages of Latin and Greek, mathematics, geometry, some Old Testament Hebrew, and lots of classical philosophy and literature. There would also be biblical theology, and a study of the Thirty-Nine Articles in the Book of Common Prayer, combined with arguments to demonstrate the superiority of Anglican Protestantism over 'superstitious Popery'. Indeed, it was then necessary for every young man who entered Oxford or the University of Cambridge to take an oath or 'test' affirming his loyalty to the Thirty-Nine Articles and the Anglican Church.

This might strike us as a painfully narrow curriculum by modern standards, though in reality things were not so constrained as they appeared at first sight. The in-depth study of ancient languages, history, philosophy, culture and theology aimed at cultivating a polished, rounded gentleman who was good with words, while the mathematics and geometry were designed to train him in logic, precision of thought and analysis. Crucial skills, indeed, in any walk of life, especially if a young gentleman planned on a career in public life, the Church, the law or Parliament.

Science in Buckland's Oxford

While there were no science degrees as such in 1801, there was quite a lot of science around, if one cared to look for it. It was, however, offered as an unexamined option for the Arts degree. For going back to the sixteenth and seventeenth centuries, in fact, there was a continuing tradition of lecture courses in *materia medica* (medical botany) in the University 'Physic' or Botanic Garden, along with lecture courses in anatomy – including the occasional dissection of human cadavers – by the Regius Professor of Medicine and his deputies.

Then in 1683, the Ashmolean Museum and Laboratory had opened in Broad Street, providing courses in chemistry, medicine, mineralogy and natural history. Modern astronomy was also being systematically taught in the Museum by the Savilian Professors of Astronomy and Geometry, while the new Radcliffe Observatory, opening in 1774, was a splendidly equipped institution of Europe-wide reputation, both for astronomical research and for the teaching of 'natural philosophy', or what would later be called experimental physics.

The eighteenth century also saw the opening of three further major scientific institutions in Oxford in addition to the Observatory. These were the Radcliffe Camera library, 1749, to house the University's growing body of scientific and medical books, the Lee Building in Christ Church, 1767, also for anatomy, medicine, chemistry and mineralogy, and the Radcliffe Infirmary, 1769, both for the treatment of non-fee-paying patients and for clinical teaching.

With active Professors and Readers in medicine, chemistry, astronomy, geometry, botany and mineralogy by 1800, the 17-year-old William Buckland would not have had to look far for scientific inspiration and instruction. Yet if no one was likely to be formally examined for a degree in any of these subjects (except for postgraduate medical students), then what was their purpose? Quite simply, they were supplementary studies that a young gentleman might take or leave, as his interests directed him. And the sciences, let us not forget, were not the only 'supplementary' disciplines on offer, for a young man might also attend endowed professorial lectures in music, poetry, Arabic, Hebrew, higher-level Greek and Latin, philosophy, law and other disciplines besides. All were seen as part of polite learning as well as the imparting of technical expertise, especially as many of these professors, be they scientists or linguists, were actively involved in research and the wider advancement of learning.

Undergraduate life, work and leisure

An Oxbridge degree course in 1800 had few of the pressures facing modern undergraduates, and young Buckland would have found quite a bit of time on his hands. As a *gentleman*, it would be assumed that he had to learn how to balance his own work and leisure, for gentlemen were not to be confined to strict routines, as would farm workers, office clerks or servants.

Formal teaching would normally take place in the morning after breakfast, with one's tutor. Then after 'dinner' – usually around noon in 1800 – an undergraduate was his own man, until 'supper' at about 6.00 p.m. followed by prayers, some Bible study and catechizing with his tutor. All meals were eaten communally in the College Hall. Then came more free time before bed. A young man might choose to spend his long afternoons reading, praying, working with the poor (as had done the Wesley brothers, John and Charles, of Christ Church, a century before), going for long walks, studying natural history, hunting, shooting, horse racing on nearby Port Meadow, singing in a choir, getting drunk, chasing local girls or attending lectures in science. Provided there was nothing excessive or – hopefully – immoral, and that he was not inclining towards Roman Catholicism, then a young esquire could do very much as he liked.

And while certain modern-day scholars have denigrated this 'open house' approach to Oxford life, it nonetheless gave great opportunities for mind broadening and self-development if one were so inclined. Many of the medical and scientific vicars whom we met in Chapter 1 had their scientific curiosity first aroused by witnessing the dissection of a criminal, a chemical experiment, plant classification, experimenting with lenses, magnets, and early electric batteries, digging up fossils or making an astronomical observation, while being 'Arts' undergraduates at Oxford and Cambridge. This laid the foundation for the lives and subsequent achievements of many of those men who would later describe themselves as 'the Revd Mr John Smith, FRS', or 'John Smith Esquire, FRS'.

While such men may not have been 'scientists' as we think of full-time, salaried scientific professionals today, they took the latest scientific ideas of their day home to their native cities, counties, Inns of Court, schools, churches, seats in Parliament or editorial desks of influential newspapers. For they were excellently placed to offer wise understanding on things pertaining to science, such as public health measures, agricultural improvement, mining and quarrying, industrial chemistry, electric telegraphy, railway safety and a host of other developments taking place in a society that was coming to involve much science and technology in its daily business. Their collective presence, moreover, demolishes the popular myth that Christian England went into shock in 1859, when Darwin published *The Origin of Species*, as supposedly up to then everybody in Great Britain firmly believed that the creation took place at 9.00 a.m. on 23 October 4004 BC, which we will discuss in subsequent chapters.

In terms of social position and attitude of mind, Buckland would have been at one with these gentlemen. The only way in which he differed from the majority of scientific vicars and county gentlemen was in his dedication and intellectual originality, and in securing salaried academic appointments in his beloved and rapidly advancing science of geology. This was wholly in the time-honoured tradition in which John Whiteside, Thomas Hornsby, Sir Christopher Pegge, Buckland's friend and older contemporary John Kidd, his contemporary Charles Daubeny and others had been appointed to Oxford chairs in chemistry, astronomy, medicine and other sciences, the generality of whom would be either in Holy Orders of the established Church, or, if medical men like Daubeny, devout Anglican laymen.

Passing the examination

In 1804, when Buckland took his BA degree, the full Honours system of classified degrees based on written examinations lay over a decade into the future. Instead, a young gentleman, while submitting some written work, would mainly be assessed orally. He would be examined *viva voce*, as his tutors and other reverend gentlemen grilled him about the prescribed classical authors, poetry, the Bible, theology, mathematics and geometry. His skill as a Latinist would be carefully assessed, as well as his

Greek, both written and oral, for they were the tongues of classical and Christian Western civilization. Cicero, Virgil, Livy, Horace and the other Roman writers gave you facility in poetics and fluent expression, while the original Christian sources and the earliest philosophy were written in Greek, which had also been the language of the pre-Christian Socrates. If a man were to be able to defend his position in public argument, he had to be able to cite, often from memory, what Socrates said in Plato's *Republic* or Virgil in the *Aeneid*, or what St Paul said to the Corinthians or Thessalonians.

Indeed, both Oxford and Cambridge were deeply oral, reading and memorizing academic cultures, and Cambridge's famous 'Tripos' examinations supposedly took their name from the three-legged stool upon which the student sat while being grilled by his tutors. In Buckland's time, academic culture was different in many ways from what it would become after the Reform Acts of the 1850s. Memory, quick verbal recall, mellifluous *spoken* as well as written Latin, mental gymnastics and a quick and ready wit were what counted.

Yet I would take issue with people today who deride this approach to both school and higher education as having no relevance to the 'real world' into which graduates would pass. For let us not forget that in William Buckland's day, an Oxbridge graduate, unless he simply intended to retire on independent means to private life, would have been a public performer. The abovementioned gentlemanly careers of the pulpit, the Parliamentary seat, the Inns of Court, the county magistrate's bench or the schoolmaster's or the professor's lectern all demanded an ability to perform in public. Verbal fluency and even fireworks were what was expected of a 'public man', be he the local vicar or the Prime Minister, for this was a universe removed from the modern culture of laptop 'presentations'. Buckland's subsequent renown as a lecturer and preacher may have drawn added lustre from his own innate charisma and extravert disposition, but such verbal facility was simply expected of a 'public man'. And if one could cite Cicero in the Latin or St Paul in the Greek, the greater the kudos accrued to a man's reputation, as one finds with Prime Ministers like William Pitt and William Gladstone, bishops such as Samuel Wilberforce and scientists like the Astronomer Royal Sir George Airy and William Buckland. (The tradition even extended well into the early twenty-first century, for I used to know an elderly Regius Professor of Medicine of great eminence, FRS and Knight, who loved to cite Horace or Virgil in the original Latin at length on High Table – a scientific 'performer' in the great tradition, proud of the thorough classical training that had preceded his world renown as a pathologist and oncologist.)

The Fellow of Corpus Christi

As we saw above, there were no 'classified' degrees in Oxford in 1804. Nonetheless, the 20-year-old Buckland was told by his College authorities that he 'had passed a most creditable examination'. Having secured an income, much, no doubt, from undergraduate teaching, William Buckland proceeded both to prepare for Holy Orders and to complete a further four years of studies to take his MA degree in 1808.

He took Holy Orders at an ordination ceremony conducted in the Chapel Royal at St James's Palace, London. In those days, however, there were no theological training colleges of the kind that came to be founded in the middle and latter part of the nineteenth century, and a young gentleman would simply tell his University of Oxford or University of Cambridge college that he intended to become first a deacon, then a priest. If his college reckoned him to be 'in good standing', a good scholar and a loyal son of the Church of England, then he was eligible to meet a bishop and receive his Orders. There were so many candidates in those days that instead of the large ordination services in a packed cathedral which we have today, it was not uncommon to use one's ecclesiastical contacts to get ordained by a friendly bishop wherever one happened to be, or at one of the Chapels Royal at St George's Windsor, Westminster Abbey and Hampton Court.

In all of the Oxbridge colleges before the Devonshire Commission's and subsequently the Ecclesiastical Commission's reforms of the 1850s and sixties, Holy Orders, at least those of a deacon, were a necessary preliminary to securing a permanent college fellowship. They would then give the reverend gentleman room and board, generally for the rest of his life, in the semi-monastic world of Oxbridge bachelor dons. Should a man later wish to marry, however, he was required by the Statutes to resign his fellowship and move out of college, and unless he had ample private means, this meant that he needed to be eligible for a college parish living somewhere in the country, a cathedral canonry or a non-residential academic professorship. In various ways, the early-middle-aged Buckland would do all of these things, for irrespective of what sum he might have inherited from the Buckland and Oke families, he would marry the daughter of a wealthy solicitor with lucrative brewery-owning connections, and hold canonical, professorial and decanal appointments, plus two country livings.

Though a naturalist from his south Devon childhood, familiar with fossils and similar curiosities, it was probably in Oxford that Buckland became a geologist proper. Here, in the relatively leisurely almost five year interval between getting his BA degree and taking his MA and getting ordained, young William Buckland immersed himself in all the life science teaching that Oxford could offer. In particular, he attended the anatomy lectures of Sir Christopher Pegge, Regius Professor of Medicine (and *de facto* guardian of his future wife, Mary Morland), and the chemical and mineralogical lectures of Dr John Kidd and others, most likely in the Anatomy School and Laboratory in the Lee Building in Christ Church, and in the Ashmolean Laboratory, as generations of young men, destined to become medical and scientific vicars, had done before him since at least the middle and late seventeenth century. I am not aware, however, of references to Buckland's attending astronomical or physics lectures in the Radcliffe Observatory and elsewhere. It was living things, especially long-dead living things, which clearly fascinated him, along with stones and chemistry.

Although an accomplished classical scholar and theologian, William Buckland was a deeply practical man, skilled with his hands and interested in how living things worked. Bones, joints, teeth, claws, digestive tracts and walking and moving postures interested him from a mechanical point of view, and this would lie at the heart of his subsequent articulations of fossil bones to enable us to see what long-extinct beasts such as his famously discovered and articulated megalosaurus looked like. As we shall see, Buckland's skills and ideas in this respect would be especially accelerated after reading the works of the Swiss-French comparative anatomist Baron Georges Cuvier, though that would be a decade into the future when the Revd Mr Buckland was a newly elected Fellow of Corpus Christi.[2]

Chemistry and mineralogy in Buckland's Oxford

But why was the University of Oxford offering classes in chemistry and mineralogy, at the hand of the young Dr John Kidd, DM, of Christ Church in the early nineteenth century, as it had in the time of Kidd's predecessor, Sir Christopher Pegge? Kidd himself would hammer home the reasons in his *An Answer to a Charge Against English Universities* (1818), where he argued that while the sciences occupied an essentially 'ancillary role' in the classical, theological and mathematical curriculum at Oxford, they imparted, as we saw above, a rounded polish to a young gentleman, equipping him for public life.

Yet in addition to being of a general cultural interest, chemistry, mineralogy and geology touched upon many important currents of ideas and activities taking place in late Georgian society, as we shall also see in Chapter 9. For one thing, coal prospecting and mining, the rapidly expanding metallurgical industry and the escalating demand for good building stone all made mineralogy important. After all, many a young Oxford or Cambridge gentleman would find such knowledge useful if he owned land under which there was coal, iron or fine limestone.

Along with the benefits accruing from mineralogy to the industrial revolution, such knowledge also pertained to the parallel revolution taking place in British agriculture, in which land drainage, soil chemistry and the recognition of the value of mineral fertilizers all played a part. It would be William Buckland, in the 1830s and 1840s, who would recognize the agricultural value of 'coprolites', or fossilized long-dead animal droppings, for in addition to giving insight into a prehistoric animal's diet and lifestyle, the ground-up phosphate-rich coprolites made excellent fertilizer for the land.

John Kidd, a devout layman and physician, further saw the strata and rock formations as providing clear indicators of the biblical Deluge, from which a clear Natural Theological lesson might be drawn.

Then hand in glove with all this, the new chemistry, in the wake of Joseph Priestley, Antoine Lavoisier, John Dalton and others, in addition to any theoretical aspects relating to atoms or 'elements', supplied valuable new techniques for the 'assay' of rocks and minerals, and the preparation of useful chemical products such as chlorine bleaching powder, fulminate explosives, improved optical glass and even pharmaceuticals.

Indeed, should an Oxford or Cambridge graduate go on to inherit broad acres, become a country vicar concerned with the profitability of his 'glebe' land, a don with college estates to manage, a City of London liveryman whose livery company owned lands across England, an MP discussing new Parliamentary Bills involving land improvement and canal or, after 1830, railway construction, a good knowledge of mineralogy and chemistry could turn out to be extremely useful. And should a clergyman rise up to become the Bishop, Dean or Chapter member of Durham Cathedral, then there was the rich profitability of the vast, extensive coal measures that riddled the diocesan estates. (One only hopes that these gentlemen, enjoying the legendary coal-rich 'golden canonries' of Durham, gave something back to the poor men, women and children who dug out the lucrative mineral for them.)

Buckland the geological inspiration

During 1804–1808, when preparing for ordination and taking his MA degree – the degree which then, as now, gives full senior status to members of the University of Oxford – Buckland was not only attending Kidd's and Pegge's lectures in mineralogy, chemistry and anatomy, but revelling in the delights of hands-on fieldwork. Oxford is blessed with an abundance of excellent building and other stone within manageable walking or riding distance, and one is sometimes surprised at the energy of these men, who might think nothing of a five-, six-, or twelve-mile walk in an afternoon to visit quarries and other geological sites at Shotover, Headington and beyond.

William Buckland, by 1812 or so, was emerging as the charismatic leader of the geological pack, and he and his friends William J. Broderip and the London and Devonshire brothers William Daniel and John Josias Conybeare would undertake geological marathons. Always willing to learn at first hand, Buckland's friendly and humorous personality enabled him to have easy conversations with quarry workmen, who had an intimate knowledge of the stones and the lie of their local land. There were also the curious quarrymen's tales that the friends picked up, such as the one about 'toad holes' in the rock. Sometimes, it was said, a quarry worker would be excavating a stone block when, all of a sudden, a live toad would leap out of a cavity in the virgin rock. Could these toads have been trapped by the waters of Noah's Flood, their mud solidifying to stone, and the toads going into deep hibernation – as toads were supposedly able to do? Then all of a sudden, in *c.*1810 when the rock was being quarried, the toad awoke after a 5,000-year sleep, and leapt out!

Many years later, Buckland attempted to test this reputed hibernation of toads experimentally and had toad-sized holes cut into a block of stone, into which he inserted living toads. They were sealed in and left for a duration. But when the block was opened, all the poor toads, alas, were found to be long since dead. Yet at least, if it were any compensation, they died in the cause of science. The 'toad stone' block, with its holes, is still preserved in the garden of the Canon's House on the northwest range of Tom Quad, Christ Church, Oxford, where Buckland and his wife, Mary, would live between 1825 and 1845, as we shall see shortly. The Canon's house has, since the late nineteenth century, been the official residence of the Archdeacon of Oxford, in whose garden I inspected Buckland's experimental 'toad stone', mercifully unoccupied by modern-day toads.

After 1805 or so, Buckland would use the long summer Oxford vacations to make lengthy and detailed geological tours of Britain and northern Europe, often with friends like Broderip and the Conybeare brothers. And in an age of rattling stagecoaches, horses and marathon walks, they must have demanded immense physical stamina, for field geology was not for delicate souls. It could also be physically dangerous: hammering hard rocks with a geological hammer could lead to eye damage from flying splinters and sparks struck from the rock. In a letter to his friend Lady Mary Cole, for example, Buckland told of a recent incident occurring while he was geologizing near Sidmouth in his native West Country, when an 'ignited spark' flew from his geological hammer and lodged in his eye. The pain and discomfort increased when the iron fragment began to oxidize, reacting with the eye's moisture, rendering it impossible for him to read or write.

Luckily, Buckland was introduced to an eye surgeon in Exeter who skilfully removed the metallic fragment. From him, Buckland gained a piece of medical information of which, quite surprisingly, he had been hitherto ignorant, although it was already well established in surgical practice; for the doctor placed a leaf of the belladonna plant (rich in the drug atropine) upon his injured eye prior to commencing the operation. This produced 'a great expansion of the pupil and iris' and made the internal structure of the eye easier for the surgeon to see. The surgeon told Buckland that it was already used in cataract surgery.[3] Buckland's friend and Cambridge 'opposite number', the Revd Adam Sedgwick, Woodwardian Professor of Geology, would also on one occasion suffer eye damage from a flying rocky fragment.

One man whose ideas profoundly influenced William Buckland was William Smith, a self-made genius, who had become fascinated by the mineralogy of certain strata. His studies would prove pivotal in the future of palaeontology and make him famous. We will be meeting Dr William Smith, DCL, Oxon., in the following chapters.

Over the years following his election to his Corpus Christi College Fellowship, Buckland's reputation both within the University of Oxford and across the wider community blossomed. His rooms in College became, in effect, the first museum of natural history in Oxford, and several visitors, such as his lifelong friend Sir Roderick Murchison, later recorded what greeted them when visiting Buckland there. Bones, fossils, mineral specimens and all manner of geological clutter were to be found, with Buckland himself 'looking like a necromancer sitting in one rickety chair not covered with some fossils, and cleaning out a fossil from its matrix.'[4] He became an expert in cleaning up fossils, knowing exactly what detritus to scrape away and how to get to the authentic bones before attempting to articulate them.

Yet central to Buckland's success as a geological and palaeontological pioneer was not only his scientific genius but also a personality that captivated people. Then in 1813 Buckland succeeded Kidd to become Oxford University Reader in Mineralogy. While John Kidd had lectured in mineralogy as an aspect of chemistry, Buckland played a central role in turning it into a science in its own right, and in developing the new science of palaeontology, where fossils might be used to construct a timeline, or history, of organic life development on earth. He discusses this in detail in his professorial Inaugural Lecture, '*Vindiciae Geologicae*, or the Connexion of Geology with Religion Explained' (1819), which, in many ways, inaugurated what would come to be seen as the 'Oxford School' of geology.

But we will return to this, especially in Chapters 4 and 5, when we examine the origins of fossil-based stratigraphic geology, based upon the Flood of Noah and other deluges. We must now, however, go back in time from Buckland's day to look at how earlier pioneers of geology framed their ideas about global history, between the Genesis creation *ex nihilo* and the days of Adam and Eve and beyond.

Chapter 3
Rocks and Ages

There is a persistent modern-day myth that before Darwin, or perhaps before Buckland 40-odd years earlier, it was universally believed at all levels of society that everything that existed came into being in 4004 BC, and that the first five days of creation encompassed the origins of everything, from the separation of light from darkness to the creation of plants and then animals. Then on the sixth day, God created 'man in his own image', Adam, and Eve, before resting on the seventh day. I have already provided some discussion of this circumstance in my *Slaying the Dragons*[1] and elsewhere, but as it is so fundamental to understanding William Buckland, his life, historical context, science and theology, I explore the topic in more detail here.

Dating the creation to 23 October 4004 BC

James Ussher, Archbishop of Armagh, is often cited as the man who defined this orthodoxy in his monumental *Annales Veteris Testamenti* (*Chronology of the Old Testament*: 1650) and subsequent works up to 1655, but this is an exaggeration. Ussher, far from being the simplistic father of modern fundamentalism that some like to claim, was a scholar of formidable Europe-wide reputation, who claimed to read and speak no fewer than 13 languages, living and dead. He was continuing a Renaissance scholarly tradition, which was a million miles away from simple fundamentalism, and walked in the footsteps of people like Philo of Alexandria and Joseph Justus Scaliger. They were not interested in geology or mineralogy, but in purely human ancient chronologies, and a 'naturalistic' understanding of the earth as a physical body was quite plainly *not* their concern. Instead, they were trying to date key events in ancient human history. For instance, how many years before the birth of Christ were the Jews carried away into the Babylonian captivity by Nebuchadnezzar? What were the dates of Solomon's temple, and of Moses, Abraham and the Old Testament patriarchs? Ussher used a sophisticated – for the 1650s – technique of trying to cross-date biblical events in Greek authors such as Homer and Herodotus.

Ussher's vast linguistic competence gave him access to Syriac, Aramaic, Hebrew, Arabic and other literary traditions as well, so that he could also attempt to cross-date biblical events from incidents recorded in other Middle Eastern literature. By the seventeenth century, European scholars travelling in the Levant and related lands were discovering manuscripts hitherto unknown in Europe, many of which were being translated into Latin, the *lingua franca* of European scholarship. As we have seen, this linguistic accomplishment still lay at the heart of a learned education in Buckland's time, hence the abundance of Latin and Greek in the undergraduate curriculum of 1800.

'A thousand years in thy sight are but as yesterday' (Psalm 90.4)

Renaissance scholars delighted in linguistic and numerological puzzles. When would the millennium, Armageddon or the end of time come? It had been widely expected in AD 1500: when the powerful pentagonal number five was multiplied by the Three in One of the Holy Trinity, one obtained 1500. Then, when 1500 passed without incident, what about 1533, for had not Jesus Christ died and been resurrected in his thirty-third year? Then what about the hidden meaning behind the prophet Daniel's visions of the contest between the Ram and the Goat? What, moreover, was the numerological significance of the Ram's and the Goat's horns, and what forthcoming events did they signify? Topping it all were St John the Divine's exotic visions on Patmos, with their complex cycles of years and days, the Number of the Beast, 666, and the Whore of Babylon, followed by the First and Second Judgements, and culminating in the descent from heaven of the crystalline New Jerusalem, as narrated in the Holy Bible's final book of Revelation.

All these visions and prophecies were taken in deadly earnest by Renaissance theologians and scholars, for they were about beginnings and endings of time itself, and God in his providence had supplied keys by which mankind might unlock and reveal these mysteries. Many Catholics and Protestants believed that the worldly creations, including men and women, were destined to last six thousand years, because if you multiplied the six days of creation by Psalm 90.4's 'For a thousand years in thy sight are but as yesterday', then it was clear for all to see. It was also held by most scholars that the world was about 4,000 years old at the time of Christ's incarnation, but there was considerable variance between the number-reckonings of different chronologists. For example, scholars who worked from the Jewish Septuagint Old Testament narrative often derived slightly different numbers from those who worked from the older Hebrew texts. Yet all must end after 6,000 years had elapsed – the real puzzle lying in calculating exactly where we were, and how close to the end, in 1600 or so.

When these essentially 'internalist' biblical texts were correlated with Greek, Syriac or Arabic narratives, by Ussher and other chronologists, one can understand that their dating enterprise, far from being simplistic or superstitious, lay at the cutting edge of scholarship in 1600 and for quite some time thereafter. This is how either Ussher, or later scholars who ransacked these chronologies, came up with the figure of 22–23 October 4004 BC for the creation date. It was a piece of highly sophisticated chronological arithmetic concerning God and his human creation, but it had nothing to do with planets, fossils, optics or what would later be called physical science. One thing that did help to enshrine 4004 BC in a genre of Protestant orthodoxy, however, was the practice of English-language Bible printers who began to place Ussher's dates in the margins of their editions of the Authorized Version, or King James Version, of 1611. Hence, a chronological myth was born: that the Church endorsed the 4004 BC creation *ex nihilo* date, and that all good Protestant Christians should do likewise.

Geology, not literary chronology

Even in Ussher's lifetime, however, there were men in Europe who were beginning to look at the earth from a different perspective: one founded not upon finding keys to ancient numerological mysteries, but on observing and trying to interpret natural phenomena. Since the first bold oceanic voyages of discovery, after *c*.1470, the surface of our planet was revealing itself to be fundamentally different from that described in Ptolemy's *Geography* of *c*. AD 150. No educated person in 1500 believed the earth to be flat (the flat earth was a myth popularized by Washington Irving in his heroic life of Christopher Columbus in 1828), but Ptolemy had taught there was more land than water on the earth's spherical surface. Yet the discovery of the Pacific Ocean, the American continent and other natural wonders had shown that physical, hands-on experience was more reliable than ancient narratives when it came to making sense of planet earth.

Then in addition to the continents themselves, explorers were discovering meteorological systems such as Caribbean hurricanes, violent earthquakes in the Andes, powerful ocean currents, volcano chains in Indonesia and the strange global behaviour of the magnetic compass needle, which in some distant places did not point to the north. All this was already going on before Scaliger and Ussher were born, and indicated the emergence of a new approach to understanding natural phenomena that went beyond the mathematical, logical, Aristotelian science of Europe's medieval universities. England's Royal Society, along with savants in Paris, Bologna and Leiden, came to adopt this new observational and experimental approach to nature by 1660, and Dr Robert Hooke was one of the earliest to apply it to 'earth-forming' processes, or geology. Between 1667–1668 and 1700, Hooke delivered a series of 27 'Lectures and Discourses of Earthquakes' to the Royal Society, which were subsequently published. The audience over these years was rich in scientifically-minded clergymen and even included several bishops: gentlemen who were looking beyond ancient manuscripts and encrypted prophecies as a way of comprehending the natural world and humanity's natural and spiritual condition – to the beginnings of Natural Theology. We will return to the Royal Society and its achievement in Chapter 7.

Dr Robert Hooke: earthquakes, fossils and continents

In many respects, Robert Hooke was William Buckland's intellectual and geological grandfather. As with Buckland 160 years later, Hooke was not a chronologist or one who sought insights into the earth's past from ancient writings, but rather from physical evidences: rocks, sea levels, strata, fossils, earthquakes and volcanoes. As a Westminster School and Christ Church, Oxford, trained scholar, however, he was fully familiar with Latin and Greek literature, such as Flood narratives in Plato. His interests were neither arcane nor esoteric: the literary sources which interested him were those narrating specific events, such as the accounts of volcanic eruptions and other natural phenomena recorded in Pliny and other early natural science writers. He was also fascinated by recent Jesuit missionary and other translations of Chinese annals which spoke of cycles of ages covering hundreds of thousands of years, and he tells us that 'the Chinese do make the world 88,640,000 years old'.[2]

Hooke, the son of a clergyman, had been born in 1635 at Freshwater, Isle of Wight, which, 60 miles further east than Lyme Regis, was still part of that same geologically rich coast that helped inspire the young Buckland (later styled the Jurassic Coast). Unlike Buckland, however, Hooke was not a naturalist by inclination, so much as a physicist. Life forms in themselves were less of a fascination to him than were the physical forces that built and constantly modified the earth, and his interest in fossils lay in their significance as potential indicators of ancient anatomical function rather than as diverse manifestations of life. Hooke was more of a geophysicist than a geologist, yet the insights which he drew and developed over four decades were truly remarkable. He pointed out, for instance, that the fossil and shell beds of the western tip of the Isle of Wight, around and to the north of Freshwater Bay, contained similar anatomical specimens to those found near Hurst Castle on the Dorset mainland, across the Solent. Could the Isle of Wight have once been joined on to the Dorset coast? If so, when had it collapsed into the sea, and why did not the most ancient historical sources record the event? The Isle also bore clear traces of drastic sea-level changes, sometimes leaving shell deposits – which must once have been on the seabed – entombed in the rock scores of feet above the present high-water mark.

Hooke studied fossilized giant ammonite shells – *Cornua Ammonis* – from rock strata around the English Channel, and some as large as coach wheels found near Bristol. They were clearly not 'sports of nature', or twirls in the rock, as some suggested. When he had a stonecutter slice them in two longitudinally down the edge, their interiors were found to be beautifully multi-chambered, just like the interiors of smaller living shells. The giant ammonites had clearly once been living things and had become extinct. Hooke was one of the very first scientists to recognize the extinction of ancient species, and to publish detailed descriptions and engravings of them.

While one could perhaps try to reconcile earthquakes and such findings with the global disruption implicit in Noah's Flood, Hooke clearly thought in terms of vastly greater timescales.[3] In his lecture delivered to the Royal Society on 26 January 1687, he proposed what was probably the first 'naturalistic' mechanism for global change in scientific history, when he suggested that, in the earth's constant encircling of the sun through vast ages, the terrestrial poles gradually wandered, or rolled about, causing latitudes and longitudes on earth to gradually change with reference to the astronomical pole. Consequently, our present continents and oceans doubtless changed as well, causing seabeds to rise, mountains to be inundated, and coastal boundaries to alter. While the Noachian Flood was no doubt a part of this process, the clear message coming from the Earthquake Discourses was that there had been numerous other such deluges, extending back many aeons of time, between the divine creation *ex nihilo* and the 4004 BC creation of the present world and its human inhabitants, as narrated in Genesis. As we shall see, Buckland's wider geological explanatory rationale would be accommodated within a similar unlimited timespan between the creation *ex nihilo* and the Garden of Eden.

Dr Edmond Halley and cometary 'shocks' shaping the earth

Hooke's younger contemporary Dr Edmond Halley, of comet fame, would also come to develop a similar model in the 1680s and 1690s. In many ways, he built upon Hooke's ideas. A pioneer of global meteorological and geomagnetic research, Halley was clearly thinking in terms of vast, pre-Edenic timescales. Comets were objects of great contemporary concern to astronomers in the 1680s and 1690s, especially in the wake of the detailed treatment they received from Sir Isaac Newton in *Principia* (1687), and were believed to be large, rocky, world-like objects, sometimes moving in very eccentric orbits. So, was it possible that in the pre-human past, comets had struck the earth, destabilizing it in its orbit, and leaving great scars on the surface, before bouncing off into space? The Caspian Sea, in western Asia, was believed by Halley to be just one such scar. He also saw this as fitting into his model for the saltiness of the oceans, for why were some vast lakes on the earth's surface, such as the Caspian Sea and Lake Titicaca in the Peruvian Andes, full of sweet fresh water, while the oceans were salty? Were they much more recent bodies of water than the oceans, and had their feeder rivers not yet been flowing for long enough to build up a significant salinity? Might it not be possible, he suggested, to ascertain some idea of the age of the earth by regularly measuring the presumed increasing saltiness of the seas?[4]

And why, asked Halley in 1715, was Hudson's Bay, Canada, so bitterly cold, despite being on the same latitude as England, with its temperate climate?[5] Could it be that in pre-Edenic times, what would become England and northern Europe were much further south in latitude, and that modern-day Hudson's Bay had then been in the Arctic polar regions? Could a comet have dealt the earth a glancing blow, knocking it over in its orbit, making a new north polar region, with northern Europe several degrees further north, and the old north polar region becoming Canada? Was this new Canadian region still semi-frozen, hence its much greater coldness than Great Britain?

After its foundation in 1660, the Royal Society began to collect and collate all manner of data about the distant regions of the earth, as supplied by returning sea captains and other travellers. Both Hooke and Halley readily availed themselves of this data from the Royal Society's growing archives, and data acquired from elsewhere in Europe. Halley then went on to do some arithmetic regarding tropical storm measurements. If, for example, it rained globally for 40 days and 40 nights at the same intensity as the most violent tropical storm then on record, how deep would the ensuing water envelope surrounding the earth be? A mere 132 feet, in fact! While this might have been sufficient to inundate the flat lands of Mesopotamia, it would have made little impression upon all the mountains and even the high ground on our planet.

In the 1690s, Edmond Halley and his Cambridge colleague William Whiston (who became Newton's professorial successor at Trinity College) even discussed whether cometary tails might be composed of frozen water vapour, which thawed as the comet approached the sun. So, might the earth passing through a watery cometary tail have occasioned Noah's Deluge in Genesis 6–8? Such a naturalistic mechanism need not in any way undermine the genuinely divine providential purpose of the Flood, although it gives us an insight into the way that 'natural philosophers' were thinking for well over a century before William Buckland became a Fellow of Corpus Christi College. It is also important to recognize that none of this work was done in secret, for it was presented before the Royal Society and published in its prestigious and internationally circulated *Philosophical Transactions*, and in other high-profile and internationally distinguished published works.

Great balls of fire: Comte de Buffon and the cooling earth

The essentially mineralogical and geophysical tradition of earth studies before Buckland's time was continued in the remarkable experiments of Georges-Louis Leclerc, Comte de Buffon. While Hooke, Halley and others had accepted that a vast period of time had elapsed between the creation *ex nihilo* and Eden, no one – perhaps with the exception of Halley with his suggested accumulative sea saltiness proposal – had any idea how one might devise a naturalistic chronometer, by which one might calculate the age of the earth from measurable physical criteria. Working on the idea that the earth had originated by being ejected from the sun in the remote past (as his fellow-countryman Pierre-Simon Laplace would also propose in 1796), Buffon surmised that the young earth, being a largely metallic world in its chemical composition, would have begun its existence in a white-hot or semi-molten condition.

In his *Introduction À l'Histoire Des Minéraux* ('Introduction to the History of Minerals': 1775), Buffon relates the details of an experiment which he devised. He took ten iron cannon balls of different sizes and heated them to just below melting point in a furnace. He then timed how long it took for them to cool to a temperature where they could be touched without burning the hand, and then to cool to room temperature. Next he compared the internal volume of each sphere to the already well-known size and volume of the earth, and thus tried to calculate how long a once white-hot earth, freshly hurled into space from the sun, would take before life was possible upon it. His different sphere sizes gave a predictable spectrum of figures, yet they averaged out to around 70,000–75,000 years. While Buffon was in no way involved with Natural Theology or any sort of physical-scriptural reconciliation, one might choose to suggest that 75,000 years or more might have elapsed between the creation *ex nihilo* and the Garden of Eden.[6] As far as I am aware, Buffon's represents the first naturalistic chronometer experiment performed to ascertain the age of our planet. Halley had suggested from his saltiness of the seas studies in 1715 that we might discover a figure if we started carefully measuring increased oceanic salinity over several centuries, but he never conducted such an experiment, nor did he ever propose a figure.

From Freiburg to Edinburgh and the 'new' mineralogy of James Hutton and Abraham Werner

Edinburgh became a leading centre of geological thought and speculation during Buckland's early days. In particular, the writings and observations of two men became the foci for two distinct and fundamentally different approaches to earth history. These were represented by the home-grown Scottish Vulcanists or Plutonists, in the wake of Dr James Hutton, the Edinburgh chemist, mineralogist and reluctant medical doctor who did not care for seeing patients, and the Neptunists, in the wake of the mining and mineralogy Professor Abraham Gottlob Werner, from Freiburg, Germany.

Dr James Hutton

Dr James Hutton was an Edinburgh Scot, born into a mercantile family in 1726. An Edinburgh University graduate, he abandoned studies for his first career, the law, then took an MD degree at Leiden in Holland. What drew him to a medical degree, however, was not a desire to practise medicine, but the excellent training in chemistry and anatomy, which were integral parts of a medical training. Having made a lot of money by the manufacture of industrial chemicals, investing the proceeds in profitable farmlands from which he drew the rentals, Hutton had an ample private income, enabling him to devote his time to his passions: chemistry and mineralogy.

Generally speaking, the theories of the earth and its mineral origin in Hutton's time tended to focus upon the cataclysmic, in which the finger of God, colliding comets, rolling poles, sudden earthquakes or violent volcanic convulsions produced sudden changes to the terrestrial surface. But this is not how he was coming to interpret mineralogical phenomena. He was impressed by the ineffably slow gradualism of earth-forming processes. Instead of talking of theoretical cataclysms in the remote past, he became the prophet of that geological school which stressed only 'causes now in operation' as lying at the root of everything. These included 'normal' tectonic trembles, such as an Italian volcanic eruption or a Caribbean or Peruvian earthquake, which, though they might be terrible in their destructive consequences to the people who suffered them locally, had no wider global significance. Likewise, storms, wind, rain and erosion would gradually wear away the hardest rocks and redeposit their chemical contents on the seabed, to be gradually transformed into limestone or sandstone through mechanical pressure and the earth's slow, baking internal heat.

Hutton would play a major role in geological history, introducing and affirming two key ingredients in the subsequent development of the science. The first was a principle of 'uniformitarianism' (not to be confused with the religious denomination Unitarianism), or the principle of 'causes now in operation' since the remotest times, with no need for dramatic cataclysms. In the process of eternal, gentle change going on within the earth, its internal heat slowly baked and fused the granitic, flint, and crystalline rocks into hard masses of the kind found everywhere in the geology of Scotland and the world's great mountain ranges. Eventually, wind and rain would wash them away to form sands, then softer sedimentary rocks, which could in turn be baked into hard crystalline masses – and so on *ad infinitum*.

The second was the earth's relentless internal heat, which caused even the hardest rocks to slowly fuse, buckle and form synclinal and anticlinal strata. Hutton drew heavily on the geology of Scotland, whose gaunt, granite Highland mountains must be the remnants of long-past volcanic and geological activity, though now they were quiet, solid and seemingly eternal in their stability. Were the Salisbury Crags and Arthur's Seat to the southeast of the city of Edinburgh the remnants of once mighty volcanoes, only the basalt and dolerite plugs of which now survived? Had countless ages of wind and rain worn them down once the local subterranean heat and pressure had subsided?

Hutton's monumental two-volume *Theory of the Earth* (Edinburgh, 1795) and its preceding papers in the *Transactions of the Royal Society of Edinburgh* presented the picture of a timeless earth '. . . with no vestige of a beginning – no prospect of an end'. It was a geological vision which – unlike Buffon's cannon ball experiments – offered no prospect of dating creation, and was based on fundamentally different criteria from those of the fossil geologists, with their concern with deluges, strata and organic progression from primitive forms to dinosaurs, through a series of catastrophes which prepared the earth for Eden and human and biblical history. William Buckland was fully familiar with the Edinburgh School of geology, but he did not accept its wider premises, though he made use of some of its observations when relevant. Hutton, however, helped to frame the geological ideas of Sir Charles Lyell during the late 1820s, whose *Principles of Geology* in three volumes after 1831 would re-establish the uniformitarian principle, though in Lyell's case, with an emphasis placed upon fossil geology. Lyell's vision of a stable, non-cataclysmic earth in turn came to influence Charles Darwin in the course of the nineteenth century, some years after Buckland's death.

Professor Abraham Gottlob Werner

Werner was born in Wehrau, now Poland, some 24 years after Hutton, and spent his entire professional life in what was then Germany. But his reputation was in many ways to reach its apogee in Edinburgh, where he and Hutton came to epitomize the opposite ends of the Edinburgh School of mineralogy and geology. Hutton, with his emphasis on the earth's internal heat, became the icon of the Vulcanist or Plutonist School, while Werner, with his stress on a vast deluge being responsible for creating all the rocks and strata, was the icon of the Neptunists. Between them, they had created the 'Fire and Water' Schools of Edinburgh geology by 1810. Werner's came from a region of Europe where metal mining was a major industry, and he became Professor at the Freiburg Mining Academy. Serious academic interest in rocks, metals and mining ran deep in Germanic culture, and Dr Georg Bauer's (pseudonym Georgius Agricola) *De Re Metallica* ('On Metals and Metallurgy': 1556) discussed and richly illustrated mines, mining methods and even the occupational diseases of mine workers. (The miners depicted in Agricola's detailed illustrations, generally stunted in size and wearing high stuffed caps to prevent them injuring their heads in the narrow underground galleries, look astonishingly like the miners in the Disney version of *Snow White and the Seven Dwarfs*.)

Central to Werner's hypothesis was a great, world-transforming deluge. This was not axiomatically seen as synonymous with the Genesis Flood of Noah (which would be fundamental to the early ideas of Buckland and the Oxford School of geology, which we will discuss anon), but something much further back in time – a deluge so great that mountains would be washed away and continents turned to murky silt. This hypothetical circumstance supplied the basis for Werner's geological model. As things settled down after the turbulence of the global deluge, he hypothesized, and the waters dried up, the swirling detritus formed five distinct sedimentary layers. The first, and heaviest, layer at the bottom became the granite, gneiss, flint, schist and similar hard crystalline rocks. The second consisted of shales, greywacke and fish fossils, and was styled the 'transitional'. Third came the limestones, sandstones and chalks, or the 'secondary' rocks. Fourth came the gravel, sand and loose alluvial strata;

and fifth, after the disappearance of the last aquatic remnants of the deluge, the volcanic lavas.

While this fivefold schema went a long way towards explaining the geology of Werner's Saxony, it failed to offer explanations for many other regions of Europe – let alone the wider world. Nor did he have any real explanation of where this prodigious volume of water came from, or where it eventually went, leaving only our familiar oceans behind. Also problematic for his theory were the large bodies of basalt rocks found in various parts of Europe, which did not appear to be near sites of volcanic activity. As more and more primary geological data poured in, from Europe, North and South America and India in particular, the harder it became to reconcile it with Wernerian diluvialism. On the other hand, while the idea of a 4004 BC creation *ex nihilo* was far from universally accepted, one could somehow try to square Werner's hypothetical deluge with that of Noah, as we shall see in Chapter 11 with the nineteenth-century scriptural geologists. One might, for example, as some of the scriptural geologists attempted to do, see the six days of the Genesis narrative not as normal days of 24 hours' duration, but as 'long days', perhaps many thousands of terrestrial earth days long apiece – as six vast epochs known only to the mind of God. But as geological data rapidly accumulated by the middle years of the nineteenth century, it was found that the earth's long and complex history could not be compressed into six convenient units of time.

The Oxford School of geology

This is where things stood, broadly speaking, when a group of geological friends came together in London to form the Geological Society in 1807. Geological opinions were diverse, and often associated with the Edinburgh and other Schools. Yet the approach of John Kidd and the young William Buckland came from an essentially different direction, and would constitute what would be seen as the Oxford School of geology. It was less concerned with theoretical global phenomena, or fundamental forces, such as internal heat. It was organic rather than mineralogical in its priorities, being more interested in extinct organic forms, their anatomy, diet and habitat, found in the fossil-bearing strata.

It was, in many respects, also much more pragmatic, dealing with what one might excavate in a specific locality rather than modelling a universal earth history from first principles. What was particularly important to the Oxford School, however, was not just the fossils in themselves, but their anatomy. How did skeletons, joints and teeth fit together, and how might one articulate fossil bones to gain a clear picture of the once-living creature – as Buckland famously did with his megalosaurus?[7] To what extent could these articulated fishes and reptiles tell us something about the direction, or *progress*, of living forms over vast aeons of time? What, moreover, could they tell us about ancient seas and climatic features, when one could excavate the fossilized remains of ancient extinct fishes in Oxfordshire quarries and luxuriant fossil ferns in the coal measures, suggesting that chilly present-day south Wales, south Lancashire and Northumberland had once been covered with dense tropical vegetation?

In this Romantic Age, with its stress on feeling, wonder and overpowering beauty, what could be more mind-blowing than the discoveries of the geologists? We will return to this in Chapter 9. This approach to geology fitted in nicely with the English love of country sports, hunting, long walks, farming and all things rural: things that were bred into Buckland's very bones, yet which had a following across all social classes, from the squire on his horse to the Lancashire and Yorkshire mill workers' Sunday afternoon treks to the Pennine slopes in search of novel plants.

Of central importance to the ideas of Buckland and his friends was the work of an older French contemporary, Georges Cuvier, whose researches from the 1790s onwards would lay the foundations of much subsequent natural history. Among his many achievements, three of his realizations would lie at the heart of Buckland's thinking and that of the Oxford School, and of subsequent progress in geology. They were (1) the interpretative significance of the anatomy, structure and functions of fossils parts and their parallels to living species; (2) that species extinction had been the norm across geological history; and (3) that the earth's surface had undergone many radical changes, or catastrophes, across vast aeons of time. These wiped out whole species of creatures, entombed them in the rock and made room for the appearance of newer and anatomically more advanced life forms.

Buckland and the Oxford School would be deeply influenced by Cuvier's ideas and insights, as we shall see. Yet one thing that was especially appealing to them was the potential for tracing the hand of God in Cuvier's model of earth history. This was by no means a simple biblical literalism, but rather a genuinely perceived connection. Unlike the uniformitarianism of the Scottish Vulcanists, with its no discernible beginning or end, or the great primal ocean preceding Noah's Deluge of Werner, Cuvier's model of earth history was much more theistic, and suggestive of a developmental grand plan for creation, extending from the simplest shells to the large lizards and beyond. And if the catastrophes rendered extinct earlier lower forms, then in due process of time the guiding hand of God restocked our planet with a higher set of forms – on and on, until one reached the Garden of Eden. Anatomy, William Smith's stratigraphy, extinction and *non*-evolutionary progress and direction were all combined with Cuvier's providential hand of God in nature, in Buckland's and the Oxford School's understanding of ancient natural history. This understanding attained particular academic consolidation after Buckland succeeded John Kidd to the Oxford mineralogy chair in 1813, and even more so when he became the first incumbent of the new Readership in Geology in 1819.

Chapter 4

Geology Vindicated and Noah's Flood Comes to Yorkshire

By the time that William Buckland was appointed to the new Readership, he had already established his reputation as Britain's most famous geologist. He had done this partly on the strength of his discoveries in the field and his drawing upon the stratigraphic techniques of William Smith and the anatomical ideas and methods of Georges Cuvier. These ideas, despite Britain's long war with France up to 1815, still came relatively easily into England, as savants on both sides of the English Channel often kept in touch with each other's work. In addition to his discoveries, Buckland possessed other, less easily defined yet very real gifts, such as great personal charm and charisma, an ability to make friends easily, a fluency with words, and a strong and distinctly eccentric sense of humour. All came together to form the brilliant teacher that he rapidly became. His style and character captivated far more people than they put off, although his appeal rarely extended to those of a highly serious disposition. Persons of this turn, moreover, were not uncommon in the Church and in the universities, where a stiff dignity was often the approved style. The Revd Dr Thomas Gaisford, Canon and later Dean of Christ Church, Oxford, might sometimes have found Buckland somewhat difficult, while the young Charles Darwin (born 1809) recorded that while he found Buckland 'good humoured and good natured' he also found him 'a vulgar and almost coarse man' and 'craving for notoriety which made him sometimes act [more] like a buffoon than a man of science'.[1] This derived, perhaps, from Darwin's own introverted temperament and delicate constitution, especially after his return from the *Beagle* voyage in 1836.

On the other hand, Buckland's charm, erudition and love of fun made him an entertaining man to be around if one were not unduly professionally serious or over-delicate. His social range spanned much of Regency society – from the Prince Regent, who had endowed his Regius Readership in Geology in 1819, to members of the aristocracy, and so on downwards. The future Prime Minister, Sir Robert Peel, was another admirer and warm friend, and both the Prince Regent and Peel, in their respective times, would help advance his career, from his Readership, to his Christ Church Canonry in Oxford in 1825, and then, in 1845, to his prestigious appointment to the Deanery of Westminster. As a university teacher, Buckland's success was great, and quite apart from the generality of future geological vicars and bishops who attended his lectures over 35 years, it would be hard to find a professional academic geologist of the next couple of generations who had not been inspired by him, even if they later rejected particular aspects of his ideas. One such admirer, who came up to Oxford in 1857, the year after Buckland's death, was William Boyd Dawkins. He would later affirm Buckland's posthumous reputation, in the insightful essay that he contributed to Buckland's *Life*, compiled and written by his daughter Elizabeth in 1894. We will return to Dawkins at the end of Chapter 14.[2]

Vindiciae Geologicae: geology defended and vindicated, 1819

Buckland had spelled out his geological credo in his inaugural lecture as the new Regius Reader in Geology at Oxford University. This was his published *Vindiciae Geologicae* ('The Vindication of Geology': 1819), in which he laid out his vision of geology, its relation to the other sciences, classical learning and theology. It would also in many respects constitute the vision of the Oxford School of geology.

Quite apart from its geology, the *Vindiciae* tells us much about Buckland the man and his approach to life, culture and the world in general. He begins by giving his fulsome thanks to the Prince Regent, (crowned King George IV in 1820, following the death of his father King George III) for the creation of the new Oxford Readership, and the clear recognition of geology as a valuable and economically useful discipline. He also thanks other influential individuals who had supported him, before driving home the value, beauty and compatibility of geology as a science, as wholly in keeping with Oxford's rich intellectual tradition. He next proceeds to emphasize the compatibility of geology with Oxford's already established and renowned excellence in classical studies. In no way does he wish to challenge Oxford's existing curriculum, stressing that he is not advocating scientific or specialist degrees, for Latin, Greek and mathematics must remain at the heart of a young gentleman's education. Without being explicit, he must have been aware of the difference between the classics and geology as instruments for cultivating the intellect, for a study of the ancient tongues and their literary culture, along with mathematics, geometry and logic, taught a gentleman (as we saw in Chapter 2) to think and express himself with clarity and precision. A clumsy sentence, a weak argument or an inability to work one's way logically through the 150 Theorems in Euclid's Geometry would make one a liability in public life, whether in Parliament, the law courts or the pulpit. And most Oxbridge graduates in 1819 would enter public life in one way or another, be it as a squire presiding in the local magistrate's court or the Archbishop of Canterbury addressing the House of Lords on some matter of national importance.

As Buckland was aware, however, geology in itself could not impart any of these skills, being based on visual comparisons and attempting to make sense of scores of scattered fragments of minerals, fossils and aquatic phenomena dug out of the earth. Unlike astronomy, for example, in which Oxford had a long-established professor (1619) and the world-class Radcliffe Observatory (1772), mineralogy and geology had no absolute standards: no 360° circle, and no Kepler's or Newton's laws against which to cross-check their findings. Even chemistry, which had a long-standing Oxford association, was fast acquiring predictability and precision with Lavoisier's chemical elements (1780), Dalton's atomic theory (1804) and the electrolytic analysis of water, salt and saltpetre; while anatomy had a venerable and unbroken classical and modern lineage that took it back through Hunter, Harvey and Vesalius to Hippocrates. But how could rocks and fossils help form a young gentleman's mind?

As a discipline in its own right in 1819, Buckland was of the opinion that it could not. What it could do, though, was provide a vital ancillary service by which a classically trained mind might be broadened further through natural knowledge. In *Vindiciae*, Buckland is also at pains to emphasize that geology and mineralogy are useful subjects, with direct connections to chemistry, agriculture and other sciences, for different minerals in given locations resulted in different soil types and agricultural resources. As we have seen, in an age when most land-owning gentlemen, Oxbridge Colleges, the Church and other bodies derived the greater part of their incomes from the land, geology possessed an obvious economic significance, from helping to improve the fertility of the soil by the spreading of pulverized, phosphate-rich coprolites to the location of new coal seams.

Buckland, however, sees the greatest value of geology and mineralogy as broadening and confirming humanity's understanding of God and his purposes, for central to his thinking is the Argument from Design and Natural Theology. Confuting those theologians who held that geology undermined religion by upsetting the simple narrative of the Genesis creation story, he argues that geology confirms, deepens, broadens and glorifies the divine narrative, to show us wonders omitted from the biblical story. Does not geology, as do the other sciences, proclaim the providence and goodness of God towards his human creation? Rock faulting, for example, exposes useful minerals in the earth's crust, while the coal measures, salt, and metals (upon which Britain was becoming increasingly dependent in the new industrial age) were conveniently close to the surface, enabling them to be mined. This was established Natural Theology, extending back in its argument to John Ray's *The Wisdom of God Manifested in the Works of the Creation* (1691). As part of his wider defence of the natural theological potency of geology to proclaim the divine hand, Buckland takes issue with the eminent Glasgow divine, the Revd Dr Thomas Chalmers, who had said that geology could lead to scepticism. Chalmers had pointed out the contrast between the simplicity of the Genesis creation story and the terrestrial complexities revealed by geology, but Buckland drives home a few key points, which suggest a different interpretation. Buckland argues that geology spells out that the earth as we now find it is recent, and quite congruent with the calculated dates of the Garden of Eden creation. Likewise, he states that the landscapes we have today bear numerous indications of the great Flood of Noah (soon to find further dramatic substantiation from Buckland's Kirkdale and other cave excavations), which clearly demonstrates the Bible-confirming power of geology. The geological landscape is rich in evidences of Noah's Flood, he argues, as river valleys, gravel beds on the tops of hills and non-fossilized animal bones provide evidence for the Deluge. Fossilized bones, of course, were ancient, and dated from before 4004 BC, whereas still calciferous bones found in shales and gravels were not old enough to have fossilized and must be from the creatures wiped out in the 40 days and nights of Noah's torrential downpour. Similarly, geology demonstrated the recent appearance of man on earth, as well as of animals familiar to us today, such as deer, for no such remains are found in the ancient strata where extinct lizard and fish remains abounded.

Yet while Buckland had no problem with the 6,000-year-old state of the present orders of life on earth, including humans, he argued that the creation *ex nihilo* had taken place long before Eden. On the other hand, it stood to reason that there was no mention of extinct lizards, or saurians, in Scripture, for these were not self-conscious, moral beings, and played no part whatsoever in God's purpose as narrated in the Bible. This purpose was to establish and proclaim his creation of a world, post-Edenic, for those beings whom God had made in his own image: Adam and Eve and their descendants down to this day. So, to put it simply, God had mentioned the *ex nihilo* creation in Genesis 1, then, saying nothing about the legions of soulless, pre-moral brutes that would dominate the earth across the ensuing millennia, he had jumped forward in the Mosaic narratives to the planting of Eden to make it ready for Adam and Eve. So, the whole divine story would begin, to run from Genesis 2 to the Last Judgement and the descent of the holy city, the New Jerusalem, in the book of Revelation. In Buckland's geological thinking, as laid out in *Vindiciae* and later writings, a vast period of time had elapsed between the creation *ex nihilo* and Eden, and this is where geology came into it and found its justification.

In *Vindiciae* Buckland also proceeds to take issue with those scriptural literalists who 'abuse' religion by trying to tie every fact and discovery in science to a specific biblical reference, for this could only lead people astray, both scientifically and theologically. He argues that the Creator's *Word*, or the Bible, could never be in conflict with his *Works*, or the natural world. And if humanity's God-given intelligence discovered that the creation had unfolded in sequence over long ages, then God would never have deceived us. As we know today, and Buckland would also have known, the 'world' to the Mosaic writer was essentially the flat desert lands of the Middle East, from Egypt to Mesopotamia. Yet as even the Greeks would discover, and Columbus and Magellan would confirm, the 'world' was not only spherical, but also very large, with the Middle East occupying only a tiny surface area of the total terrestrial land mass.

So, what had taken place between the creation *ex nihilo* and the final clearing of the mists that preceded God's planting of the Garden of Eden? As we have seen, some geological thinkers spoke of there having been six 'long days', each of potentially vast duration, during which God had brought the earth from its primal chaos to Eden. Buckland dismissed this model, preferring instead to see a period of unspecified but vast duration between the *ex nihilo* creation and the first day of Eden. During this vast period, God had formed and re-formed the primal earth through a series of global catastrophes, after each of which the Almighty had restocked the earth with new and more advanced life forms on the new continents. It was a manifestation of the grandeur of God and his providence, as the divine hand had constantly moulded and remoulded both the mineral planet and the fauna living upon it, in a series of interventions over an incalculably vast period of time. Crowning it all would be Eden, and man in God's own image, whose mischievous free will had led to evil, and necessitated the last great catastrophe: the Flood of Noah. This was the 'catastrophist' geology, developed from the discoveries and ideas of Buckland's greatly admired inspiration, the anatomist and fossil geologist Baron Georges Cuvier in France. And 'catastrophism' would become the hallmark of the Oxford School of geology. *Vindiciae Geologicae* would stamp an unequivocal seal of approval on Buckland's ideas, both geologically and scientifically.

Hyenas in Yorkshire and the 'Relics of the Deluge'

In 1821, his reputation, both at home and abroad, would ascend to new heights in the wake of a chance discovery made by workmen at Kirby Moorside, in the Vale of Pickering, Yorkshire, in 1821, which chimed in perfectly with Buckland's *Vindiciae* of two years before. He was not the first scientific gentleman to look at Kirkdale Cave, however, as a local physician had done some excavating a few weeks before, and had even sent anatomical specimens to the Royal College of Physicians and elsewhere. Edward Legge, Warden of All Souls College and Bishop of Oxford, who had attended Buckland's lectures, had also picked up on the significance of Kirkdale Cave, and now urged Buckland to go north and investigate.

The discovery of Kirkdale Cave opened up a world of rich possibilities for geology after 1821. Its significance derived, first of all, from its status as a hitherto undisturbed 'virgin' cave, discovered by quarrymen, meaning that its contents were fresh and untouched since time immemorial. Second, it was a bone cave, and when excavated was found to contain the anatomically identifiable bones of hyenas, elephants, bears and around 22 other exotic animals, most of which, by 1821, were only to be found alive in Africa, India and other distant lands. Bone caves were by no means a geological novelty in 1821–1822, as Buckland had excavated caves in Germany, especially at Gailenreuth, in 1816, and the remains of bears, such as *Ursus spelaeus* – cave bear – and such animals were already familiar. From page 99 onwards in *Reliquiae Diluvianae* ('Relics of the Deluge', 1823), after discussing excavations in other British caves beyond Kirkdale, Buckland looks at a variety of caves in Germany and elsewhere, displaying his wide and impressive first-hand speleological knowledge. There was, however, already a perfectly respectable explanation for the appearance of exotic tropical beasts in north European caves: Noah's Flood. As the waters of the deluge swirled around the planet, they would inevitably sweep up elephants and rhinos and carry them thousands of miles north, their remains ending up in mud and shale deposits and in caves.

Very significantly, though, while Kirkdale Cave contained the jumbled and broken remains of tropical and other exotic beasts, these were all fragmentary. But the hyena remains were fairly intact. Could this mean that Kirkdale Cave was what Buckland styled *antediluvian*, or predated the Noachian Deluge? Could it have been an established hyena den, into which generations of hyenas (estimated to be some 200 individual animals over their time of residence) had dragged in chunks of their prey to eat? When it was pointed out that hyenas would have been incapable of killing elephants and other large beasts, Buckland responded by arguing that hyenas had no trouble in eating rotting meat, so could whole limbs of dead and decomposing elephants, rhinos and bears have been ripped off and taken back to the cave for supper?

This would lead Buckland to a novel idea of the Noachian Flood as the last great geological agent. In pre-Flood times, could hyenas, elephants and such have been indigenous in the northern latitudes? He became more confident of this idea when he saw a travelling animal show, which contained a living hyena. He fed the animal with ox bones, and was fascinated to observe that the living hyena bit and chewed the ox bones in precisely the same way as its ancient ancestors had done. Likewise, it seemed to rub its fur on the side of its cage in a way that matched the rubbings on the cave wall at Kirkdale. So had all manner of tropical animals walked the Kirkdale moors, when suddenly a great surge of water came crashing over the landscape, effectively entombing the hyena tribe in their cave along with the fruits of their latest hunting expedition, then sealing everything up for millennia to come? Such an explanation for the cave begged a whole host of questions. Exactly how strong and extensive had the biblical flood been, especially in distant places like north Yorkshire? The basic underlying landscape appeared to be vastly ancient and antediluvian, formed by a succession of much more violent catastrophes in the remote, pre-Edenic past, leaving the Flood of Noah to merely deposit gravels, entomb hyenas and wipe out local wildlife.

Furthermore, what did Kirkdale Cave tell us about earlier animal ecology and climate? If elephants and rhinos had once lived in the region and geographical latitude of Kirkdale Moor, it must have been very much warmer in antediluvian times than it is today. There was nothing new in the idea of historic climate change, such as in the jungles and swamps that had subsequently formed the coal measures, although Noah's Flood had been much more recent, perhaps only 4,500 years ago, and by its very nature well within the human time frame. What seems to have evolved in Buckland's geological thinking, therefore, was that instead of Kirkdale Moor and other places far from the Holy Land being remodelled through a single 40-day deluge, a great flood tide had rolled across these distant places. It had occasioned a sudden, local extinction and change of ecology, entombing the old livestock, such as the hyenas in their cave, and allowing God to repopulate these regions with the postdiluvian plants, animals, gravels and sands which we find today. Buckland also pointed out that climatic and ecological swings had left their marks elsewhere in the northern hemisphere. Giant hairy mammoths and shaggy-coated elephants had been found in Siberia, their thick coats well preserved and their flesh even edible. In 1825, Buckland was even sent some red mammoth hair from St Petersburg. No such beasts lived anywhere on earth today, although they had clear anatomical parallels to modern elephants.

In Kirkdale Cave, Buckland drew attention to the thin layer of stalagmite deposition covering the cave floor. Stalagmite deposition, it was fully understood by 1821, was very slow in its formation, and many caves had layers of the mineral up to several feet thick. Kirkdale Cave's relatively thin floor layer was seen as an indicator that its current sealed geological status was relatively recent. It was also a dry cave, its ancient mud-based depositions below the stalagmite displaying no stratification, as one would expect if ordinary rain-based local floods had washed animal bones in over time. Buckland drew powerful arguments from his Kirkdale time capsule, relating to animal ecology, climate, extinctions, catastrophes and the sheer suddenness of the inundation. His findings and conclusions also chimed in most elegantly with Georges Cuvier's ideas of global history, of the suddenness of catastrophes that remodelled the earth and wiped out its ancient antediluvian animal inhabitants, along with his use of careful comparative anatomical techniques both to articulate extinct animal skeletons and even to understand their dietary habits.

Buckland's Kirkdale findings and published *Reliquiae Diluvianae* were very favourably received by Cuvier and others in Continental Europe, as well as by scientists closer to home. They elevated his reputation to the highest level in Britain, and won him the prestigious Copley Medal of the Royal Society in 1822 – as near to a Nobel Prize as existed at that time. But it would be wrong to assume that everyone was won over by Buckland's way of interpreting both the fossil record and Scripture, as presented in *Reliquae Diluvianae*. A number of highly reputable naturalists and geologists, such as Granville Penn, George Eastman and others, still held to a more straightforward interpretation of the six-day creation, as we will see in Chapter 11.

'Billy' the celebrity hyena

As a disciple of Georges Cuvier's anatomical approach to fossil geology, the Kirkdale Cave discoveries led Buckland to search for modern hyena remains in anatomy museum collections to compare them with the antediluvian animals, and he obtained a live young hyena, captured in South Africa by William Burchell, the African traveller.[3] By the time the 'Baby Beast' or 'Tiger Wolf' had arrived at London Docks, he had won the hearts of the sailors and all those who had encountered him, for 'Billy', as he was named, was a perfect pet. He was friendly, affectionate and had a human sounding 'laugh' (a true laughing hyena) that delighted all who heard it. The thought of Billy being killed so that he might be dissected, and his skull and teeth in particular compared with those of his Kirkdale ancestors, was too much. Buckland's friend Mr Cross and others pleaded for Billy's life, and when a modern hyena skull was found in a museum fossil collection, his life was saved. The living, laughing Billy proved more useful in life than he would have if consigned to an early death. Domiciled in the Surrey Gardens Zoo, much was learned by watching him. He cracked open his marrow bones, just as his forebears had done, even leaving similarly placed teeth marks on bones. He only cracked marrow bones, seemingly ignoring the others. After eating, Billy's droppings – known as *album graecum* – on the floor of his cage were visually identical to the fossilized coprolites found at Kirkdale. Upon analysis, they were found to be chemically identical as well. And as we saw above, the way Billy rubbed himself on his cage bars corresponded perfectly with the rubbing marks on the Kirkdale Cave walls.

The good-humoured Billy became a true favourite with the Zoological Gardens visitors, and so sociable was he that his keepers felt perfectly safe when entering his cage to clean up or do repairs. He finally died on 14 January 1846, after suffering from a large goitre in his throat. At a good 24 or 25 years old, he was probably the longest-lived hyena in history, from his capture as a cub to dying a venerable celebrity. Billy's cadaver went to the Royal College of Surgeons for dissection, after which his skeleton and stuffed and articulated coat and skin were preserved.

Other caverns

As we have seen, Buckland had excavated caves in Germany back in 1816, but Kirkdale gave them a new geological significance. While returning to do excavations into the floor of Gailenreuth Cave in Franconia, and study the remains of *Ursus spelaeus*, or cave bear, Buckland undertook further excavations in several other British caves. Exploring and excavating a cave demanded physical fitness of the highest order. All had cramped, back-breakingly awkward interiors, as is clear from careful cross-section survey drawings of these caves, while the Paviland, or 'Goat Hole' Cave in south Wales required mountaineering skills as well, as we shall see below. All exploration had to be performed with no more than the light of a candle or an oil lamp, with flames that were often blown out by the air currents moving through the cave. This was 'extreme caving', and much had to be done by touch, long before modern safety helmets and electric headlights were even dreamt of. It was not an occupation for the timorous or the physically delicate, and while this is not especially obvious from his portraits, Buckland must have been very fit, strong, courageous and something of a daredevil to undertake his geological marathons.

Once inside the cave, with one's picks, shovels, crowbars, sledge hammers and other implements, one had first to attack the cave floor, usually covered with hard limestone stalagmite deposits, before gaining access, hopefully, to less hard diluvial mud below which might contain the fossils of extinct creatures. These potential fossil-bearing regions might then go down some six or a dozen feet, every square inch and every trowel-full of which had to be carefully removed and analysed for teeth or small bones, all by the light of a flickering flame. Hyenas were not always to be found, however, although other wonders appeared. At the Dream Lead Mine Cave at Wirksworth, Derbyshire, a relatively accessible cave with two surface openings, the ancient cave chamber was found to be largely filled with hardened mud sediment. When this dense mass was carefully excavated, a complete rhinoceros skeleton was found. Had it, and other bones, been washed down the surface opening by the Deluge? One interpretative problem with many caves was working out the difference between bones washed down sinkholes all of a sudden, in relatively recent times, and bones that might have belonged to the antediluvian residents of the cave.

The Red Lady of Paviland

One post-Kirkdale cave, which both fascinated and puzzled Buckland, was the Paviland Goat Hole Cave, some fifteen miles west of Swansea in south Wales. The local land was owned by Mr Christopher Talbot of Penrice Castle, who became a friend of Buckland's, along with Miss Jane Talbot, a naturalist who corresponded with Buckland, and a local gentleman named Mr Lewis Weston Dillwyn, whose work Buckland acknowledges. Buckland sometimes stayed at the Castle. First getting access to the narrow mouth of Paviland Cave, and negotiating its interior once inside, required gymnastics and daring of the highest order. The only entry points were from the rock face of a precipitous cliff, with the sea directly below. Once one had swung into the cave mouth on a rope, the initial passage necessitated a tight crawl, before it suddenly opened above a dead drop enclosing a space the size of a small church.

What made the 1822 Paviland Cave excavations remarkable, though, was the discovery of what were obviously human remains in its interior, along with worked flint implements and what appeared to be decorative items. Finding hyena bones in a cave was one thing; but finding those of a human posed serious questions, especially after Buckland discovered half the skeleton of what was thought to be a woman in Paviland Cave. At this time, scientists elsewhere in Europe were suggesting that some humanoid bone remains were vastly ancient, but Buckland defends the 4004 BC date for human creation. He introduces 'her' in *Reliquiae Diluvianae* as 'Man. Portion of a female skeleton, clearly postdiluvian.'[4] Very curiously, the 'female' skeleton seems to have been deliberately dyed red, no doubt with the iron mineral content of the local rocks. She was a puzzle, and Buckland suggested a solution. The Red Lady of Paviland, as she came to be christened, was 'modern', maybe an ancient Celt or Briton, a contemporary of the Romans.

'From all these circumstances', Buckland argues,' there is reason to conclude, that the date of the human bones was coeval with that of the military occupation of the adjacent summits, and anterior to, or coeval with, the Roman invasion of this country.'[5] As there had been a known Roman settlement in the area, she was no doubt a camp follower, or prostitute, buried in the cave with red materials, perhaps to symbolize her profession. Was she an indigenous Briton, belonging to one of those tribes who were here before the Roman invasion in AD 55?

Modern pathological studies combined with carbon 14 dating, however, would show that 'her' bones were actually the remains of a man, who had lived in the last Ice Age, around 30,000 BC, at a time when the Paviland cliff was many miles inland from the sea. Yet one cannot blame William Buckland for drawing the conclusions that he did from the very limited research technologies available in 1822, which his work would ultimately help to advance. We will return briefly to the Red Lady of Paviland in Chapter 14, when we look at the post-Buckland fascination with human prehistory.

The beginning of human prehistory: the Torbay caves

By all appearances, though, the Lady had been properly interred: laid out, and not just deposited. She was also accompanied by bits of worked flint and decorative items, probably intended as funerary offerings. In the mid-1820s, other human ancients in new cave excavations joined her, both in Britain and in Europe. In 1824, for example, the local south Devon naturalist Thomas Northmoor began to excavate the already well-known Kent's Hole or Kent's Cavern at Wellswood, Torquay. Father John MacEnery, the Roman Catholic Chaplain to the landowning Cary family of nearby Torre Abbey, was also a keen naturalist and carried on his work. Buckland soon learned of the Kent's Cavern investigations, as he did all aspects of Devon geology. Although no human bones were found in Kent's Cavern, the discovery of knapped and worked flint implements made it clear that humans had once lived in the cave and, from the surviving animal bone evidence, may have been contemporary with mammals that were now either extinct or had never been known to live in England. Yet how could this be, for surely, that could only have meant that they predated Adam and Eve?

Considering its long albeit sporadic human occupation, I recall the cave tour guides speaking of Kent's Cavern as 'Torquay's first hotel'. Two years after Buckland's death, in 1858, a hitherto sealed cave would be discovered across Torbay in Brixham, and as we shall see in Chapter 14, beneath its thick stalagmite floor, it contained human artefacts that clearly ante-dated 4004 BC.

The dating of possible human remains and artefacts apart, it cannot be denied that William Buckland was one of the pioneers of speleology, or the scientific study of caves. That study would also play its part in the science of hydrology and the tracing of subterranean watercourses, and would be furthered by the daring adventures of the Frenchmen Édouard-Alfred Martel and Norbert Casteret into the early twentieth century. Every mod-ern day weekend caving enthusiast must pay homage to the memory of Buckland for having shown them the way.

Buckland, the hyena skull, and the alarmed undergraduate: a glimpse of Buckland's lecturing style

An incident occurred in Oxford around 1840, which provides an exam-ple of Buckland's dramatic lecturing style, pertaining directly to hye-nas, caves and Kent's Cavern. Sir Henry Acland, then Regius Professor of Medicine at Oxford, sent the account to Mrs Elizabeth Oke Gordon when she was preparing her father's *Life and Correspondence* for pub-lication in the early 1890s. Like the Bucklands and Okes, the Aclands were an old Devonshire gentry family, and William Buckland was a good friend of Sir Thomas, Henry's father. On the occasion in question, Buck-land was lecturing – pacing 'like Franciscan Preacher up and down' – in his teaching room in Oxford's Clarendon Building, adjacent to the Old Ashmolean Museum (now the History of Science Museum). He was discoursing on the Kent's Cavern and other related finds, some of which were on display before him, when with a dramatic flourish, he suddenly descended from the platform to his audience, brandishing a large fossilized hyena skull which he held before a 'terrified' and dumb-founded undergraduate, demanding 'What rules the world?' Getting no answer, Buckland presented the skull, and repeated his question, to the undergraduate Acland, who replied, 'Haven't an idea'. Re-ascending his rostrum, Buckland exclaimed, no doubt with true dramatic flair, 'The stomach, sir, rules the world. The great ones eat the less, and the less the lesser still. '[6]

With performances like the above, along with equally vivid displays mentioned elsewhere in this book, one comes to understand how Acland, the Reverend William Tuckwell, Sir Roderick Murchison and many other men, now elderly, recalled the style, mannerisms and antics of William Buckland many decades after his death.

Chapter 5
Geologists in the Landscape

By the early nineteenth century, several factors were driving the new science of geology, especially in Britain. One, of course, was intellectual curiosity combined with Natural Theology, though economic factors were also conspicuously present. This was the age of the industrial revolution, where the newly invented steam engine was king, and its relentless appetite gave a special urgency to coal prospecting and its vital adjunct water and then rail transportation from mine to factory or domestic hearth. Coal was not the only subterranean substance to drive the new science: prospecting for iron, lead, copper, lime and other minerals became a major requisite. So did the voracious demand for fine building stone and brick- and pottery-making clays for the rapidly expanding city of London and other cities, including the north Midlands pottery industry. As most of this mineral-rich land, from Cornwall to the Scottish Highlands, was privately owned, either by individual or corporate proprietors, such as Oxbridge colleges and City of London livery companies, the subsoil became quite literally a commercial gold mine.

Knowing how to locate and extract this mineralogical cornucopia gave rise to a major branch of the surveying and cartographic profession: the mineral surveyor. Yet once the minerals had been found, in rural Somerset or somewhere else, far removed from the steam engines or factory or housing developments, how were they to be conveyed? Since James Brindley's world-changing six-mile canal had been built between the Duke of Bridgewater's coal mines at Worsley, Lancashire, and coal-hungry Manchester after 1761, the canal became the obvious big-bulk conveyor of industrial materials. By 1800, canal building was going on across England, focusing largely on Birmingham's Grand Junction system. Building a canal, however, required slicing through the landscape to maintain levels of flat waters, punctuated by locks, bridges, aqueducts and tunnels. Slicing through the landscape involved exposing numerous hitherto largely ignored rock strata, and also learning new things about the hydrology of that landscape, and how water could be managed so as to keep canals full yet not flooded, drained away from where it was not wanted, and taken to where it was. A similar hydrological knowledge was needed to constantly top-up the 'lodges' or small artificial private lakes alongside the textile and other factories, which ensured a constant supply of water for the ever-thirsty steam engines inside.

As we have seen, these demands would give an opportunity to a highly intelligent and ingenious young blacksmith from Oxfordshire, who, by the time of his death in 1839, would have earned the soubriquet of 'Strata', and become an honorary Doctor of Civil Laws, the father of field geology and an early teacher of and inspiration to William Buckland. This was William Smith.[1]

Dr William Smith

One might say that William Smith's career really came about as a result of the rapidly developing economic geology of the late eighteenth century. Born in 1769 and entirely self-taught following his rudimentary education in Churchill, Oxfordshire, village school, Smith went on to become a land surveyor. The key to his subsequent geological ideas was coal mining, especially around Rugbourne Farm, in north Somerset. Here in the 1790s he became involved in underground surveys for coal prospecting, and proved so good at it that he greatly impressed several local landowners. After displaying his skills at reading the landscape for the purpose of locating coal measures, he was next invited to survey a route for a Somerset coal canal, by which the mined coal might be conveyed to market in London and other towns. This survey work would become instrumental in framing William Smith's subsequent geological ideas, because of his successful identification of fossil-bearing rocks.

Working in 1796 in two adjacent valleys a couple of miles apart, Smith found a key to identifying a strata type as it dipped and re-emerged from the lie of the land. This lay not in the often confusing mineralogical character of the rocks, but, as he recognized, in their unique fossil content, or signatures. Smith made the profoundly influential discovery that specific fossil types did not simply occur anywhere, but only in their specific and unique strata. A host of geological possibilities lay in this discovery, such as the ability to trace a particular mineral- or fossil-bearing rock stratum across great distances in the landscape. This method would also come to be used to study the way in which the strata, all of which would originally have been laid down flat on the sea or a lake bed, had become bent and twisted as the landscape had evolved over vast aeons of time, even leading to some strata being subducted or folded under other strata, perhaps across hundreds of miles. The unique fossil types would provide the key to understanding the landscape and its history.

It is impossible to over-estimate the significance of Smith's discoveries, for they would shape the future of palaeontology and allow geologists to establish precise criteria for rock and fossils identification, be they in Somerset, Spain, or America. And William Buckland would sing his praises.

Crucially, William Smith's discovery made geological mapping possible, in which strata and mineral types could be drawn and coloured on maps covering hundreds of miles of country, using their fossils as a benchmark. This technique would prove invaluable not only in future coal and mineral prospecting, but also in establishing geology as an empirical, as opposed to a speculative, science. Smith was excellently qualified to undertake the drawing and colouring of such a map, being a highly skilled surveyor who had surveyed, land-drained, mineral prospected and geologized across much of Britain. He perhaps knew the field geology of England better than any other single individual by 1810. In his geological and surveying journeys around Britain, he assiduously collected fossils, each clearly labelled. In 2019, to celebrate the 250th anniversary of his birth, 23 March 1769, the Geological Society put on a special exhibition of some fossils from his own collection in the Society's apartments in Burlington House, Piccadilly, with their accompanying labels. It was fascinating to be able to see some of the very specimens collected by Strata Smith on his travels. Beneath his portrait in Burlington House are preserved some cuttings of his white hair, set in a glass roundel.

Eminent gentlemen of science from 'humble' origins

William Smith's social position has intrigued many historians. Recognition took a long time in coming, and many have tried to argue that this was because of the genteel character of the membership of the Geological Society (1807), of which, as we saw above, William Buckland became Royal Charter President in 1824. Smith, we are told, spoke with a pronounced local Oxfordshire accent, and had the powerful physique and bearing of a prizefighter rather than that of a refined gentleman.

Yet one need not go far into the lives of many renowned and honoured British scientists of Smith's time and before to find numerous individuals who were the sons of small farmers or tradesmen, and whose formal education, at best, had been a village school and a year or two in a local grammar school, but who had nonetheless won social acceptance. Think of precision engineers and instrument-makers such as Thomas Tompion, George Graham, John Bird, John Harrison, Jesse Ramsden, and Edward Troughton and the opticians John and Peter Dollond. Then there was the anatomist and surgeon John Hunter, the explorer Captain James Cook, RN, the astronomer Sir William Herschel (Knight Guelph), the engineer James Watt, the chemist and physicist Sir Humphry Davy (Knight Baronet) and the young Michael Faraday. All of these men, with the exception of Tompion, became Fellows of the Royal Society, and some winners of the Society's prestigious Copley Medal and other major awards. Their humble origins were no fundamental impediment in a society that valued enterprise, civility and ingenuity. Nor was Smith always hard up. Indeed, in his early days as a renowned surveyor and economic geologist, he could command fees of two guineas per day, and on one appointment, a salary of £450 per annum – sums of money that would have made many a country clergyman, Oxbridge professor or provincial solicitor or doctor distinctly envious.

I would suggest, rather, that Smith's long haul to proper recognition and acceptance derived from other factors. For one thing, he seems to have been a bad businessman, investing in commercial enterprises that crashed, losing money, and even being imprisoned for debt. His marriage to a lady named Mary Ann was also something of a disaster, for the poor lady suffered from long-term mental illness, was confined in the York Asylum, and drained both Smith's emotional and material resources. As an honourable and God-fearing husband, however, he did his duty in caring for her as best he could. I also suspect he lacked the adaptive social instincts of Herschel (an immigrant German bandmaster's son) or Davy (son of a Cornish wood carver and gilder of yeoman farmer ancestry, though he had received a grammar school education), and of the other scientists mentioned above. Many not only became social successes in Georgian London, but also were positively lionized by fashionable society, ranking earls and baronets within their circle. Brilliant and gifted artisans turned gentlemen, yet possessing an ability to pick up the correct social skills.

True recognition came to William Smith as he approached the end of his life. He received the prestigious Wollaston Medal of the Geological Society in 1831. The newly established national British Association for the Advancement of Science (BAAS) founded in York in 1831 was quick to recognize him, and at the Association's Oxford meeting in 1832, William Buckland played a major role in honouring the 65-year-old Smith. When the Association met in Dublin in 1835, Trinity College conferred a Doctorate in Civil Laws (LLD) upon him, confirming him as 'Dr Smith', while a £100 per annum Civil List Pension had already been bestowed on him in 1832, to assure his future financial security. Dr William Smith possessed plenty of well-connected genteel friends and admirers by his middle age, and they were active in obtaining both academic recognition and financial security for him. Buckland was foremost here, making no bones about geological science's huge debt to Smith, who would later have a very successful nephew and protégé, John Phillips, of whom more will be said below.

Yet one eminent geological cartographer and writer, George Bellas Greenough, disagreed with Smith and his followers about the interpretation of stratification and the use of fossils as geological indicators.

George Bellas Greenough

Like Sir Charles Lyell, Greenough was originally a lawyer by training. Christened George Bellas after his Doctor's Commons lawyer father in 1778, he was orphaned as a small child and partly brought up by his grandfather Thomas Greenough, an entrepreneurial and wealthy London apothecary, who had made his fortune by the successful sale of a variety of commercially manufactured pharmaceutical products. Young George took his grandfather's surname, to become Bellas Greenough, and went to Eton, Cambridge and Göttingen before becoming MP for the rotten borough constituency of Gatton, Surrey. Greenough's politics, however, were far from rotten, for he was a reformer and a hater of slavery and social oppression, who resigned his own commission in the London and Westminster militia following the use of military force to break up an otherwise peaceful assembly at the Manchester Peterloo Massacre in 1819. His geological interests came about through a fascination with mineralogy, which was probably strengthened during his student days in Germany, where he visited the mineral-rich Harz mountains and came to admire Abraham Gottlob Werner. An instinctive empiricist, deeply sceptical of theoretical interpretations in geology, Greenough could not accept Smith's crucial realization that specific fossils could be used to indicate and trace the lie of the strata across the landscape.

Empirical in his science, Greenough was a natural organizer, collector and collator in other respects. In 1807 he became the driving force behind the founding of the Geological Society, becoming its first President. Yet while Greenough would geologize with the young Sir Humphry Davy, Buckland, William Daniel Conybeare and others, he was never an active field geologist. Instead, he was a gatherer and organizer of geological information, and perhaps most of all, a cartographer. Much has been made by certain twentieth-century geological historians of Greenough trying to sideline Smith for reasons of snobbery, and of Greenough having produced a geological map that was somehow a deliberate rival to Smith's. But as we saw above, the snobbery case against Smith, the village blacksmith's son, is undermined by the sheer number of eminent contemporary scientists coming from humble backgrounds. More significant, I suspect, were the fundamentally different principles upon which Smith and Greenough interpreted the landscape and made their maps. For as we have seen, Smith's map was based upon a specific fossil and strata correlation, whereas Greenough's was much more mineralogical in its underlying logic. Smith's map, too, was founded upon exhaustive professionally conducted field work, across the length and breadth of Britain, while much of Greenough's derived from collected data and data sent by distant correspondents. Both maps, however, are highly prized possessions of the Geological Society, and now reside in Burlington House, Piccadilly, London.

Greenough was more than just a drawing office collector, however. In 1816, he, Buckland and William Conybeare had undertaken a grand tour of European field geology, going through Germany, Poland, Hungary, Eastern Europe, Italy and France. One wonders, however, how far Buckland's gift for friendship played a part in keeping everyone happy. In many ways, Greenough was a physical geographer rather than a geologist, and he would later go on to found and preside over the Royal Geographical Society, and produce the first geological map of British India. All the evidence suggests that Buckland and Greenough got on well, differences of geological interpretation notwithstanding.

It was an English surveyor who taught geologists how to read the lie of the land and to locate and excavate fossils. But it would be a French, largely self-taught, anatomist, (whom we have already met) who would teach them how to interpret fossilized fish, lizards and other beasts and to articulate them, displaying what in 1840 would be christened 'dinosaurs' to an enchanted international audience. Like Dr Smith, the Frenchman exerted a profound influence upon William Buckland's geological thinking, and received his fulsome acknowledgement and praises. The Frenchman was Georges Léopold Chrétien Frédéric Dagobert, universally known under the name preferred by his mother – Georges – Baron Cuvier.

Baron Georges Cuvier

In the way that William Smith was regarded as the stratigraphic 'father of geology', so Georges Cuvier would be heralded 'the father of palaeontology'. In many respects, Buckland drew these two vital strands together to create modern geological science.

The son of a Lutheran bourgeois family in Montbéliard in southeast France, formerly a part of Westphalian territory in the Holy Roman Empire, Georges Cuvier received his higher education at the German Caroline Academy, Stuttgart. Fascinated by natural history as a child, he became an early disciple of the taxonomic principles of the Swedish botanist and medical professor Carl Linnaeus, who had died in 1776. In Linnaeus's system, life forms, as exemplified in plants, were created in a precise order of species, genera and such, and were by their very nature fixed. Thus, Cuvier would become a major opponent of early evolutionists, such as Jean-Baptiste Lamarck and Étienne Geoffroy Saint-Hilaire. Cuvier would win renown in Paris during the Napoleonic period, becoming, among other things, Professor at the Jardin des Plantes in Paris. For him the key to classifying and understanding living forms was not in speculative attributes, but in their morphology and the structure and function of their parts. His approach was that of the anatomist. His early work was directed towards the study of invertebrates, fishes and molluscs, although his enduring fame, and his relevance to geological history and especially his significance for William Buckland, derived from his comparative work on fossilized and living animals.

Although earlier anatomists had drawn attention to occasional structural parallels between fossilized and living animal parts, Cuvier took the matter much further, and in 1800 his publication on the close comparisons between fossilized and living elephants caused something of a sensation.[2] Cuvier supplied a key to the understanding of extinct animals, which made it possible, for the first time, to identify and articulate fossil parts to create three-dimensional long-dead beasts.

Cuvier's law of correlation

Based on fossil and living comparisons, Cuvier went on to develop a rule of correlation of parts, making it possible, for example, to identify which individual bones scattered in the mud of the Seine valley belonged to which kind of animal. Did its eyes look semi-sideways, or did their skull sockets show that the eyes looked directly ahead? What sort of tail, if any, did a fossilized animal possess? How long were its legs, and did its joints suggest speed and flexibility of motion, or were its legs like pillars, supporting a large, slow-moving body? Did the creature have horns, cloven hoofs, flexible toes or claws? Most important of all, what were the teeth like? Were they sharp fangs, incisors and flesh-tearing teeth, or were they flattened grinders? Buckland also grasped the significance of teeth, as he taught his Oxford pupils how to assemble and articulate scattered fossil bones using Cuvier's congruence idea. But how did Cuvier's anatomical congruence approach work?

The teeth were fundamental, for they provided the key to the fossilized animal's diet, and therefore its lifestyle. Sharp, strong, tearing teeth, set in a powerful jaw, with a large bite capacity, a widely opening mouth such as in the hyena, dog or tiger, indicated a carnivore and hunter. A herbivore, by contrast, would have a mouth and teeth adapted to harvesting and masticating grass and leaves rather than biting, as in the cow or elephant. These features would predicate the rest of the animal's skeletal anatomy. Broadly speaking, a carnivore would have biting teeth, a large, powerful jaw, forward-looking eyes, a rib cage indicating a relatively small body volume, a flexible spine and, quite likely, a long, flexible tail, to help balance it in the chase. Its legs also would probably be quite long, with flexible joints and paws with toes and claws, but not cloven hoofs without claws. It would have a smaller body volume because meat can be digested through a shorter length of gut than can grass and leaves, and a carnivore would be unlikely to have horns.

The herbivore, on the other hand, would have masticating teeth and skull eye-sockets giving plenty of side vision, to look out for potential predators, not the forward-focused eyes of the hunter. Its ribs would indicate a large body volume, accommodating a long gut, and it would have legs that in many cases acted as supporting pillars rather than being suited to running, jumping and springing. The legs would generally terminate in cloven hoofs, and the leg joints would be much more limited in their flexibility than those of hunters, while tails would be either vestigial or relatively thin and inclined to hang down. When fighting, herbivores would tend to push and shove each other, an activity for which horns could be very useful, whereas carnivores when in competition for mates or territory would use claws to scratch or teeth to bite their opponents. Just think of how modern-day dogs and cats fight with their own kind, in contrast to how sheep or wild cattle do. While all animals can run, sheep and cattle tend at best to manage no more than a brisk trot over a short distance, whereas a dog or wolf will race along. There were interesting variants: long-legged herbivorous deer could often outrun a big cat predator, whereas omnivorous creatures such pigs, rats and mice had sharp teeth, big body masses and little legs, enabling them to scurry along, but not to race.

These variants apart, Cuvier's law of correlation would become a foundational technique for palaeontology. His inspired comparative anatomical work provided a method by which scattered bones could be scientifically articulated, joint matched with joint and structure matched with structure, to give breathtaking insights into the remote past and make long-extinct animals visual, historic realities.

There is an amusing anecdote that may or may not be true relating to Cuvier's law of congruence, which suggests that the eminent anatomist, like his protégé Buckland, was not without a sense of humour. It seems that one night, Cuvier's students decided to play a trick on him. One young man dressed up as the devil, with all the Prince of Darkness's traditional attributes. The aroused Cuvier stared closely at the snarling apparition that was threatening to drag him down into hell, and said: 'Since you have horns and hoofs, you are completely harmless. By the law of correlation, you must feed only on plants.'[3]

Cuvier's catastrophes

As we have seen, lying at the heart of Cuvier's approach to animal and earth history was his 'catastrophist' geology. Like the law of correlation, it would exert a profound impression upon William Buckland's thinking and provide a viable alternative to 'transmutational' or early evolutionary thinking, to which we will return in Chapter 12.

There were two long-standing scientific caveats concerning transmutationalist thinking, extending even into the very decade following Darwin's *Origin of Species* (1859), both of which were taken on board by Cuvier and Buckland. The first was the well-known inability of different living species to cross-breed with each other. The second was the absence of any cross-bred or transitional fossil creatures in the rock strata. Strata, after all, seemed very fixed and definitive, with what were then understood to be unique organic forms: plant, invertebrate and vertebrate, specific to given strata. This came not from biblical interpretation so much as from the best observed physical data available in *c.*1820.

By the time of writing his paper on extinct elephant fossils in 1796, Cuvier was coming to see fundamental changes in terrestrial fauna. Most crucially, had species extinction been caused not just by one universal flood, but by a sequence of catastrophes extending back into the remote geological past? This view would draw further substantiation from Cuvier's and Alexandre Brongniart's detailed studies of the rock strata of the Paris Basin, in which (like William Smith in England) they noticed that specific fauna types were only to be found in their unique strata. Like Robert Hooke in his 'Lectures and Discourses of Earthquakes' delivered before the Royal Society over a century before, Georges Cuvier began to collect non-biblical flood stories from travellers around the world, as they came to be translated into European languages by ethnologists. What emerged from all this was, that while a great flood of some kind might have occurred globally or in given regions well within human historical time, it had been preceded by many great global catastrophes long beforehand.

Cuvier was reluctant to go into too much detail about the precise causes of these catastrophes and appearances of new species, but tended to confine himself to collecting, ordering and interpreting the physical data. For William Buckland, however, these catastrophes and the creation of new continents and species were clear signs of the guiding hand of a benign providence, gradually preparing the planet for Eden and the creation of Adam and Eve. By 1820, therefore, one sees many of the components of Buckland's mature geological thinking clearly in place. For the study of caves, fossil-bearing strata identification and the anatomical techniques by which one could articulate fossilized bones to create strange creatures from 'antediluvian' times supplied geologists with the conceptual tools for creating a coherent history of the ancient earth and its 'progressive' life forms. Then to complete the picture, one could see the 'catastrophes' as driving agents by which changes came about.

Yet rising to prominence within the Geological Society and community were three men in particular, two of whom, in terms of temperament

74

and attitude, formed a strong contrast to William Buckland, whereas the third was in many ways very similar. They were Sir Roderick Impey Murchison, Sir Henry Thomas De la Beche and the Revd Professor Adam Sedgwick.

Controversy about the rocks

Sir Roderick Impey Murchison was descended from the ancient Scottish Highland clan of that name, who in the eighteenth century had lost land and local social influence following the abortive Highland risings against the anti-Stuart, new Hanoverian Georgian government in London. Roderick's father, Kenneth, had trained as a doctor and gone on to make a fortune in India, marrying Barbara Mackenzie, also of ancient Highland lineage. Henry De la Beche's parents, Thomas and Elizabeth, were originally named Beach, but his army officer father, assuming a rather far-fetched connection with the medieval Barons De la Beche of Berkshire, changed the family name to De la Beche. Both men had military connections: Murchison had been a young army officer serving during the Napoleonic Wars, while De la Beche had been educated at the Royal Military College, Marlow, Buckinghamshire, although his expulsion for espousing radical Jacobin views meant that it was unlikely that he ever carried the King's Commission.

Both men were outdoor types, and Murchison in particular, after leaving the army, became devoted to foxhunting. Yet what a cavalry officer, a huntsman and a geologist all needed was a quick eye for reading a landscape, be they looking for approaching French dragoons, hiding places for foxes or topographical features that might suggest interesting rock forms. Social pretentions apart, both individuals were born gentlemen and would become longstanding stalwarts of the Geological Society.

Birth, money and social connections, of course, were important for proper gentlemen, but perhaps more important was knowing how to act the part: a thing which William Smith never managed to do. Marrying the right girl also helped enormously, even when marriages fell apart. Like William Smith, Henry De la Beche suffered a matrimonial misfortune. After a few years of marriage, and an extensive

Continental honeymoon, Lady Letitia (as she would otherwise have become in 1842) left Henry to run off with Major-General Henry Wyndham. He never remarried. Murchison, on the contrary, married Lady Charlotte, a general's daughter, whose intelligence, devoted affection, encouragement and support in many respects made her husband's career. Charlotte seems to have inspired Murchison, jogging him out of a tendency to idleness and giving him determination and focus. He would go on to win the highest acclaim and become Director of the Geological Survey.

The controversy that would erupt between Murchison and De la Beche concerning the validity of the technique of using fossils as key markers of geological strata would, in part, be resolved following the efforts of the Revd Professor Adam Sedgwick of Cambridge. Sedgwick would also come to play a major role in one of geology's great early controversies, along with his friends Murchison and De la Beche. We will be looking in more detail at Sedgwick's geological achievements and friendly relations with Buckland in Chapter 9.

The great Devonian Controversy

As we have seen above, in 1825 geology as a 'natural history' science, unlike astronomy, physics and chemistry, lacked hard, measurement-based criteria against which to test new claims and discoveries. Geology was a comparative and not a precision instrument-based, experimental science, and its criteria could not be repeatedly verified in the laboratory or observatory. And while reliable and repeatable chemical tests could be conducted upon specific rocks and minerals, such tests told one nothing about the mineral's age, sequence or place in earth history. Such an 'absolute' test in geology would really have to await the twentieth century and a new understanding of the atomic, molecular and palaeo-magnetic structure of rocks. Consequently, geology was always susceptible to disputes about comparisons: about what came first, what overlaid what, and how fossil anatomy related to fossil mineralogy. One such controversy, centred on the interpretation of the ancient rocks of Wales and the west of England, came to be known as the Devonian Controversy.[4]

Like so many controversies, however, the 'Devonian' was not just about science: it was also about individual reputations, Geological Society and government patronage, politics and prestigious appointments. While William Smith had produced his geological map of Great Britain in 1815, geological discovery had moved so fast by the mid-1830s (to say nothing of the growing importance of economic geology to the world's first 'industrial nation') that wider official interests beyond those of intellectual curiosity were now becoming involved. This would lead to a full geological survey of Great Britain, in close collaboration with the already well-established Ordnance Survey of 1791. While the Ordnance Survey mapped the land surface, the Geological Survey would chart the rock and mineral measures beneath, and both surveys took on a political and economic significance. As geologist to the Ordnance Survey, and in many ways a scientific bureaucrat, Sir Henry De la Beche was aspiring to establish himself as the nation's official geologist, becoming Director General of the new Geological Survey. This placed him on a collision course with Sir Roderick Murchison, who saw himself as the correct person to occupy that position, and who was watchful for any incidents or statements that might signify De la Beche's lack of competence in geology.

The Controversy erupted in 1834, when De la Beche, Murchison and Sedgwick were working on the ancient rocks of western Britain, including the Lake District, north and south Wales and the Bideford area of north Devon. Sedgwick was in north Wales, Murchison in south Wales, and De la Beche in Devon. The question that especially occupied Sedgwick was the nature and sequence of the rocks below the old red sandstone.

De la Beche was surprised to find botanically identifiable, pre-Carboniferous plants in the Culm, or proto coalbeds, near Bideford. Yet they were in the strata of the greywacke or early 'transitional' rocks which lay well below the botanically rich Carboniferous coal strata. How could this be? Were William Smith's methods of using fossils to sequentially 'date' strata wrong, or – as Murchison claimed in 1837 – was De la Beche simply incompetent as a government-backed geological surveyor? Murchison's accusation was especially embarrassing as, in these years immediately following the passage of the great Reform Bill of 1832, government 'jobbery' was in full public gaze, and reformers were after any recipient of government money who did not seem to fully earn it. Indeed, all this had the power to cast the whole Geological Survey under suspicion, especially as Thomas Spring Rice, Chancellor of the Exchequer, appears to have taken a serious interest in the new geology.

Neither De la Beche nor any other geologist in the public eye turned out to be either incompetent or falsely in receipt of public funds. Quite simply, the geology itself was much more complex and multi-layered than anyone had credited in 1830. The fossil strata described by De la Beche were genuine, leading to new authentic strata layers being identified. These would come to be christened the 'Devonian', and then in Wales in the 1870s the 'Ordovician', named after the ancient Welsh tribe the Ordovices, in the same way that Sedgwick's and Murchison's Silurian system took its name from the ancient Silures. All of these early geologists knew their history and were familiar with ancient tribal names from Roman writers such as Tacitus.

William Buckland, however, eschewed controversy as far as possible, preferring amicable relations with all, and he stayed on good terms with De la Beche, Murchison and, of course, Sedgwick. By the late 1830s, when the Devonian Controversy was raging, Buckland was, in many ways, the most senior and most highly respected geologist in Britain, his *Vindiciae Geologicae*, *Reliquiae Diluvianae* and, as we shall see in Chapter 8, his monumental Bridgewater Treatise, *Geology and Mineralogy*, representing benchmarks of achievement and authority in the sciences.

Professor John Phillips FRS

Another man involved in the Devonian controversy was John Phillips, nephew of Strata Smith. Orphaned while still a child, young John Phillips was taken under the wing of Uncle William, and after some formal schooling, was trained up by Smith as a land and mineral surveyor. In spite of several financial mess-ups in Uncle William's professional life, including his doing a stint in a debtors' prison, John worked with his uncle on extensive surveys in Yorkshire. This brought him to the attention of Vernon Harcourt and the gentlemen of the Yorkshire Philosophical

Society, who gave John Phillips the job of classifying and arranging the Society's extensive collection of fossils, and soon after the Keepership of the Museum. Phillips would thereafter play a leading role in the framing and organization of the fledgling British Association for the Advancement of Science in 1831.

John Phillips was undoubtedly a gifted taxonomist and organizer, but in addition to his own surveys, especially of the geology of Yorkshire, he introduced new techniques into palaeontology, such as the use of the statistical sampling of given types of fossils in given strata. This led to his involvement in the Devonian Controversy, and his introduction of three new sequences in strata classification: the Palaeozoic, Mesozoic, and Cainozoic.[5]

John Phillips, unlike William but like many of the other figures mentioned above, was an adroit learner when it came to acquiring social style and polish. He would not only be elected FRS by the time that he was 34, but also become Professor of Geology at the new King's College, London, and a famous teacher, writer and lecturer. After 1856, he would succeed William Buckland as Reader, then in 1860 Professor of Geology at Oxford, also becoming Keeper of the University's Ashmolean Museum. He died after falling downstairs after a good dinner in All Souls' College in April 1874. There are, one might say, worse ways in which a devout lay son of the Church of England can be called away to meet his Maker. All this was a very fair achievement for the son of a tax officer and grandson and nephew of blacksmiths, who picked up the social rules and recreated himself as a university gentleman.

There was, however, one geologist in the landscape who was truly outstanding, and whose work and reputation resounded across scientific Europe. For this geologist was not only a woman, but a local Lyme Regis, Dorset, girl, who worked in the family shop, and was self-educated. She was Mary Anning, and we will meet her again and discuss her work in more detail in Chapter 9.

In 1825, William Buckland's life underwent two major changes. First, his achievements won him a truly 'star' academic and ecclesiastical appointment, when, in the summer of 1825, he was preferred to a

Canonry of Christ Church, Oxford. Second, he was now able to marry Miss Mary Morland, and within 18 or 20 months, would go from being a bachelor don to a cathedral dignitary, a husband and a doting parent.

Chapter 6
The Geological Canon of Christ Church and Miss Mary Morland

By 1825, it was felt by many in high places that William Buckland was a national asset and warranted official recognition. While the British government did not formally employ or pay scientific, literary or artistic individuals (as we shall see in Chapter 7), it did bestow honours, Civil List pensions and ecclesiastical preferments where appropriate. Famous as the 41-year-old William Buckland was by 1825, his Oxford Geological Readership and Corpus Christi College Fellowship did impose some significant limitations. For one thing, his official academic income was only around £200 per annum, although on the positive side, his College Fellowship gave him a spacious set of rooms and High Table food and drink for life as part of the job in Corpus Christi College. On the other hand, it was a *bachelor* Fellowship, and by 1825 all the signs were that Buckland had a young lady in mind, whom he wished to marry. What is more, this lady not only shared his geological and anatomical interests, but also was of considerable and established scientific accomplishment. She was the 28-year-old Miss Mary Morland.

Miss Mary Morland, fossil anatomist and artist

They had first met, as prolific diarist Miss Caroline Fox recorded in her journal for 1839, under distinctly romantic circumstances. Crossing Dorset on a public coach, according to Caroline Fox, who wrote up the anecdote passed on by Davies Gilbert, Buckland found himself facing a young lady studying a hefty volume of Cuvier's researches into fossil anatomy. Knowing already by repute who such a young lady from Oxford might be, he politely inquired, 'You must be Miss … [Morland], to whom I am about to deliver a letter of introduction?'[1] Replying in the affirmative, she recognized her travelling companion as Professor Buckland. No date is given for this original meeting, but it could have been around 1819, so it is likely that they had known each other for some time by 1825. But who was she?

The future Mrs Mary Buckland had been born on 27 November 1797 in St Helen's parish in the beautiful and prosperous county town of Abingdon, some eight or nine miles down the Thames from Oxford. She was the daughter of Benjamin and Harriet Morland, though tragically, Harriet died when her daughter Mary was a little less than two years old. Benjamin Morland was a wealthy solicitor, political agent and businessman, and a member of the prosperous West Ilsley brewery-owning family (a firm which still brews beer today). Benjamin Morland was also a promoter of and investor in various geologically-related enterprises, such as canal building and coal prospecting, and one wonders how far his interests in commercial mineralogy, the lie of the land and the mineral riches lying beneath the soil might have helped to form his daughter's fascination with things geological.

Of course, little Mary was brought up to be a county lady, receiving part of her education at a ladies' boarding school in Southampton, though one of Benjamin's friends was to play a decisive role in her early life. This was Sir Christopher Pegge DM, FRS, Regius Professor of Medicine at Oxford, a leading local physician, a senior lay member of Christ Church and predecessor of Dr John Kidd. Sir Christopher and Amy, Lady Pegge, quickly took to Mary, in consequence of which she appears to have spent part of her early life in the Pegge household in Oxford.

It was here that the young lady who might otherwise have been perfectly at home in a Jane Austen novel displayed unusual interests and capacities. For Mary acquired a passion for things geological, anatomical and medical, and Sir Christopher gave her the run of his extensive private museum of bones, fossils and things preserved in spirits, along with his library. Although there is no record of such an event, I have often wondered whether Sir Christopher and the teenage Miss Mary made private visits to the Anatomy School in the Lee Building on the south side of Christ Church to view dissected cadavers. The Lee Building was, of course, the official laboratory and lecture room of the Regius Professor of Medicine, with cadavers wheeled in through the back gate following a hanging after the Assizes. I suspect that had young Mary been taken into the building by Sir Christopher, she would have been fascinated. After all, Mary Morland subsequently became an internationally acknowledged draughtswoman of fossil anatomy, her scientific and artistic skills combining, and one would not have been surprised to learn that such an intellectually enquiring young woman had seen how recently living bones, joints and muscular appendages worked together, no less than those of long-dead animals.

Mary Morland was clearly an enterprising young woman, and by her early twenties was corresponding with none other than Georges Cuvier himself, so it seems, and was sending him drawings. One might also dare to suggest that her unusual interest in bones and fossils, her reading of French anatomical books and her familiarity with cutting-edge Continental science indicated not only self-confidence and independence of mind, but even a touch of eccentricity in one of her sex and social position in the days of *Sense and Sensibility*. If this was indeed the case, it could well have been one of Mary's attractions for Dr Buckland, and a major factor behind their subsequent long and very happy marriage. It might also have something to do with their production, after 1826, of five – surviving, that is, out of nine births in total – brilliant and in some cases distinctly eccentric children. By far the most famous of these five children was Francis Trevelyan Buckland, or Frank, to whom we will return in due course.

Caroline Fox was clearly very impressed by Mary Buckland née Morland when they dined together in October 1839, recording: 'Mrs Buckland was a most amusing and animated woman, full of strong sense and keen perception. She spoke of the style in which they go on at home, the dust and rubbish held sacred to geology, which she once ventured to have cleared but found it so disturbed the Doctor that she determined never again to risk her matrimonial felicity in such a cause.'[2]

It is likely that William's wish to marry Mary Morland had already led him to consider resigning his bachelor College Fellowship and taking a country parish living, which would have given him the freedom to marry. In fact, by 1825, Buckland had already been presented with the living of the delightfully named parish of Stoke Charity not far from Winchester. Had he left Oxford to become a country clergyman, it needed in no way impede his work as a geologist, for as we saw in earlier chapters, scientific clerical gentlemen were everywhere. Yet such a remove would have been a big loss for the University and for its geological teaching. But who spoke to whom to set the wheels of patronage in motion is not clear, although Buckland certainly had influential admirers. Then in the summer of 1825, the Prime Minister, Lord Liverpool, offered Buckland the glittering prize of a Canonry of Christ Church, one entailing few official clerical duties. As Sir Charles Lyell wrote on 20 July 1825 to fellow geologist and surgeon Gideon Mantell, 'Buckland, as you know, is made by Lord Liverpool a Canon of Christ Church, a good house, 1000 L (£1,000) per annum, and no residence or duty required.'[3]

One cannot help but wonder how many feathers Buckland's open-ended appointment initially ruffled in Christ Church. His new Regius stipend was considerably more than that of the residentiary Canons of the Cathedral and the Canon Professors of Divinity, and more than double that of his old teacher and friend John Kidd, the married, unordained Regius Professor of Medicine based at Christ Church, who did not even enjoy a residence in College, but had his own house in Oxford city.

The 'residence' duties from which Buckland was exempt would have been those of a regular 'Canon Residentiary' in an English cathedral, who would have been required, with his colleagues, to have been part of a residentiary cycle, to conduct services at his allotted times in the Church year. On the other hand, so we are told, Buckland and his family were regular attenders at Cathedral services, and William, with his gift for friendship and fellowship, no doubt played his part in Bible-reading, prayers and preaching in the Cathedral. Evidence suggests he was soon enjoying good relations with his Canon colleagues, including, among others, the Dean, Thomas Gaisford, and Canon Edward Pusey, the Oxford Movement High Church theologian and Regius Professor of Hebrew.

Over the summer and autumn of 1825, Buckland set about adapting the large Canon's house to suit his geological needs, to house collections and for performing experiments. These modifications included the construction of Buckland's famous 'toad stones', mentioned in Chapter 2. The Canon's house itself was on the far west end of the north range of Tom Quad, Christ Church: a grand and spacious residence that would later become, and to this day remains, the residence of the Archdeacon of Oxford. On 31 December 1825, he married Miss Mary Morland in the parish church of Marcham, near Abingdon, just a few miles from Oxford.

The long geological honeymoon

Having scarcely time to settle into their new home in the Christ Church Canonry, William and Mary set off for an extensive nine- or ten-month honeymoon early in 1826. Such long honeymoons were by no means unusual for the better-off classes of late Georgian Britain, especially as the opening up of Continental Europe after the Battle of Waterloo made it possible for the British to travel abroad for the first time since before the French Revolution in 1789. The Bucklands' honeymoon, however, was relatively short compared with that of Florence Nightingale's wealthy parents, who had two daughters born to them abroad before returning home from their two-year Continental honeymoon. Florence was named after the Italian city of her birth.[4]

Naturally, in February 1826 Paris was to be the first major destination for the Bucklands, and where they met everybody who was anything in French science, or in European science if they were then in Paris, such as Alexander von Humboldt. Mary was thrilled to meet Baron Cuvier, whom she had admired since her teens. Cuvier seemed, however, while warmly welcoming the Bucklands, to have been a rather 'taciturn', socially withdrawn gentleman.[5] But they were fêted by François Arago, the Director of the Paris Observatory, who struck Mary as being very 'English' in his manner, for a Frenchman. Especially admirable about Arago was his concern with what we today style 'educational outreach', and his delivery of popular scientific lectures to the citizens of Paris. William and Mary also visited the Jardin des Plantes with Cuvier and saw exotic beasts in the zoo, and met Pierre Louis Antoine Cordier, the leading field geologist in France. The newly-weds also attended parties, soirées, the opera and Mary, no doubt, visited the fashion houses for which Paris even in 1826 was internationally renowned. Both William and Mary had an easy command of the French language.

From Paris, the Bucklands travelled southeast, via the steep and geologically fascinating valley of the river Sorgue, which, so Mary's journal recorded,[6] began underground, like many springs around the Alps. Mary, who was a skilled conchologist, picked up several types of land shells with which she was unfamiliar. On this honeymoon journey, it was not so much a geologist and his bride as two geologists travelling and working together.

The couple travelled and geologized their way down Italy, seeing all the great sites of European civilization, before arriving at Palermo, in Sicily. There a memorable incident took place, reported some years later by a British official at the Court of Naples: this dated from the time when Naples and Sicily were parts of a separate kingdom prior to the unification of Italy after 1871. In 1624, Palermo had been in the grip of a terrible plague epidemic, which was stayed by the intervention of the twelfth-century St Rosalia. So relieved were the people for this mercy that Rosalia's bones were re-entombed in a special casket, where many subsequent generations came to venerate them and to beseech the saint to grant some private miracle. The Revd William Tuckwell, a friend of the Buckland family and especially of Frank and his brother Edward from childhood onwards, recorded many stories about William and Mary, which were clearly doing the rounds from the 1830s onwards. One of these involved St Rosalia and an incident that took place during the couple's honeymoon. Entering St Rosalia's shrine, Buckland cast his sharp anatomical eye over the bones, and declared (presumably in Italian), 'These are the bones of a goat, not a woman'. One can imagine the consternation that must have ensued, and it is hardly surprising that on future occasions St Rosalia's bones were not directly visible, but enclosed in a casket.[7]

On another occasion, Buckland entered a 'foreign cathedral', where the supposed blood of a martyr often appeared on the floor. 'The Professor dropped on the pavement, and touched the stain with his tongue: "I can tell you what it is; it is bat's urine".'[8]

Returning home, William and Mary were keen to see the caves of Lunel, near Montpellier in southern France, which were famous for their beautiful stalactite formations, especially the Grotte d'Osselle. But in the Lunel caves Buckland was struck by their parallels with the English and German bone caves, and particularly Kirkdale Cave. The Lunel caves contained the remains of ancient hyenas, which Buckland thought were of the Abyssinian type. Once again, as at Kirkdale, many generations of hyenas appeared to have resided in these caves, and they had gnawed their marrow bones in the same way as their Yorkshire cousins, as could be seen from the fragments of other beasts that had been dragged in for meals. The Lunel caves also contained many specimens of *album grae-cum*, perfectly preserved fossilized hyena droppings, of the kind found at Kirkdale.[9]

It may strike some people that the Bucklands' long honeymoon was as much a research expedition as a romantic interlude in two busy lives, but that, quite simply, is what William and Mary were like. It is clear that their long sojourn in Europe had not been lacking in romance, though, for when she arrived home at their Christ Church Canonry, Mary was in an advanced stage of pregnancy, and would give birth to their first child, Francis Trevelyan, or Frank, on 17 December 1826, some 14 days short of his parents' first wedding anniversary. The 41-year-old former bachelor don took to married life with gusto, and his commitment to domesticity now ran parallel with his commitment to geological science, as did that of Mary. The Bucklands were perfectly matched: evident from what they said and did and wrote, and from what dozens of friends, colleagues and visitors said about them. Very noticeably, both Bucklands had keen, and one might almost say slightly crazy, senses of humour. Both also possessed warm, outgoing personalities, and loved entertaining and welcoming guests into their grand house in Tom Quad. Be the guests old friends, such as William Daniel Conybeare and Richard Whately, or distinguished visitors from abroad, such as Justus von Liebig, the German father of organic and agricultural chemistry, or Louis Agassiz, the Swiss geologist and prophet of 'Ice Ages' geology, all received the same warm welcome. It is also recorded that foreign guests whose long journeys had left them exhausted and hungry by their time of arrival at Christ Church were given their fill, and their hosts were sometimes amused by the succession of platefuls of food that they could polish off in the Canonry dining room.

In addition to her scientific gifts and skills as a hostess, Mary Buckland was a born museum curator: Sir Christopher Pegge bequeathed his geological and mineralogical specimens to her when he died in 1822. Possessed of great manual dexterity as well as artistic and technical illustrative gifts, Mary was an expert in repairing damaged and broken fossils. Very few fossils came out of the earth in a neat and whole condition, and she was sometimes presented with little more than fossil bone fragments. But her acute eye, gift for shapes and ability to see what once came from where when beholding a medley of fossil fragments on the tabletop made it possible to reassemble whole bones and parts of skeletons. She even developed her own special cements and glues for this work, after which the bones would be classified, catalogued and put in special cardboard boxes, often made by the children as they grew up. Mary's neat and exact handwriting is still to be seen on the specimens preserved in Oxford's Natural History Museum archives and in other collections where the ever-growing array of Buckland specimens came to reside.

The tragedy of the death of children

As we saw above, William and Mary produced nine children, yet only five lived to adulthood. This sad fact must inevitably have cast something of a shadow across the otherwise happy lives of the family, as comes over in their daughter Elizabeth's account of her father published in 1894. Tragic as all these child deaths were, one wonders whether Victorian parents were psychologically prepared for such regular tragedies in a way that people today are not. In a deeply Christian age, irrespective of denominational allegiances, one wonders how far a shared cultural belief in heaven and the almost certain salvation of child innocents would aid in alleviating the suffering of bereaved parents in a way that may be less common in a more secular time.

Although vaccination after 1798 had hugely reduced the age-old dread of smallpox, there were plenty of other potentially lethal fevers that could suddenly scythe through a family in a matter of days. Cholera epidemics, most notably in 1832 and 1848–1849, caused devastation, leading people like Buckland, Dr John Snow and others to recognize a link, in that pre-bacterial age, between cleanliness, lifestyle and susceptibility. It was generally recognized that cholera was always at its worst in the congested, insanitary slums of the big cities, although the well-to-do could also go down with it, and even elegant cathedral cities, such as Exeter in Buckland's native Devon, were ravaged by the 1832 epidemic, as Dr Thomas Shapter's description makes clear.[10]

Children were especially susceptible to scarlet fever, though that disease was also quite democratic in its social catchment. In June 1839, for instance, Sir George and Richarda Airy, the Astronomer Royal and his lady, who knew Buckland and were good friends of Adam Sedgwick, lost two sons in one week from scarlet fever, the first boy dying at the Greenwich Royal Observatory. While the family accompanied him to the Airy grave plot in Playford churchyard, Suffolk, a second son sickened and died at Chelmsford on the way to the funeral. Sir George, Richarda and their other children were also touched by scarlet fever, though mercifully, no one else died.[11] Scarlet fever, diphtheria and various agues carried off the young of all classes, be it in a Christ Church Canonry, the Carlisle Deanery (where Archibald Tait, later Archbishop of Canterbury, and his wife lost several daughters over a few days), or in a labourer's or miner's cottage. It was an unpredictable horror mercifully unknown to modern Western people, at least until the Coronavirus pandemic in 2020, but still all too common in present-day 'third world' countries. What was truly exceptional, however, is that the astronomer Sir John Herschel and Lady Margaret Herschel, who also knew the Bucklands well, produced 12 children, all of whom survived. We will be looking at Buckland's work as a public health reformer in Chapter 13.

So, when reading of the joy of the Buckland family and their delightful, loving routines, one must be aware of that awful grim shadow of death by epidemic that hung over every Victorian household, irrespective of wealth, distinction or culture. One wonders how the surviving children themselves felt, as six-years-and-eight-months-old Adam Conybeare Sedgwick Buckland and three of his siblings were each ceremonially conveyed from their house across Tom Quad, with the College bell Great Tom tolling, to be sealed up in their own vault beneath the floor of the north transept in Christ Church Cathedral (a white marble slab, almost two feet square, marks the location of the grave). Amid their tears and prayers, they must have wondered who was to be next.

Among those who comforted the Bucklands in their loss was William's fellow Christ Church Canon Edward Bouverie Pusey, Regius Professor of Hebrew, who lived directly across Tom Quad on the southwest side, and had a rather different theological approach. As we have seen, Buckland's theology owed much to a sheer delight in the natural creation and in what

God taught us by contemplation and rational study. It was, in many ways, a joyful theology and appealed to persons of an instinctively optimistic outlook. Pusey's, on the other hand, was a theology focusing rather upon constant prayerful repentance, strict spiritual discipline, an awareness of one's sinfulness, a rejection of the gaudy joys of this world and a direction of one's focus towards judgement, redemption and heavenly salvation.

It is said that Dr Pusey once regarded it as a sort of rebuke when someone commented upon his smiling, and resolved thereafter not to smile any more. Likewise, he is said to have resolved always to look humbly downwards and not to presume to look up. A leading figure of the Oxford Movement with his friend John Henry (later Cardinal) Newman in the 1830s, Pusey, while never converting to Roman Catholicism like Newman, was a leader of the new Anglo-Catholic tradition within the Church of England. Yet Pusey attracted, and still attracts, a strong following in certain sections of the Church of England, his followers being surnamed 'Puseyites'. One wonders how these two Anglican clergymen, Buckland and Pusey, related to one another, especially within Christ Church, for temperamentally they seemed so far apart. Yet the Bucklands, especially Mary, benefited greatly from Dr Pusey's 'spiritual Ministry'[12] following the deaths of their children, especially that of Adam. I would suggest, quite simply, that while Buckland's optimistic Natural Theology (of which we shall say more in Chapter 8) worked well in the good times, Pusey's deeply earnest and prayerful Christian spirituality was much better equipped for dealing with grief and tragedy. One can easily imagine the grave Dr Pusey, who would be distraught following the death of his beloved young wife Maria Catherine in 1839, walking across Tom Quad to the Buckland house to pray and extend his Christian compassion to the grief-stricken Buckland family. (Dr Pusey and his wife lie below a large white memorial slab in the floor of the nave of Christ Church Cathedral. I, like many others, always try to avoid walking upon it.)

I would suggest, however, that no Georgians or Victorians, no matter how temperamentally merry-hearted they might have been, would have been unschooled in how to cope with tragedy and suffering; scientific erudition apart, practical medicine was pitifully feeble when it came to dealing with serious illness, pain and suffering, and the spectre of death was everywhere present. Prayer, spiritual reading and conversation, and a commitment to good works were just as much a part of the Buckland household as they were of that of Dr Pusey, even if one family was more naturally inclined to jokes and laughter and the other to earnest intro-spection. For while one household might perhaps place more emphasis on the merriment of the wedding feast at Cana and the joy and exhila-ration of the Resurrection and the other on the Good Friday suffering of the crucified Jesus, what they both shared was a deep, Christian com-mitment and a strong sense of humanity's fallen nature and the need for redemption.

A commitment to serving the poor

In addition to wining and dining visiting scientific and academic dig-nitaries, Mrs Mary Buckland was committed to the service of the poor, especially in the parish of St Ebbe in Oxford city centre, only a five-minute walk away from the grand Tom Tower gate of Christ Church, for in early Victorian Oxford wealth and poverty lived cheek by jowl. Instead of attending the Cathedral on Sundays, Mary Buckland would often walk over to St Ebbe's Church with their family, where they would have met and chatted with the other half of the Oxford city community. She also liked the simpler service of St Ebbe's Church, especially for the children, for St Ebbe's was in 1835, and still is today, an active evangelical city par-ish, much given to outreach, Christian teaching and the spread of the gos-pel to all people.

Also living in St Ebbe's parish was a community of poor Jews, whose lives were severely afflicted by a fire, which burned down several of their houses. The Bucklands quickly sprang into action to help them, including loaning the distressed Jewish families valuable items of glassware for use in their religious ceremonies. Mary also paid sums of money to help get several of their devastated small businesses back on their feet. Her kind-ness, in particular, clearly won the hearts of the local Jews, and at Passover time they would come round to make a gift of 'half a dozen of the large, thin wafer-biscuits, about twelve inches across' as a 'token of respect and gratitude from the Jewish community.'[13]

In this pre-railway age of the 1830s, the Bucklands were also on friendly terms with the itinerant bargee families, whose narrow canal boats supplied Oxford with coal and many other bulky items. The Buckland children especially enjoyed visiting the bargee families, living in the tiny, brightly painted cabins at the stern end of each barge. Assured as they were in their secure status as upper-middle-class Christian gentlefolks, the Bucklands were more than willing to cross social divides and do their duty in helping the poor and marginalized. While some people today might accuse them – and folks like them – of being patronizing, one must face the question of what was the alternative: to leave poor Jews, bargees, quarry workers and others to suffer without any aid from 'above'? Rather, one might say, the well-to-do Bucklands were doing their best to live out their Christian commitment in an age that was very different from our own. For whether one read the Old or the New Testament, what was quite plain was that the prosperous owner of the fertile vineyard had a sacred duty to help the poor folks at his gate.

Undoubtedly happy and fun-loving as they were in their Christ Church Canonry, the Buckland children grew up to take life seriously. In addition to visiting the poor and being made aware of their social duty as gentlefolks, time was always seen as precious. Idleness and time-wasting pursuits were not tolerated, as Mrs Elizabeth Gordon in the 1894 *Life* of her father makes abundantly clear. Reading, learning, making things and recycling old things to suit new needs were all part of the daily routine. Whether her brothers ever played cricket or other sports is not known, as Mrs Gordon does not mention them. There was, however, ample opportunity for exercise, such as family rambles around Bagley Woods, Headington and Port Meadow near Oxford. A didactic element was invariably present, for they were taught to identify particular trees, flowers, stones, birds and wild creatures, and to bring choice specimens home to go into their organized childhood collections. The children were even taught how to fold old and discarded letters to make tapers for lighting lamps and candles around the house. Creativity, thrift and self-discipline were all taught as life skills, and one suspects that had not Mary and William been so full of fun and humour, the children's routines might have been rather over-earnest.

But fun was never far away, at least when the family was not in mourning for a child's death. Great pleasure, for example, was had by all in looking after and studying a veritable army of pets, which could include more unconventional creatures, such as rats, mice, hedgehogs, toads, snakes and even a donkey – which latter pet the children sometimes rode into the house and around the drawing-room, seemingly with full parental approval. And there was at least one small pet crocodile, which involved both father and eldest son, Frank, in a truly schoolboy-standard prank.

In the middle of Christ Church's great Tom Quad is a large fountain in a wide, lead-lined circular stone basin of water about five feet deep, known as Mercury, from the statue of the Greek god which stands in its midst. Father and son, it appears, were keeping watch through a window to see when the Dean's carriage drove out of College. Upon witnessing the departure, they carried the pet crocodile out of the Buckland Canonry and took it for a swim in Mercury's deep pool. On another occasion, a live turtle had been brought up from London to be killed and prepared in the kitchens for a College celebratory dinner. Wishing to study how a turtle swam, and if its leg movements corresponded to those of fossilized turtles, not only did they give the poor creature its valedictory swim in Mercury, but, it was said, young Frank got into the water with the turtle and had a ride on its back![14]

Rats, squirrels, toasted mice and tiger steaks for all

Mealtimes in the Buckland Canonry could be truly memorable occasions, as all manner of meats might be served. Crocodile, rat, mouse (tasty on one's breakfast toast, apparently), dog, cat, squirrel, badger, a piece of tiger and other animals appeared not only on the family's plates, but on those of visitors as well. The exotic dishes served up at Mary's ever-hospitable table became legendary and were commented upon by numerous visitors. It was found, however, that mole flesh was unpleasant, and bluebottle flies downright awful! Yet Buckland's experiments with these bizarre foods were most definitely *not* just a personal eccentricity. In addition to his genuine scientific curiosity about these meats, the socially conscious and humane Bucklands were all too aware of a crisis unfolding across Britain in the decades between the end of the Napoleonic Wars in 1815 and the late 1840s, as the country experienced food shortages. A rapidly growing population combined with arable farmland being enclosed, often for more profitable sheep farming for wool, combined with a succession of bad wheat harvests, meant that, for the poor, bread was dear and food often scarce. Then the hated Corn Laws (until Buckland's fellow reformer Prime Minister Sir Robert Peel abolished them in 1846) kept the price of bread at a high level, which benefited landowners and cereal farmers but punished the labourer and factory workers.

When eating fried mice or toasted squirrel, Buckland was also attempting to find cheap, or free, and easily available foodstuffs that might help to nourish the poor, though it might have proved more difficult for an Oxfordshire or Dorset farm labourer to come by crocodile and hyena steaks. Deeply humane intentions lay behind several of William Buckland's apparent eccentricities.

The Buckland children

Though all five of the Buckland children who survived childhood were highly intelligent, it was perhaps Frank, the eldest, who was the most remarkable. 'At two and a half years of age, he never forgets either pictures or people he has seen four months ago', recorded his mother Mary, while Frank's lifelong passion for all aspects of natural history was taking organized shape at about the same time.[15]

When Frank was no more than a little boy who could not yet even speak clear English, a visiting Devonshire clergyman left the Christ Church Canonry 'crestfallen'. The clergyman had travelled up to show Buckland some curious fossils he had found. As Buckland and the visitor were talking together, little Frank happened to be playing in the room. Buckland offered the clergyman's fossils to his son, with the question, 'Frankie, what are these?' to which the little boy replied, 'they are the vertebrae of an ichthyosaurus'.[16] It is hardly surprising that the visitor, who believed that he had made a significant discovery, was crestfallen.

We saw above how the teenage Mary Morland might well have been acquainted with the interior and contents of the Christ Church Lee Building Anatomy School and Museum, and we know for certain that young Frank Buckland sampled its grizzly delights as a small boy. Suspended by a rope in the Anatomy School was the articulated skeleton of a hanged murderer. Little Frank was entertained when William, the elderly caretaker of the building, untied the rope, and by pulling upon it made the skeleton's feet 'dance' on the floor below. The skeleton may well have been that of a big, powerful man who, after being condemned to death many years before by the Oxford Assize Judge for one murder, took a swipe with his fist at his accuser standing nearby, killing him with one blow, satisfied that he could only hang once. The giant dancing male skeleton had a female companion, and they could be made to dance together by means of their ropes. It is not clear whether she had been the woman who, being sentenced by the judge, took off her shoe and threw it at him, almost sending him reeling from his bench.[17]

Elizabeth Gordon's *Life* of her beloved father and George Bompas's *Life* of his brother-in-law Frank Buckland are rich in stories about what their childhoods were like in William and Mary's busy, hard-working, socially-reforming and deeply Christian household. What perhaps comes through most conspicuously is the ongoing sense of joy. William and Mary were perfectly matched in so many ways, and their marriage was truly companionable. This joy in each other's company shone through for their children, whose formative years, when they were not mourning for the latest sibling recently entombed in the Cathedral vault, appear to have been hard-working, amusingly eccentric and extremely happy.

Chapter 7

'Gentlemen, Free and Unconfin'd'. Paying for Geological and Other Scientific Research in Buckland's Britain

It is important to understand how British geology operated within the wider scientific, cultural and official worlds in which William Buckland lived and worked. For British science, be it geology, astronomy, chemistry or medicine, was structured very differently from that of Continental Europe. In Britain, for example, there was little or no formal government funding, largely for political reasons, which will be mentioned below. The great majority of scientists were financially independent gentlemen – working alongside a significant minority of intellectually influential ladies – who paid for their researches out of invested or earned wealth. While nearly all of the men (but not, before the 1860s, the women) were educated at Oxford, Cambridge, the Irish or Scottish universities, teaching hospitals, dissenting academies or in the military, thereafter on an official level their relationship with these institutions tended to be tangential. With no government ministers, research grants or academic assessors to bother about, scientific research and communication hinged upon personal relationships: generally friendly and sociable, but occasionally tinged with bitter rivalry, as in the case of Sir Henry De la Beche and Sir Roderick Murchison regarding the Devonian Controversy discussed in Chapter 5.

British science's operational bases, therefore, were essentially social, self-regulating and in many ways informal. They consisted of gatherings in members' London residences or country houses, the gentlemen's clubs of Pall Mall, most notably the Athenaeum after 1824, and their members-run metropolitan learned societies. These scientific gentlemen saw science (as did Buckland) as an integral part of liberal culture rather than a profession or basis for a structured career, and not infrequently they were members of more than one society. A geologist might also be a member of the Society of Antiquaries, or after 1820 the Royal Astronomical Society, each with its own social and dining circles, for they did not see their disciplines as rigid and exclusive.

One can rightly say, therefore, that British science, throughout Buckland's lifetime and beyond, was essentially club-based in its social structure. In the Athenaeum or Travellers' Club, for example, one might meet William Buckland, the engineer Isambard Kingdom Brunel and the astronomer Sir John Herschel, along with physicians, lawyers, Archbishops, Members of Parliament and even a Prime Minister. Each had come in to dine or meet friends, and a literary gentleman might share a bottle of madeira with a fossil geologist, or see the increasingly solitary artist J. M. W. Turner sitting quietly by himself in the Athenaeum, with his candle and glass of wine.

On the other hand, this informality of organization in no way impaired the quality of their scientific work, for Buckland and his colleagues (including those in the non-geological sciences) were highly respected across Europe. Anglo-European scientific relationships were amicable and egalitarian, and these men regularly crossed the Channel both ways, visiting each other, exchanging medals and granting membership of each other's learned bodies, all in a quite unxenophobic fashion. One will recall from the last chapter how Elizabeth Gordon (Miss Buckland) mentioned the regular stream of foreign visitors who dropped into her parents' Christ Church Canonry to eat or to stay. But how did this peculiarly British mode of scientific organization come about?

The British learned society

Britain's first major learned scientific society was the Royal Society of London, founded in 1660, and chartered by HM King Charles II in 1662. Its purpose was to advance all branches of natural knowledge, not by abstract speculation, but by observation and hands-on collection and classification of natural things, and by disciplined quantitative experimentation, backed up, where appropriate, by mathematical analysis. It had an open-ended, and in many ways a democratic, approach to science, and was open to all people, anywhere, who had the time and inclination to undertake the research. There were no arcane requirements comprehensible only to the cognoscenti, and affairs were generally conducted, and proceedings published, in the vernacular. Research papers from overseas scientists were accepted both in the language of their countries and in the still international learned language of Latin.

The *Philosophical Transactions*, published continuously from 1665 down to today, along with books and lectures published by the Royal Society, contained mineralogical and geological items as a normal part of its spectrum of sciences. These included articles or observations about crystals and minerals, the inflammable or 'dead damps' airs found in coal, lead and copper mines, local economic geography such as coal seams, the nature and possible causes of mineral springs and accounts of fossils dug up in various places. Earthquakes and volcanic eruptions were reported, as witnessed by travellers or sea captains, along with unusual meteorological phenomena like aurorae, which were sometimes believed to be occasioned by the release of something from the earth. For the deeply maritime British, as for the Dutch savants, there was a long-term fascination with geomagnetism and what particular internal terrestrial phenomena might lie behind the westward drift of the compass needle and its baffling non-north-facing twists, as witnessed in the south Atlantic. Edmond Halley's three long-haul voyages in HMS *Paramore* between 1698 and 1701 were made with the explicit purpose of examining and collecting data about geomagnetic phenomena.

As was shown at some length in Chapter 3, Robert Hooke's far-reaching 'Lectures and Discourses of Earthquakes' delivered to the Royal Society between 1664 and 1700 represented the most complete and sustained geological study conducted within the early Royal Society, containing Hooke's conclusions about a vastly ancient pre-Deluge earth, complete with fossils, extinctions and changing continents.

All of this research discussed before the Royal Society, however, either in papers delivered to meetings or published under the Society's imprimatur (with the exception of Halley's naval voyages), was the work of private gentlemen. The Royal Society, unlike the academies of Paris or

Bologna, was a private self-funded body, its members part of a Fellowship of equals who were free to elect new Fellows without seeking permission from a monarch or patron. Their pattern was in many ways the self-electing Fellowship of an Oxford or Cambridge college, and they paid for and published their researches out of their own pockets. As a corporate body, they were, as Bishop Thomas Sprat styled them in his *A History of the Royal Society* in 1667, 'Gentlemen, Free and Unconfin'd'.[1] While the King had given them a title and two Royal Charters, he gave them no money or resources beyond some ceremonial items, and hence did not attempt to exert any control upon their researches.

This 'Gentlemen, Free and Unconfin'd' model became the pattern for future British learned societies. The same format was used in 1707 when a group of gentlemen came together to form the Society of Antiquaries. Their charter would be granted in 1751, and King George II, and his royal successor, would serve as their patron. By 'antiquaries' was meant individuals fascinated by what would later be called archaeology, who devoted themselves especially to the study of British ruins, such as Stonehenge, Roman and medieval ruins and surviving ancient manuscripts. One can also see in the antiquaries a connection to geology, for both early archaeologists and geologists had a fascination with the lie of the land and the excavation of what was buried beneath the ground. Besides, as most early antiquaries were landowners, they shared with the geologists an interest in good land management and the exploitation of mineral resources.

The next major society to be founded was the 1768 Royal Society of Arts, in which the connoisseur King George III had an active interest. Once again, this society, which also had the educative function of training up young painters and draughtsmen and in running practical art classes, was self-funded, and its famous annual summer exhibitions had an overt commercial dimension in so far as the newly exhibited pictures were offered for sale, in part to recompense the young painters themselves and in part to finance the Society.

The Geological Society, 1807, and an enterprising apothecary's apprentice

Then came the Geologists, in 1807. On 13 October, a group of 13 gentlemen met at the Freemasons' Arms, Covent Garden, London, with the aim of founding a society devoted to the study and advancement of geology. Among their stated aims was to regularize geological nomenclature, and such was the interest in geological science that by 1815 it had around 400 members on its books.

One of the original 13 founders was the 29-year-old Humphry (later Sir Humphry) Davy, the already famous chemist. But who was Davy, with his partiality for dandy fashions and fondness of moving in London's most elite social circles? In 1807, Davy was Professor at that hub of upmarket West End science, the Royal Institution in Albemarle Street, near Piccadilly. In addition to his already acknowledged major chemical discoveries, such as the use of electrolysis to discover the new elements sodium and potassium, Davy was the Institution's big draw, and his brilliant and theatrically powerful lectures delivered to hundreds of fee-paying ladies and gentlemen rivalled anything on offer at the Drury Lane or Covent Garden West End theatres.

When one looks at Davy's origins, one finds that they were not a million miles removed from those of his geological contemporary William Smith. Both were the sons of provincial working tradesmen and artisans: Smith's father, as we saw in Chapter 5, being an Oxfordshire blacksmith and Davy's a Cornish wood carver. So how did Smith come to be considered an 'outsider' in the upmarket world of the Geological Society, whereas Davy was a founder member and very much part of the inner gang, with his interests in the chemistry of minerals and agriculture?

As indicated in Chapter 5, I would put it down to knowing how to get on in the world. Unlike Smith, with his pronounced rural Oxfordshire accent and prizefighter demeanour, Davy soon shed his Cornish talk. From first working as a Penzance apothecary's apprentice, then as assistant to a high-profile Bristol experimental physician, Thomas Beddoes, he was firmly ensconced in the equally self-made creation of the American loyalist Count Rumford (Benjamin Thompson), the commercially-based Royal Institution, by the age of 23. From there, the road was open: a marriage to Jane Kerr (a rich landowning widow, formerly Mrs Apreece), friendship with everybody who was anybody right up to the Prince Regent, a knighthood and independent wealth. While William Smith was a man of fossils, fields and the rural landscape, Sir Humphry was an adroit social climber, accomplished self-promoter and entrepreneur – in addition to being a scientific genius and discoverer.

William Buckland joined the Geological Society in 1813, and during 1824–1825 he became 'Charter President', holding the presidential office in the year that King George IV, the former Prince Regent, presented his Royal Charter to the Society. Buckland was something of a hybrid social type in the Society, however, being neither a straightforward gentleman of independent landed means nor a working professional in a non-geological profession, such as Sir Roderick Murchison, the soldier, or Gideon Mantell, the doctor. Instead, he was an opulently beneficed Anglican clergyman of old Devonshire ancestry, and a Cathedral Canon 'without portfolio', as it were, who held what was effectively a personal Chair in Oxford, with a magnificent house thrown in free of charge. While I am not aware of Mary's personal financial settlement from her father, Benjamin Morland, I suspect that, from Benjamin's landed and commercial interests, it would have been worth having.

So, when one considers the open-ended, more or less 'duties free' nature of his Christ Church Canonry, Buckland certainly would have qualified as a '*Gentleman*, Free and Unconfin'd'.

Politics, finance and science

This 'Unconfin'd' model characterized British science from the Renaissance to the late nineteenth century, and stood very much in contrast to that of Continental Europe. In France, Germany, Austria and most other European states, patronage for not just the sciences but also the arts operated in a vertical as opposed to a horizontal direction. In these much more autocratically governed states, emperors, kings, cardinals, archdukes and ministers of state decided who got the rewards, the free space and the encouragement to be creative – invariably on the taxpayers' money. Think of the court composers Haydn and Mozart, painters such as El Greco, and the hosts of literary, artistic and scientific savants of King Louis XIV,

Frederick the Great, the Russian Czars and Czarinas or even the favoured intellectuals who clustered around Napoleon Bonaparte: men such as the artist David, the mathematician Laplace and the geologist Cuvier.

Perhaps the only possible exceptions were the mercantile Dutch – in Amsterdam, the Hague, and the University of Leiden. Gerard Mercator, the pioneer cartographer, for example, was a commercial engraver and publisher, yet even the landowning astronomical brothers Christiaan and Constantijn Huygens were willing to be lured by royal patronage. Protestant Christiaan found himself in a not always easy relationship as a pensioner and Académicien of the French King Louis XIV in Paris, while Constantijn worked on a high ministerial level with Stadtholder Willem; when his boss became King William III of England in 1688, he became effectively the King's trusted personal secretary. In England, things were very different, and this derived essentially from political circumstances, especially following the English Civil War of the 1640s, and most of all from the Parliamentarily circumscribed monarchy which came in with William III, an arrangement that would lead to the constitutional monarchy with limited powers of modern Britain. Having fought a civil war, then effectively forced the potentially absolutist Stuart King James II to abdicate in 1688, Parliament established itself as the dominant power in the land, and crucially, this meant full control of the nation's public finances.

The courts of William, Anne and the Hanoverian Georges after 1714 were hard up, relatively speaking, compared with the absolute sovereigns on the Continent. There were the independent royal estates that generated revenue for the sovereign, along with debated Parliamentary grants of supply, but compared to one of France's Louis or Russia's Peter and Catherine, British monarchs were kept on a tight leash. What is more, the seemingly all-powerful Parliament was also obliged to watch its back, if any given party or faction wanted to win the next election. The real whip in Britain was held not by the King or by the aristocracy, itself relatively modest in Continental terms, but by those city and county freeholders who could vote in Parliamentary and city elections. Ever watchful of the conduct of European governments, these people were all for small government, where taxation was minimal and wholly controlled by Parliament, and only basic security was funded from the public purse, which primarily meant the Army, Navy and Civil Service. The sciences, arts, education and culture in general were to be funded by private individuals, from the money that they were free to make and keep, through a system of low taxation and (hopefully) good fiscal management. Hence, the '*Gentlemen*, Free and Unconfin'd' ethic.

This lack of regulation and emphasis upon personal and economic freedom made possible the initiative-taking that produced the industrial and agricultural revolutions. While this laissez-faire economy could lead to exploitation, it also provided enormous opportunities, and it is interesting to note how Continental visitors to England were often struck by the freedom and relative prosperity enjoyed by the English poor, compared with the permanently half-starved feudal peasant classes of Europe. Even the English working and poorer classes, it was often noted, openly scorned and attacked unpopular figures in the street, demanded meat and not just vegetables, and wore leather shoes (even if second-hand) rather than wooden *sabots* or clogs. While the rapid industrial mechanization which generated vast numbers of low-skilled, low-pay factory workers in the north had become a national scandal by the 1830s, it also paved the way for non-revolutionary social reform, largely driven by Christian Evangelicals on all social levels, from Lord Shaftesbury's Factory Acts at one end to the Rochdale workers' self-help Cooperative Movement at the other.

By 1800, however, while the Royal Society was continuing to play a pre-eminent role in scientific organization, there were many who felt that it had become too set in its ways and too narrow in its range. This was in part a consequence of the apparently eternal presidency of Sir Joseph Banks, who had sailed with Captain Cook on his first voyage of 1769–1771, been elected president in 1778, and remained in that office until his death in 1820. Sir Joseph's primary concern was botany, and while it is true that he, Buckland and Sir Humphry Davy got on well, Banks's relative narrowness, at a time when all the sciences were expanding and advancing greatly, was seen by many as a problem – one only partially relieved when the former Cornish woodcarver's son Davy succeeded him to the Presidency. In part, it had been Banks's conservatism that had led to the formation of the Geological Society in 1807 and the Royal Astronomical Society in 1820.

Things were developing fast in the 1820s, and there was a growing need for a new type of non-specialist scientific society, much wider in its range and personnel than were the existing societies, yet which would work in harmony with them. As many towns and cities across Britain, such as York, Manchester and Dublin, were becoming active scientific centres, it was felt necessary to break what seemed like the metropolitan stranglehold upon British science. This would lead to the founding of the British Association for the Advancement of Science in 1831: an association within which William Buckland would be an active force and charismatic presence from 1831 down to the late 1840s.

The British Association for the Advancement of Science

The British Association for the Advancement of Science was the brainchild of a group of Fellows of the Royal Society, and it was modelled, ironically, on the Gesellschaft Deutscher Naturforscher of Germany, that country which epitomized academic state-related science. The driving force behind it was the Revd Dr William Vernon Harcourt, one of that dynasty of powerful York city, Minster and county families, along with, among others, Sir Charles Babbage, Edinburgh's Sir David Brewster and the Revd Dr William Whewell, Master of Trinity College, Cambridge (the scholarship boy son of a Lancaster carpenter).

They were thinking in terms of an *association*, much more open-ended and broader in membership than a specialist society, and one that would, on principle, never meet in London. Instead, the new British Association for the Advancement of Science after 1831 would be itinerant, moving around the country, and holding a large annual scientific jamboree at some major centre within the British Isles: a grand scientific conference, no less. Over the days when the Association was holding its meeting, there would be specialist sessions devoted to different sciences which subscribing members could attend. Then, when the more focused scientific papers had been given, there would be a variety of social events laid on, such as dinners, excursions to local places of interest and band concerts, which the wives and families of attendees could enjoy. The British Association would rapidly evolve into a holiday for the thinking classes, spread out over several days but generally avoiding Sundays, so that the many clerical Association members could get home to perform their spiritual duties on the Lord's Day.

The first, 1831, meeting was held in York, largely hosted by the already well-established Yorkshire Philosophical Society and organized by the young John Phillips. It was such a runaway success in its range, openness and popular appeal that it was decided to hold another the following year, this time in Oxford. William Buckland had been unable to attend the York inaugural meeting owing to the tragic death of one of his children. But he was the natural choice for the office of President for the June 1832 Oxford meeting of the Association.

The Oxford meeting was an even greater success than the original launch in York. Crowds poured in, and not just gentlemen of science, but also journalists, scientifically-minded members of the public and clergy, including their wives and daughters. The Buckland Canonry in Tom Quad became a social centre in its own right, and the Royal Duke of Sussex, President of the Royal Society, was their houseguest. Buckland, with his instinctive flair for oratory and sociability, and his unquestioned status as a scientist of the front rank, played a major part in turning the 1832 meeting of the British Association into a thundering success. Oxford played its own part in adding ceremonial touches, the opening taking place amid the grandeur of Sir Christopher Wren's Sheldonian Theatre. It was in the Sheldonian that Buckland straightened the record of the gentlemen geologists' slighting of William Smith, when he presented the now elderly man with the Geological Society's prestigious Wollaston Medal, to rapturous applause.

In addition to the academic papers read before the geological and other specialist sections of the Association, there was no shortage of pleasurable diversions, with dinners, teas, music and social activities, which could also appeal to the ladies accompanying their husbands. Oxford, in its full June glory, with its ancient college buildings, beautiful gardens, woods and three converging rivers, was the perfect setting. These midsummer delights included outings into the countryside to see things of interest, one memorable such outing being to the summit of nearby Shotover Hill. Here, to a mixed audience including ladies as well as savants, Buckland delivered a memorable lecture on the lie of the land, particularly agricultural improvement. He discussed how a knowledge of geology could lead to the more effective drainage of wetlands and peat bogs, not only to improve the economic value of the land, but also to produce more food in a time of bread shortages and the dangerous riots that might result.

Buckland's brilliant and resounding concluding Presidential Address was about the importance of geology. Much was also said about the early 'dinosaur', the megatherium. It too was delivered to a mixed audience of ladies as well as scientific gentlemen, and various people afterwards left written record of the power of Buckland's lecture, and his ability to make the technical, anatomical and dietary features of this great extinct beast comprehensible to a lay or popular audience, as reported by Sir Charles Lyell to his friend the doctor-geologist Gideon Mantell, in June 1832. As we have seen, Buckland was an instinctive and brilliant teacher who captivated audiences.[2]

But what was the role played by the ladies in the early British Association meetings, and especially that of 1832? Why were they excluded from the formal sessions?

The ladies at the British Association

By 1832 there was a small yet very significant body of women in British science, the oldest of whom was the astronomer Miss Caroline Herschel, now living in retirement in her native Hanover. In 1835, she would be awarded the Gold Medal of the Royal Astronomical Society. Also, in mathematics, there was Sir Charles Babbage's friend and Lord Byron's daughter, Lady Ada Lovelace. Living in London was Jane, the wife of the Genevan exile physician Dr Alexander Marcet, herself famed as a writer and scientific expositor. In Lyme Regis, there was the 21-year-old Mary Anning who, with her mother, ran a curiosity shop in the town, and already had a rapidly growing reputation as a palaeontologist. We will meet Mary Anning again in Chapter 9. Nor must we forget Mary Buckland, who combined the duties of a busy housewife, mother and hostess with being a serious and creative colleague of her husband, William.

The most famous and widely known and published scientific woman in 1832 was, perhaps, the 52-year-old Mary Somerville, who, while an

Thompson, Pinx.

Walker & Boutall. Ph.Sc.

ætat 62.

1. William Buckland in Doctor of Divinity gown holding a large fossil bone. (From a portrait by T. C. Thomson, reproduced from Gordon, *Life and Correspondence of William Buckland*, frontispiece.)

EXPEDITION TO SHOTOVER.

2. Three sketches, unattributed but perhaps by Buckland's friend Revd Dr William D. Conybeare, of geological jollifications in the field at Shotover, near Oxford, *c.* 1820. *Top*: Clowning around with large hammers, carried in mimicry of the ceremonial maces of the Oxford University Bedels. *Middle*: An excavated fossilized beast, rather like a small mammoth, is joyfully carried home. *Bottom*: Buckland on horseback describing the lie of the land, using a large bone as a pointer. (Gordon, *Life and Correspondence of William Buckland*, p. 29.)

3. William Buckland delivering a geological lecture in 1822 inside the Ashmolean Museum, Oxford (founded 1683; now the History of Science Museum). Buckland's audience appears to be composed of senior University members. The seated gentleman in the old-fashioned wig on the left is probably the elderly Revd Dr Martin Routh, Provost of Magdalen College, while the young man standing beside him is probably Buckland's friend Dr Charles Daubeny MD, chemist, botanist, and Fellow of Magdalen. (Gordon, *Life and Correspondence of William Buckland*, facing p. 32.)

KIRKDALE CAVE.

4. Kirkdale Cave, north Yorkshire, *c.* 1821, showing the newly-made opening to this virgin bone cave recently discovered by quarrymen. Here, Buckland discovered complete hyena skeletons, along with fragments of other animals long since vanished from Yorkshire. (Gordon, *Life and Correspondence of William Buckland*, p. 57.)

5. William Buckland entering Kirkdale Cave, only to find it full of living hyenas hungrily
tucking into their supper! Cartoon by Buckland's lifelong friend Revd Dr William D.
Conybeare, *c.* 1823. This and other surviving cartoons convey a sense of the merriment the geological gentlemen enjoyed together, combining science, religion, and fun.
(Gordon, *Life and Correspondence of William Buckland*, p. 61.)

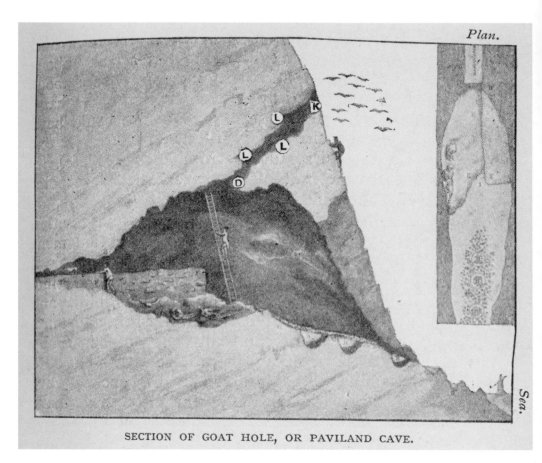

Plan.

Sea.

SECTION OF GOAT HOLE, OR PAVILAND CAVE.

6. Section through the Paviland Cave, Gower, south Wales. Access was only possible through two small apertures high up the cliff face, with a dead drop into the rocks and sea below. One gets a sense of the sheer intrepidity, to say nothing of the physical strength and agility, displayed by Buckland and his fellow field geologists and cave explorers. (Gordon, *Life and Correspondence of William Buckland*, p. 67.)

SECTION OF CAVE IN DREAM LEAD MINE, NEAR WIRKSWORTH, DERBYSHIRE.

7. Section through the Dream Lead Mine cave, Derbyshire, with opened-up vertical shafts, giving access to the rich fossilized bone treasures awaiting excavation. (Gordon, *Life and Correspondence of William Buckland*, p. 71.)

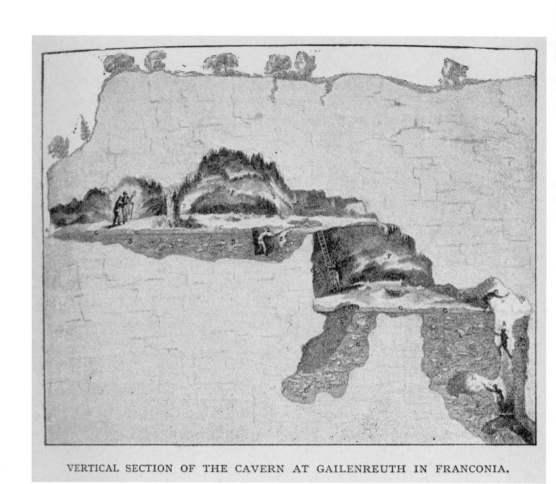

VERTICAL SECTION OF THE CAVERN AT GAILENREUTH IN FRANCONIA.

8. Section through the Gailenreuth bone cave, Franconia, Germany. (Gordon, *Life and Correspondence of William Buckland*, p. 72.)

9. William and Mary Buckland and their son Frank in their Canonry in Tom Quad, Christ Church, Oxford, surrounded by some of their fossil treasures. (Silhouette by Auguste Edouart, 1829; reproduced from Gordon, *Life and Correspondence of William Buckland*, p. 103.)

10. 'Awful Changes': cartoon by Sir Henry De la Beche, 1830, depicting a bespectacled Professor Ichthyosaurus giving a lecture on the fossilized skull of a presumably extinct human being to his fellow-beasts in their primordial ocean. It presents an amusing inversion of the modern geologist lecturing on an extinct ichthyosaurus, and reminds us, yet again, of the humour and playfulness that so many of these geological researchers shared. (Reproduced from Gordon, *Life and Correspondence of William Buckland*, p. 127.)

ANCIENT DORSETSHIRE.

11. *Duria Antiquior*, or prehistoric Dorset. Reconstruction by Sir Henry De la Beche, 1830, from fossils discovered on the Jurassic coast by Mary Anning: the first such pictorial representation of a prehistoric scene based on fossil evidence. Originally in watercolour, the picture was reissued in lithograph and used as a teaching aid, by William Buckland among others. (Reproduced from Gordon, *Life and Correspondence of William Buckland*, facing p. 116.)

William Buckland
From a Picture painted about 1843

12. William Buckland carrying his famous 'Blue Bag' of recent geological finds. (From a painting by Richard Ansdell, *c.* 1843; reproduced from Gordon, *Life and Correspondence of William Buckland*, facing p. 85.)

13. William Buckland in 'Ice Age' field costume. Following his 'conversion' to Louis Agassiz's glacial theory of landscape formation in 1840 and abandonment of his earlier diluvial theory, Buckland heads north to look at the Lake District and the Scottish Highlands with fresh eyes. He has clearly just got off the stagecoach in the middle of nowhere, and the coach, in the distance, carries on its way. (Cartoon by Thomas Sopwith; reproduced from Gordon, *Life and Correspondence of William Buckland*, facing p. 145.)

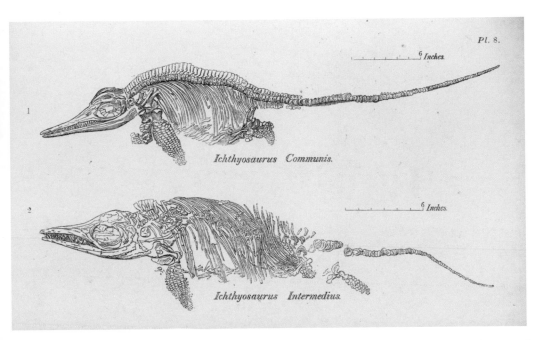

Pl. 8.

Ichthyosaurus Communis.

Ichthyosaurus Intermedius.

14. Ichthyosaurus skeletons. These could be twenty feet long. (Buckland, *Geology and Mineralogy*, vol. 2, pl. 8.)

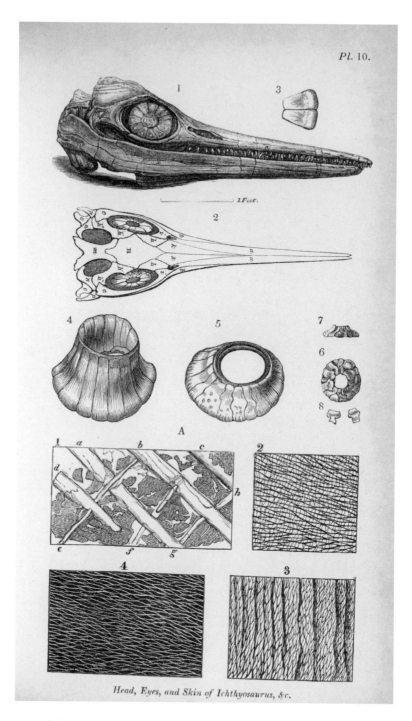

Head, Eyes, and Skin of Ichthyosaurus, &c.

15. Ichthyosaurus skull, about four feet long, with detail of eye sockets and skin. The individual fossilized 'leaves' surrounding the eyeball – an early form of iris – could by changing their shape vary the beast's vision and protect the eye from pressure in very deep water. (Buckland, *Geology and Mineralogy*, vol. 2, pl. 10.)

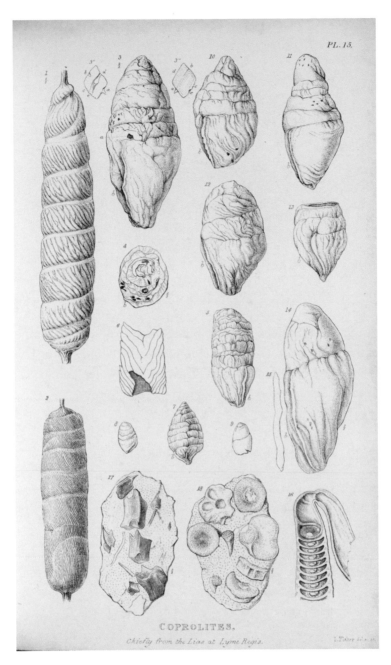

COPROLITES,

Chiefly from the Lias at Lyme Regis.

I. Fisher del. st.

16. Coprolites. Buckland recognized the crucial significance of these fossilized lumps of excrement. When found inside an ichthyosaurus or other prehistoric creature, they indicate the location of the digestive tract. Twisted or 'barley sugar' coprolites suggest the peristaltic action of the gut. When coprolite beds (the beds of ancient seas) were excavated, the ground-up lumps were found to be rich in phosphates and invaluable as agricultural fertilizer. (Buckland, *Geology and Mineralogy*, vol. 2, pl. 15.)

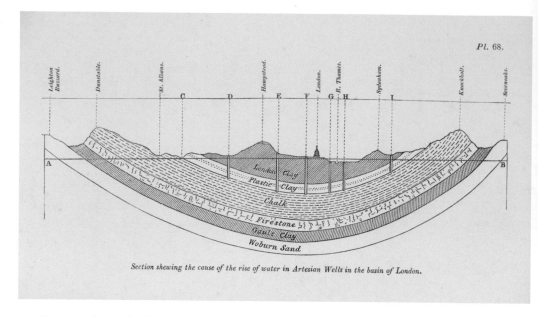

Pl. 68.

Section shewing the cause of the rise of water in Artesian Wells in the basin of London.

17. Section through the Thames Valley. Note the dome of St Paul's Cathedral marking the bottom of the valley, with the land rising to the north and south. The dipping sections of sands and clays deep underground trapped pure water, and made artesian wells possible. (Buckland, *Geology and Mineralogy*, vol. 2, pl. 68.)

18. 'Faraday Giving His Card to Father Thames': cartoon in *Punch* magazine, vol. 29, p. 26 (21 July 1855). (Author's collection.)

internationally renowned and respected gravitational dynamicist and astronomer, also shared interests with the geological community. Though not especially concerned with excavating fossils in caves and quarries, 'Mrs Somerville', as she was always politely called, accepted all the latest ideas about a pre-Edenic world and the geological significance of floods. On the other hand, her instinctively mathematical mind was most inclined to crystallography and the planes, angles and structures encountered within crystal.

It is all the more surprising, therefore, that Buckland and the organizers of the 1832 British Association decided not to permit ladies to sit in on or even contribute to the formal learned papers sessions of the meetings, where it was believed they would take down the tone. Ladies could, of course, attend the social events with their husbands, and the 'popular' lectures, such as President Buckland holding forth on Shotover Hill. What might strike us as very paradoxical, however, is that Mary Somerville and some other thinking ladies not only fully endorsed the exclusion of the scientific sisterhood from the Association's research papers sessions, but were even willing to stay away altogether. In some ways, the reason is easy to see, for science had become fashionable in London's West End, and the Royal Institution, Surrey Institution and similar venues not infrequently had almost 50–50 male-female attendance at their lectures. The picture of a chemistry lecture at the Surrey Institution, probably delivered by Friedrich Accum in 1813, for example, shows a crowded audience, a good half of whom were fashionably attired in flowing dresses and big hats.

Caroline Fox, whose journals have been cited already, was one early Victorian lady who had a serious interest in science and was certainly no fashionable dilettante. The daughter of a West Country Fellow of the Royal Society, her journal records social meetings and dinners with numerous scientists of the day, such as the Bucklands, and she clearly understood what these men were doing. Among other things, this Quaker lady records aspects of the Bristol meeting of the British Association in 1836, when she was aged 17, though it is clear that she never attended any of the formal sessions.[3] Yet Caroline, highly intelligent and socially perceptive as she was, seems to have simply accepted this as the natural way of the world. Perhaps she, Mrs Somerville and the other 'thinking' scientific ladies were afraid of the Association attracting the wrong sort of women:

namely, ladies of rank and fashion who might open it up to being no more than 'a sort of Albemarle [Royal Institution] dilettanti meeting instead of a serious philosophical union of working men'.[4]

This attitude of Mary Somerville and others might strike us as strange today. But this was an age when a lady's place was seen as the drawing room or nursery, and not the laboratory, and where it was felt by many that the enlightened Dr William Somerville FRS, MD, was playing with fire in allowing his wife to occupy so much of her time in such potentially brain-damaging activities as gravitational physics. Surely, she would go mad, as female brains were not up to such rigorous activity! When Mary Somerville's formidable *Mechanism of the Heavens* came out in 1831, a West Country MP thought it unnatural for a woman to write such a book, denounced her before Parliament, and said that she needed to be taught her proper place.[5] On the other hand, the Somervilles' more enlightened friends, Lord Chancellor Henry Brougham and the Revd Dr William Whewell, warmly applauded her achievement. What is more, Whewell and his Cambridge mathematician friend, the Revd Dr George Peacock, who in 1839 would be appointed Dean of Ely Cathedral, wrote to say that they were going to use Mary's *Mechanism* as a textbook for the Mathematical Tripos course in Trinity College, Cambridge, thus making it the first book by a woman to be used in high-level university science teaching.[6]

So were Mary Somerville and her learned sisters willing to exclude more 'normal' ladies from tough scientific meetings as a way of preserving their own intellectual integrity as 'natural philosophers'?

By the 1870s, however, Bedford College and Royal Holloway, London, Cheltenham Ladies' College, Cambridge's Girton and Newnham, Oxford's Somerville and Lady Margaret Hall, and other colleges had opened up serious academic education to women, and things were all set to change, though the awarding of degrees took longer. But either with or without active women participants, the British Association began to open up science, and to some extent to democratize it.

The Geological Survey

The Geological Survey began in 1832, as an adjunct to the work of the much older, especially post-1791, Ordnance Survey under Major-General William Roy FRS and then the inexhaustible Colonel Thomas Colby FRS, part of a growing band of scientifically minded soldiers, usually in the Royal Engineers or the Royal Artillery, and often connected with the Royal Military Academy, Woolwich. The Ordnance Survey's purpose was to survey the whole of the British Isles to a new and staggeringly exact standard of cartographic accuracy: a standard which would later be extended to the Indian and other British imperial surveys. As the cartographers measured and quantified the lie of the land, so the companion Geological Survey set out, at a time when economic geology was becoming increasingly important to industry and agriculture, to do the same for what lay beneath the soil.

As we saw in Chapter 5, Sir Henry De la Beche became the first Superintendent, beginning with the Devon survey, which would give rise to the Devonian Controversy. The Survey aimed to take a geological map of the type first drawn by William Smith in 1815 a stage further in terms of scale, detail and accuracy. Such a map, it was recognized, would have not only academic cartographic value, but could be vital from a national economic perspective as well, and such an exact chart, printed and coloured on many sheets, could be used to identify the likely locations of new mineral resources, lands that could be drained and improved for agriculture, and the best routes for new canals, or, as was becoming much more important by 1840, new railways.

While the Geological Survey did have an official, government-backed dimension, it was nonetheless funded in what was by 1835 a characteristically British fashion: the government might provide capital funding, but still assume that private individuals would routinely give their time and their own resources on a day to day basis. (This public-private partnership still operates today in what is now styled the British Geological Survey, where one half of its budget comes from the government science budget, and the other half from private sector commercial commission work.)

This semi-official, semi-Grand-Amateur pattern was also in operation at the Kew Observatory, both in Buckland's time and long thereafter.

King George III's once private astronomical observatory, with its physics instrument collection at Kew, took on a new role in the early nineteenth century. Instead of astronomy, it would co-operate with private institutions at home and public ones abroad to monitor changes in the earth's magnetic field. Kew Observatory would become a pioneering institution in geology's sister science of geophysics, to which meteorological recording would soon be added. Yet the man who drove it on for many years was a scientific military man, the unsalaried Colonel Edward Sabine, who was often in conflict with Sir George Airy, the very professional, and salaried Astronomer Royal at Greenwich. Right into the early twentieth century, Kew Observatory would be largely obliged to pay its own way on a daily basis, and its staff would undertake the precision calibration and testing of scientific instruments, such as thermometers, for commercial manufacturers to help generate a regular income.[7]

Buckland's entire geological career would be spent in this world of '*Gentlemen*, Free and Unconfin'd'. The same would apply to the next generation geologist and naturalist Charles Darwin, whose entire achievement stood on the foundation of his and his wife, Emma Wedgwood's, ample private resources. Darwin never held a paid job, and even on his famous HMS *Beagle* voyage, he was effectively a passenger and guest of the Captain and was expected to pay his own bills.

Scientists were mainly self-funded at this period, but there were some specific exceptions: one of those was a bequest that enabled Buckland, through the Royal Society, to publish a magnificent two-volume work which would epitomize the state of things geological by that date. The work would also contain one of the classic statements of science-related Natural Theology. This would be Buckland's Bridgewater Treatise, *Geology and Mineralogy Considered with Reference to Natural Theology*.

Chapter 8

Buckland's Bridgewater Treatise and Natural Theology

In 1829 the Revd Francis Henry Egerton, eighth Earl of Bridgewater, died and left an important bequest. A sum of £8,000 was entrusted to the President of the Royal Society, Davies Gilbert, for the writing of eight books by leading men of science and the Church (including the Church of Scotland), both lay and ordained, on the 'Power, Wisdom, and Goodness of God as manifested in the Creation'. This would lead to the commissioning of eight major works to argue the case for Natural Theology, in eight different departments of nature.

Eight men were commissioned to write the Bridgewater Treatises, encompassing a range from the moral nature of mankind (Thomas Chalmers), to anatomy and physiology (Charles Bell and John Kidd), to chemistry (William Prout), to astronomy and physics (William Whewell).[1] William Buckland wrote *Geology and Mineralogy Considered with Reference to Natural Theology*, which was published in 1836 in two handsome volumes, with cheaper printings eventually following. Volume II was primarily devoted to over 700 exquisitely engraved plates of fossils, skeletons of extinct beasts and geological sections through the landscape, illustrating, for example, the north to south section of the Thames Valley in London and showing the rock and clay formations on either side of the river.

Geology and Mineralogy would be Buckland's *magnum opus*, and was truly a magisterial work, both scientifically and theologically. As many reviewers commented, and one can easily see for oneself today by opening the volumes, it was beautifully and clearly written, encapsulating Buckland's well-known capacity for combining the highest erudition with clarity and elegance of expression – as he did in his lectures. Yet Buckland was apologetic for having taken so long in writing *Geology and Mineralogy*, and in a letter to Sir Roderick Murchison, he made some illuminating comments about himself and his working methods. Buckland reveals himself to have been a 'night owl' and joked with Sir Roderick that, not being a soldier as Sir Roderick had been, he was no early riser and 'as I have not your valuable military talent of early rising, I cannot steal a march upon the enemy by getting over the ground before breakfast.'[2] Buckland preferred to work deep into the night when all was quiet, and as we know from their son Frank, 'my mother sat up night after night, for weeks and months consecutively, writing to my father's dictation.'[3] So the dawn would frequently steal in around the window shutters of their Christ Church Canonry heralding a new day, to find husband and wife still busy writing, and the candles almost burned down to their sconces.

The structure, content and argument of *Geology and Mineralogy*

Buckland's was perhaps the biggest and most detailed of the eight Bridgewater Treatises. Its two handsome volumes were finally signed off from Christ Church on 30 May 1836. The first volume, of 600 pages, carried the text of the argument and detailed descriptions of numerous specimens, along with a powerful and sustained defence of the science of geology. Bound up with this argument was Buckland's equally cogent defence of traditional Natural Theology, and a clear elucidation of how modern geological research was wholly congruent with that theology, tracing the divine hand not only through present-day nature, but through the 'millions and millions' of years which had rolled before. But more of the Natural Theology anon.

Buckland begins the first of the 24 chapters comprising Volume I by looking at the formation and state of the archaic earth, which preceded all life forms. First, after the creation, came the crystalline rocks, formed from the primary chemical elements. This is mineralogy. He then goes on to discuss the formative processes that shaped the archaic globe, such as volcanic eruptions, earthquakes, and pre-Noachian flood action.

Then came the earliest forms of life, simple shell creatures in the oceans, which went on to make the sediments on the seabed from which the chalks and limestones would form. Those in turn would be followed by a progression of higher or more anatomically complex forms, such as great reptiles, and even great flying pterodactyls, found in the Stonesfield quarries near Oxford and elsewhere in Europe.

Each new type of living form would follow after the deliberate extinction of the earlier form, when the Great Creator decided to repopulate the globe with higher forms. This was quite different from evolution, for new forms and species did not *evolve* out of earlier ones, but were entirely unique creations in themselves. The agents through which these changes came about were Buckland's famous catastrophes, direct interventions of the divine will: an idea originally proposed by Cuvier and borrowed with acknowledgement by Buckland, as we have seen.

Having outlined his geological mechanism, Buckland next goes on to illustrate how diverse the geological creation was, even in a land area the size of Britain. Imagine, he tells us, that three foreign visitors landed on our shores: what kind of country would they find, to report back to friends at home? The first visitor, coming ashore in Cornwall or north Devon, would be greeted by a landscape of primary, largely volcanic, rocks, as he travelled around Dartmoor and crossed St George's Channel to arrive near St David's in south Wales. Travelling north through Wales, then across into Cumberland and on into Scotland, he would see primary mineral rocks and mountains, but little agriculture, and conclude that Britain was no more than a thinly populated sterile place, where mining and quarrying were the sole activities.

The second visitor, however, might come ashore in south Devon, near the river Exe (not far from Buckland's own family and childhood haunts) and travel northeast over Somerset and into the Midland counties, and on up to the River Tyne. What a different terrain would greet him, causing him to report that Britain was a fertile land, with rich agriculture, a dense population, abundant coal and widespread industrial activity. Instead of primary mineral rocks, this second visitor would traverse a landscape composed predominantly of the New Red Sandstone, with fossils and, ensuing from them, rich soils. Buckland's third hypothetical foreign visitor might land on the coast of Dorset and travel across country to the Yorkshire coast, a terrain of Oolitic limestone, chalk and compacted limestone. While the visitor would see no coal, iron or heavy industry, he would see a rich agricultural landscape with fertile soils and a population devoted to husbandry.

Yet these three diverse terrains fall in three contiguous south to north bands of no more than 200 miles across from, let us say, Wales to the Yorkshire Dales. The three landscapes would have been formed by differences in rock and soil chemistry from the ancient physics of the once hot crystalline rocks through their relations with erosive water, and the consequent production of sedimentary strata had resulted in the drainage patterns and lie of the present-day land. To Buckland, this was a clear indication of divine providence, placing foodstuffs, metals and building materials within convenient reach of each other.

We will turn to the more explicitly theological chapters below, but we will first examine Chapter III, which deals with 'Proper Subjects of Geological Enquiry', and discusses the mineral chemistry of the crystalline rocks. Here, and in Chapter VI, Buckland explores mineralogical chemistry and physics, in what was still in 1836 the new chemistry of specific reactive chemical elements: an approach to matter that had developed within his own lifetime, extending back only to the element theories of Lavoisier, Dalton and Davy, in and after the 1780s. In Chapter VI, Buckland reminds his readers that the early earth had passed through a long period after the creation when no organic life had existed, only mineral and physical activity. During this period, the granites, schists and crystalline rocks were laid down, after which the changes in chemical and physical activity led to the earliest sedimentary rocks being formed from their detritus, by the erosive activity of water and reactions with atmospheric gases, to form oxides, nitrates and carbonates. The crystalline rocks formed the most ancient parts of the landscape, and the cracking and faulting, which they displayed, was a clear indication of their vast antiquity. Buckland concludes that 'it is demonstrable from Geology that there was a period when no organic beings had existence'.[4]

Chapters VI to IX explore the earth's earliest developmental stages, the 'Transitional', 'Secondary', and 'Tertiary' Series of rock. Following the mineral first phase, God had populated the planet with molluscs and other forms, such as the Carboniferous coal measures, and other forms 'coeval with the commencement of organic life upon our globe'.[5] In the 'Secondary Series' one encounters flying lizards, or pterodactyls, while yet higher forms appear in the Tertiary. Georges Cuvier and Alexandre Brongniart, Buckland tells us, did early work on these Tertiary strata, in the Parisian chalk beds. As an indication of Buckland's generosity of spirit and willingness to acknowledge the work of others, he cites Sir Charles Lyell who, in *Principles of Geology*, Volume III (1830–1833), had divided the Tertiary Series into the Eocene, Miocene, and Older and Newer Pliocene.

Buckland's generosity of spirit, I would suggest, is manifest here because Lyell in his *Principles of Geology* had presented a fundamentally different, non-catastrophic model of earth action from his own. As we shall see in Chapter 12, Lyell's earth history is not one punctuated by profound cataclysms and disruptions, but one that evolved by constant small tweaks and changes, or by 'causes now in operation', such as wind, tides, erosion and 'normal' earthquakes, extending over vast periods of time. Lyell's argument was, rather, that given enough time, the accumulation of tiny changes would remodel the entire globe many times over.

Then in Chapter X Buckland recapitulates and amplifies his five principal agencies that had formed the earth: the ancient crystalline rocks, water-deposited strata, catastrophes, violent inundations and volcanic eruptions. Next, in Chapter XI, Buckland addresses himself to a potentially worrying subject which, he felt, needed to be put into proper context: namely, the 'Supposed Cases of Fossil Human Bones'.[6] By 1836, cave explorers in particular were discovering evidence of possible human remains deep underground. We saw in Chapter 4 how Buckland's discovery in 1823 of a human skeleton, carefully laid to rest at Paviland, south Wales, posed questions about the age of humanity. His explanation for the Red Lady of Paviland was straightforward: the red staining of 'her' bones and the adjacent simple funerary artefacts indicated that she had been a prostitute connected with the well-known nearby Roman garrison. The extinct animal bones also found in the excavation were clearly vastly older than the body. Buckland dated her, however, not only to the period following Adam and Eve, but also safely within the period of high European civilization of post-AD-55 Roman Britain.

In Vol. I, p. 598 of his *Geology and Mineralogy*, Buckland adds a Supplementary Note, relating to his visit to some caves near Liège, made after the text of his book went to press, in which not only human bones but also flint knives and other human artefacts had been discovered. He remained confident, however, that these human bones were in a 'state of less decay than those of the extinct species of beasts'. He points out that while Philippe-Charles Schmerling, who had excavated the Liège caves, believed that they were 'coeval' with the extinct beasts, and hence pre-Adamite, he, Buckland, from examining Schmerling's collection, 'entirely dissents' from this opinion. It was perhaps fortunate for his peace of mind that William Buckland died when he did in 1856, for during that same decade a series of discoveries were made that would radically challenge his idea of the recent appearance of humanity. They would open up a whole new world of human prehistory in the same way that he had opened up a new world of geological and animal prehistory. More will be said about the rapidly unfolding world of Victorian prehistory in Chapter 14.

Geology and Mineralogy: a treasure house of fossil wonders

As we have seen, Buckland ascribed the slow completion of his treatise to the sheer volume of detailed description and illustration upon which he hung his geological case. While Buckland could not conduct experiments or provide meticulous measurements in geology, as could his fellow Bridgewater Treatise authors William Prout in chemistry and William Whewell in astronomy, he could provide instead a rich abundance of comparative data. He does this in a quite spectacular sweep across the five concluding chapters with their subdivisions of vol. I, which themselves take up 460 printed pages. Here, Buckland systematically works his way through the realms of fossilized molluscs, bivalve shells, saurians, pterodactyls, vertebrates, articulated animals, fishes, plants and so on. His range is formidable and displays to the world Buckland's (and no doubt Mary's) great command of fossil anatomy and natural history. Nowhere are we allowed to forget that through all of it, the guiding hand of the Creator was there for all to see.

Buckland possessed a highly visual mind and was renowned not only for the formidable array of specimens with which he illustrated his lectures, but also for his drawings, pictures, maps and landscape sections. This visual dimension is carried over into Volume II of his treatise to provide accompanying pictures, spread across 69 whole-page plates and including large fold-out sheets on which several individual illustrations were included, to total, as he claimed, over 700 fine-art specimens. In the production of these pictures, especially the woodcuts, where the original ink drawings would be engraved on wood blocks for mass printing, he gives acknowledgement to a Mr Webster and a Mr Fisher in particular. Surprisingly, there is no mention of Mary Buckland, despite her artistic and organizational skills, to say nothing of her long nocturnal assistance to William across the years during which the *Geology and Mineralogy* volumes were in the making, though her contribution was later acknowledged by their children.

The plates in Volume II are of breathtaking beauty and works of art in their own right. Plate 1 is a fold-out, hand-coloured 'imaginary' composite section of the earth's upper crust, with a large, granite mass with volcanic fissures, showing the progression from the Primary to the Transitional and Secondary periods, in which the strata and their preserved fossil forms become increasingly complex.

Artesian wells and their geology

The plates, 65–69, conclude with some detailed landscape geological sections of the Somerset and Newcastle coalfields, demonstrating the presence of faulting, cracking and collapse in the earth's crust, while similar sections of the Thames Valley in London are also shown. Here we see the mechanism at the heart of London's extensive artesian wells, on both the north and south sides of the river. We are shown, for example, how the whole geological substructure of London dips down, from Leighton Buzzard in the north to Sevenoaks in the south, reaching its lowest point in north London. Six major strata sections are included, from Woburn Sand deep down to gault clay, firestone, chalk, plastic clay and finally London clay at the top. As the subterranean water is trapped between the chalk and the plastic clay, Buckland shows how wells dug down to these levels will not only reach the water, but that the geological pressure will make it spontaneously rise to the surface without any need for pumping. 'The water from the lowest stratum rises to the greatest height.'[7] In addition to London's artesian wells, he cites the work of French geologists and engineers on the 'Artesian Fountains' at St Ouen and elsewhere, pointing out that the term 'Artesian' derives from the ancient Latin name *Artesium* for the French region of Artois.

Between these stratum plates, Buckland illustrates a truly impressive range of fossilized forms, including tiny shells, teeth, scales, botanical remains and a whole array of fishes, reptiles and even spiders. They bring home most forcibly how far geology had progressed from its infant days of his early career down to 1836. While the instinctively generous Buckland cites with full chapter and verse the discoveries and contributions of fellow geologists and fossil anatomists at home and on the Continent, especially in France, one cannot fail to hold one's breath when reviewing Buckland's own discoveries and contributions. One wonders when he ever rested, and how many thousands of miles he must have ridden and walked across every part of the British Isles, to say nothing of France, Germany and Italy. Buckland's geology is profoundly empirical, built upon myriads of individual observations of everything fossiliferous, from microscopic shells embedded in limestone to ichthyosaurus and megalosaurus skeletons that were longer than a double-decker bus. All are recorded and illustrated in minute detail. One also stands in awe of the part Mary Buckland played in this vast enterprise (alongside bearing nine children, running a busy household and countless acts of charity), for in addition to her curatorial and organizational skills, she was an expert microscopist, with a particular interest in marine zoophytes and sponges. More will be said in Chapter 14 about Mary's and her daughter Caroline's microscopical researches.

Flying dragons, adaptive eyes and footprints in the sand

Of all the exotic and extinct prehistoric creatures and life forms discussed by Buckland, one is especially captivating: the 'flying dragons', or pterodactyls. While Cuvier originally described these, Buckland added greatly to our knowledge of these creatures, describing specimens from that rich treasure trove of fossilized species excavated from the quarries of Stonesfield, near Oxford. Palaeontologists and comparative anatomists disputed about what exactly these strange 'flying dragons' were. Were they bats or lizards? Either way, they were clearly not birds, because not only did key points of their anatomy differ from that of all the bird species known at that time, but the pterodactyls, instead of simply having a beak, also had a set of very sharp teeth. Were they insect eaters, and were extinct insects much bigger than those living today, and required to be bitten and chewed?

Buckland, Cuvier and other researchers up to 1836 had identified several species of pterodactyl, some the size of buzzards or snipes, though some might well (judging from remaining fossils) have had wingspans of up to 27 feet. They must have been terrifying beasts, especially as Buckland suggested that the pterodactyl was a nocturnal creature. This he deduced from the large eye sockets in pterodactyl skulls, from which he concluded that their large eyes must have enabled them to hunt at very low levels of light. It stood to reason that all of these creatures had existed well *after* God had separated the waters from the land, and had created light, as they all not only possessed eyes, but eyes of great sophistication, specificity and adaptability.

One of the most fascinating ophthalmic systems that Buckland encountered in the fossil realm was that of the ichthyosauri. These great reptiles had eyes 'sometimes larger than a man's head',[8] and while the soft matter of the eyes had long since perished, their skull apertures and related features could tell us a great deal. Most remarkable of all in the ichthyosaurus was the ring of bony plates surrounding the eye on the external sclerotic coating. This ring was not solid, but was composed of a series of beautifully fitting bony plates that formed a ring when closed, yet when opened, in the manner of the petals of a flower, exposed an additional surface area of the eye. Buckland points out that this adaptation was shared by some modern-day creatures, such as certain birds and crocodiles, but not by modern fish.[9] The close-fitting circle of outward-folding bony plates would give the creature both telescopic and microscopic vision, when its search for food required them. When the plates were folded inwards, they would have applied pressure to the eyeball, thus changing the shape of the central, uncovered region around the pupil to make it thicker and rounder. This would have given the ichthyosaurus a sort of high-definition close-up or microscopic vision, enabling it to obtain a magnified image of something close, in exactly the same way that a magnifying glass with highly convex curves gives the highest magnification.

Conversely, when the plates were folded outwards, the pressure would be released, and the eyeball and pupil would become flatter, admitting more light, which would produce an excellent long-distance 'telescopic' vision. So, the ichthyosaurus, in common with other, modern creatures possessing this capability, such as certain birds of prey, would have had very versatile eyesight. As ichthyosauri were deep water diving creatures, this would allow an enhanced deep-sea vision, while the folding plates could close up when necessary to protect the large eyeball from sudden changes in water pressure. It is hardly surprising that Buckland saw the hand of a beneficent God at work here, for how could such a piece of beautiful ophthalmic engineering have occurred by chance?[10]

No less fascinating is what we can learn about long-vanished creatures from the remains of their crawling trackways, or full footprints upon once wet sand or clay which had subsequently turned to stone. Buckland captures the sheer wonder of detecting, reconstructing and understanding the activities of long-extinct tortoises in one of the many lyrical passages which one finds in *Geology and Mineralogy*.[11] It was these fossilized footprints that led to William and Mary's experiment, in the 1830s, of making their pet tortoise walk across a piece of freshly-made pastry, rolled out on the kitchen table, in an attempt to reconstruct such footprints. It was an ingenious and inspired experiment, connecting the primarily observational science of geology with the experimental approach found in contemporary chemistry and physics.

Buckland's Natural Theology

William Buckland never wrote a specific treatise on Natural Theology, although one may say that its inner principles flow so effortlessly through all his major writings, such as the *Vindiciae*, *Reliquiae*, and most obviously *Geology and Mineralogy*, as to render explicit discussion superfluous. He was not inclined, either intellectually or theologically, to speculative or abstract thinking, for at every turn he uses a specific piece of physical evidence – a tooth, eye or wing bone – as examples of a benign Providence. In this respect one sees how very differently his mind worked from that of many contemporary theologians, such as John Henry Newman, his Christ Church neighbour Edward Bouverie Pusey and other members of the post-1833 Oxford Movement generation. Deep spiritual probing in search of sinless purity did not come naturally to Buckland as it did to them, yet examining the wonderfully engineered eye of an ichthyosaurus did – and spoke of the love of God in framing such a beautiful creation.

Although not everyone by any means concurred with Buckland's interpretation of the Mosaic narrative of creation, as we shall see in Chapter 11 when looking at the scriptural geologists, Buckland was firmly of the opinion that the creation story in Genesis had to be interpreted, or read in context, rather than taken literally. He points out in *Geology and Mineralogy,* Chapter II, for example, that the creation narrative is imperfect on points of detail. It does not, for example, mention Jupiter's satellites, or Saturn's rings. For science progresses: Copernicus was ignorant of Newton's Laws, whereas Newton in turn was ignorant of Laplace's cosmological ideas, and so on.[12] This idea was far from new even in the early nineteenth century, for Galileo, in his published *Letter to the Grand Duchess Christina* (1615), cites the wise dictum of Cardinal Cesare Baronio, that the purpose of Scripture was to teach us how to go to heaven, *not* to teach us how the heavens (or sky) *go.* In other words, Scripture reveals God's creation to mankind, but then it is our job to use our God-given intelligence to work out the details for ourselves. In short, don't read your Bible for science. It is true that Buckland does not cite Cardinal Baronio's dictum, but Galileo's *Letter to the Grand Duchess* was well known, and would almost certainly have been familiar to the widely read William and Mary Buckland. My suspicion is that Buckland did not want to risk undermining his wider geological argument by citing a Roman cardinal at a time when anti-Catholic prejudice was never far below the surface in deeply Protestant England.

Where Buckland's Natural Theology is perhaps at its most original is in its long-term developmental emphasis. Unlike most earlier Natural Theologians, Buckland is not simply concerned with tying specific examples of divine beneficence to given natural phenomena, such as agriculture to the seasons, in the here and now. Instead, he traces that beneficence across 'millions and millions' of years, to show how God's creative power was at work through now extinct life forms and catastrophe-based upheavals of the earth's crust and all that was on it, from the smallest microscopic crustaceans to the mountain ranges and ocean depths. Within this sweep of creation, Buckland even argues for what might be seen as mercies extended to sick, injured or infirm living creatures. While not the first natural theologian to suggest this idea, Buckland argues in Chapter XIII that animal pleasures are maximized and pain minimized by the existence of carnivorous animals. Carnivorous beasts will deliver a quick dispatch to the weak and feeble, thus shortening their suffering, while on the other hand providing nourishing meat for the living, as we have seen. It is a grand vision, in every sense.

Yet one looks in vain in *Geology and Mineralogy* for a full-scale treatment of Noah's Flood, which seems all the more remarkable as it played such a fundamental role not only in the *Vindiciae Geologicae* (1819–1820) and *Reliquiae Diluvianae* (1823), but in the whole Oxford School of geology which Buckland inspired. Noah's Flood is there, in Chapter II, but now there is a lack of explicit detail regarding its agency. Had almost two decades of intense new geological research and field discoveries by Buckland and others across Europe, the eastern USA, South Africa, Australia and parts of India modified and widened the worldview of *c.*1820? How far had new evidences presented in Sir Charles Lyell's *Principles of Geology* (1830–1833) required older certainties to be re-examined? As we shall see in Chapter 12, Lyell proposed a gradualist, catastrophe-free mechanism for the development of the earth. Yet as we have seen above, Buckland was remarkably open-minded, always amenable to new ideas and admired Lyell, who in many ways saw Buckland as his mentor.

By 1836, therefore, had Noah's Flood become, for Buckland, less globally formative and much less violent than he thought it was in 1820, and perhaps even relatively local. Indeed, on pp. 17–18 of *Geology and Mineralogy*, Buckland is pretty well arguing against the scriptural geologists, and examining the exact Hebrew meaning of words like heaven (*shamayim* or higher regions), created (*bara*), made (*asah*) and formed (*yatsar*), with acknowledgement to his Christ Church colleague Canon Pusey, Regius Professor of Hebrew, and others in a detailed footnote.[13] Buckland's long-term, developmental Bible-interpreting Natural Theology was also made manifest in his treatment of the creation of light and the complex eyes of fossil trilobites, ichthyosauri and other creatures. While Scripture tells us that it was not until the fourth day that the sun and moon first appeared in the sky, Buckland argues that light itself must have been there from the beginning, because of the teeming abundance of creatures with eye sockets – some very sophisticated – and also of extinct fossil plants, which clearly had needed light to make them grow. So 'the darkness described on the evening of the first day was a temporary darkness, produced by an accumulation of dense vapours "upon the face of the deep"': a sort of dense fog, perhaps?[14]

In the way that Buckland unfolds it, God's majesty as manifested in the drama of creation is even grander than in the terse first few verses of Genesis 1: Natural Theology at its most inspiring, as geology and the other sciences put flesh on the bones of the creation narrative, thereby rendering its truth even more compelling. Buckland not only brings to bear his erudition as a scientist and a theologian in *Geology and Mineralogy*, but also his powerful command of language and even of drama; the reader gains a glimpse of what the geological Canon must have been like before a live audience.

Yet perhaps nothing sums up Buckland's idea of the essentially common-sense nature and nobility of Natural Theology better than a statement reported by Caroline Fox in October 1839. It appears to have been part of a lecture on geology delivered to a general audience at the then new (1838) West End venue, the Royal London Polytechnic Institution in Regent Street. Buckland is reported to have said: 'Shall we who are endowed by a Gracious Creator with power and intelligence, and a capacity to use them – shall we sit lazily down and say, Our God has indeed given us eyes, but we will not see with them; reason and intelligence, but we will exert neither? Is this our gratitude to our Maker for some of His choicest gifts, and not rather a stupid indifference most displeasing in His sight?'[15]

Geology and Mineralogy was a masterpiece by any standards, and with its clear text and 705 individual detailed illustrations, it was the most exhaustive treatment of practical fossil geology and anatomy to date. It would continue to be used as a textbook of practical geology and mineralogy long after later geologists, and Charles Darwin, had supplied new evidence for the agents of geological change and the origins of living things, as evidenced by Professor William Boyd Dawkins, who wrote what was effectively a eulogy to Buckland in 1894.[16] Buckland's *Geology and Mineralogy*, therefore, would stand as one of the classic texts in the development of the natural history sciences, as well as a definitive statement of British Natural Theology.

Chapter 9

A Passion for Minerals and Mountains: Geology and the Romantic Movement

Modern geology, the geology of William Buckland, forms an integral part of what is generally styled the romantic Age. Although most modern people associate romanticism with literature and art, with William Wordsworth, Keats, Shelley, William Blake, Henry Fuseli and the English watercolourists, one must never forget that the inner principles of romanticism also extended to science.

Minerals, gases and steam engines in the Romantic landscape

Romanticism was about awe, wonder, heightened emotional states and bursting the boundaries, and all of this fitted in closely with the science of the age. The cosmological vastness explored by the large telescopes of Sir William, Caroline and Sir John Herschel, with its mysterious nebulae and dense star clusters, represented one aspect of science-based romanticism. Likewise, the new chemistry of post-Lavoisian atoms, in which unique chemical elements combined in very exact ways to create salts, oxides and carbonates, opened up new material wonders unimagined in 1760, and was actively promoted before fee-paying popular audiences by Sir Humphry Davy and others at the Royal Institution, the Surrey Institution, the Regent Street Polytechnic and elsewhere. The newly invented chemical 'voltaic' and 'galvanic' electric batteries demonstrated a strange, powerful force of nature, which generated terrifying sparks and was another source of wonder. The 'galvanic fluid' could ignite gunpowder, reduce common salt to a gas (chlorine) and a strange, unstable, hitherto unknown white metal (sodium). It could even break down the ancient Greek element water into two new gases, hydrogen and oxygen, in perfect proportions: H_2O. These were measured proportions no less exact than the measured and calculated movements of the sun and moon. Davy did much of this pioneering electrochemical work at the Royal Institution after c.1803, while his protégé Michael Faraday went even further, discovering the laws of electromagnetic induction in 1831 and devising an experiment to make an electrified wire rotate: the ancestor of the electric motor. Some even speculated whether electricity could be the life force itself. Mary Shelley's classic gothic horror novel, *Frankenstein* (1817–1818), explored this possibility in fiction. Then in November 1818, the anatomist and chemist Dr Andrew Ure in Glasgow electrified a freshly executed criminal, but found that while he could induce terrifying pre-*rigor-mortis* muscular contractions and grotesque facial grimaces, 'Clydesdale the Murderer' remained firmly dead.

While today we might think of industrial technology as the antithesis of romanticism and feeling, the people of Buckland's time did not: for Boulton and Watt's powerful steam engines after 1776 took one's breath away. Just imagine, if you were born into an age of horsepower, watermills and windmills, seeing a great steam engine draining a mine, powering a new textile factory or pulling hundreds of tons of Welsh or Newcastle coal in waggons behind an engine on rails. What is more, the engine never got tired or needed a day of rest: you just kept shovelling in the coal and pouring in the water, and it went like a Trojan. Only the men who serviced it needed rest, never the machine. Familiar as we are in our modern world with all manner of self-acting, inexhaustible machines, it is all too easy to forget the emotional impact that a great steam engine had on a Georgian viewer. It seemed as though our God-given ingenuity had enabled us to make something that breathed and gasped like a living being: a wonder still evoked today when people see preserved steam railway locomotives in full force.

Artists such as Joseph Wright of Derby and J. M. W. Turner painted blast furnaces glowing at night and early steam trains battling against the stormy elements, epitomizing the way industrial machines, mines, foundries and trains fired the romantic imagination. All of these new forces were both created and controlled by man, and unlike wind and water, were not laws unto themselves. And as steam engines were made of iron and consumed vast quantities of coal, they had a direct bearing on geology, as Buckland was all too aware: in the opening chapters of *Geology and Mineralogy* (1836) he discusses the significance of the coal and metal deposits as part of the earth's wider natural bounty and usefulness.[1] He concludes Volume I of his great treatise by giving a more detailed exposition of the bountiful nature of minerals and metals in Chapters XIX–XXIII.

Buckland saw all this as fitting into a wider natural theological framework. Not only had God made his created world abundant and fruitful, but he had given the crowning glory of that creation – mankind – the power to 'think God's thoughts after him' (as the seventeenth century German astronomer Johannes Kepler had put it), to make discoveries and use the divinely bestowed gift of intellect endlessly to improve the human condition through science and technology.

In the half-century following 1780, the whole of physical science and practical technology seemed to undergo a profound change, with new theories of cosmology and the nature of substance, and new electric forces – each of them dramatically changing our ideas about the nature of natural knowledge. Was not all this as mind-blowing as anything that came from the pen of a poet or the brush of an artist? One should not be surprised to discover that many of these new scientific researchers – most notably Sir Humphry Davy – also saw themselves as poets and men of letters, and socialized with them. Unlike today, there was no arts versus sciences divide in 1830. A poet might attend chemistry lectures and collect fossils, and an anatomist discuss the poems of Wordsworth; while that quintessential romantic poet, John Keats, was a qualified doctor, a graduate of Guy's Hospital Medical School, fully informed about dissection and the mechanical functions of the human body.

Taking its rightful place in this age of wonder was geology: just as the astronomers were bursting the limits of space, and the chemists and physicists the bonds of substance and harnessing energy, and the engineers advancing our creative powers through great industrial machines, so the geologists were bursting the bounds of time. They took readers who thought initially of global history in terms of thousands of years, with a continuity of animal species extending only from the Garden of Eden to the present day, to Buckland's 'millions and millions' of years, populated by successive races of creatures that could have been imagined only in exotic folktales of sea monsters or dragons, but which they now knew had really existed and walked the earth or swam in its oceans.

A Romantic summer excursion through late Georgian Britain

Imagine a summer touring holiday in, let us say, 1832, the year of the Great Reform Bill. Our tourists might travel by carriage north from London on well-laid turnpike roads, making numerous crossings of the many canals that criss-crossed England by that date. Every canal had its boats laden with coal, industrial goods or fine Staffordshire pottery: each foot of canal standing as a testament to the practical geologists, such as William Smith, who had first surveyed and mapped the strata to ascertain how to use the lie of the land to maximum advantage in digging a waterway. Their first port of call could well be Oxford, where they would see the native terrain and landscapes of 'Strata' Smith, and perhaps even meet and be entertained by the illustrious Canon Buckland and Mary in their Christ Church house. They would see the renowned ichthyosaurus, megalosaurus and other breathtaking fossilized beasts, hear the five-year-old Frank Buckland speak about fossils, and even partake of mouse on toast in the dining room. Then there would be the wonders of the Anatomy School and Ashmolean Museums, along with Dr Daubeny's Oxford Botanic Garden, to capture both their minds and their senses.

Entertained and delighted, they would head north, visiting Birmingham and the Midlands to witness the wonders of their blast furnaces, iron-rolling mills and steam-engine manufactories, such as those of Boulton and Watt. Going north, they might next head for Staffordshire, and see the blazing pot banks at night, where Josiah Wedgwood II and his competitors turned out millions of pieces of fine bone china porcelain crockery to grace dinner tables in London, Paris, Philadelphia, Calcutta and Sydney. Where did the fine clays and firing coal come from? From inside the earth – the fruits of practical geology. Next, our tourists would go to witness what was often referred to as 'the Manchester phenomenon', where steam engines and automatic looms turned out thousands of yards of textiles each day in the new Cottonopolis, with each giant steam engine driving two or three hundred looms. They would make an excursion six miles to the north on the Duke of Bridgewater's Canal to Worsley (Britain's first canal, surveyed by James Brindley and opened in 1761), then see John Gilbert's underground canal, blasted out from the living rock to the coal strata inside the hill, enabling coal boats to be filled deep underground, floated out, and taken to market in one smooth operation; carried from coal face to fireplace, almost, and drastically cutting the cost of coal.

Back in Manchester, why not take a ride on George Stephenson's new (1830) Manchester to Liverpool railway, hauled by the legendary Rocket at the breathtaking speed of more than 25 miles per hour: some three or four times faster than a stagecoach? Stephenson's railway line stood as another triumph of practical geology and engineering, as he laid his tracks upon a flexible causeway across the ancient Chat Moss Peat Bog. Getting out of their train at its original Crown Street terminus, on the Lancashire plain some way out of central Liverpool, our tourists might well have seen surveyors and engineers making preparations to cut and blast that deep, mile-long inclined trench through the Mersey Permian and Triassic sandstone and mudstone to carry the tracks down the long gradient to what, in 1836, would become the Lime Street terminus, in the very heart of Liverpool.

Our travellers might next have a cruise in a new steam-powered paddle-steamer sailing independent of wind or tide from Liverpool to Bangor, viewing the grandeur of the north Welsh mountains on their left-hand, or port side. From Bangor and its bustling slate-exporting docks, they might cross Thomas Telford's recently finished (1826) and truly spectacular great suspension bridge across the Menai Strait. In Anglesey, they could see great metal mines and slate quarries, where once again God's bounty was being used to benefit mankind, thanks to our God-given human ingenuity. Then why not travel back towards Lancashire on that magnificent piece of engineering, Telford's new coach road, hugging the sheer rock face of the Welsh mountains? En route, they might make a detour to climb up to the summit of Mount Snowdon, not only to have their breath taken away by the spectacular rolling mountain and seascapes spread out below, but also to independently measure Snowdon's altitude from the fallen mercury level displayed by a portable barometer. Travellers often did this, combining romance with science.

Continuing to roll eastwards back on Telford's road, they would be bowled over by Conway's grand medieval castle and the quaint beauties of Chester and its magnificent cathedral, before being struck by the dense pall of factory chimney smoke that generally hung over Manchester. A decade into the future, this pall would lead the Germany-trained Scottish-Manchester chemist Dr Robert Smith to conduct the first quantitative scientific researches into air quality, smoke pollution and acid rain, comparing samples of Manchester air with that of Snowdon and the Lake District.

So far on their journey, our imaginary tourists might have been reading Adam Smith's iconic *An Inquiry into the Nature and Causes of the Wealth of Nations* (1776), with its implicit praise of organizational and industrial ingenuity, along with humanity's ability to take control of and improve its natural condition. In tandem might be read William Paley's *Natural Theology* (1801) with its emphasis on God's designing power in nature. But as our tourists travel up through Lancashire, with its coal pits and cotton looms left behind, a new mood sets in north of Lancaster, and especially as they arrive in Kendal and Westmorland. As they enter the Lake District, industrial ingenuity has been replaced by the new romance of lofty mountains, plunging waterfalls and lakes, such as Windermere. The romance of 'Mountain Gloom and Mountain Glory', with all its spectacular geology and emblems of Noah's Flood still to be traced in its plunging valleys, deep lakes and rubble moraines, such as the one at the foot of Lake Windermere. Was not this the sort of thing to send hearts fluttering, especially if one called at Dove Cottage to say 'Hello' to the now elderly and almost sacred William Wordsworth?

Our awestruck tourists now put away Adam Smith and unpack their boxes of watercolours and sketch books to catch the light, shade and grandeur of the lakes and high fells. Wordsworth's *Lyrical Ballads* (1798) is now the reading of choice, although geology lies at the heart of it all.

Continuing north, our travellers enter Scotland; and while the river Clyde is picturesque and Glasgow has its glories and industrial wonders, they head for the Great Glen and the Highlands, which make the heart pound even faster than Windermere and Cat Bells in the Lake District. It was the Age of Romanticism that transformed the Scottish Highlands in the public imagination, from a cold, damp inaccessible place to the apotheosis of feeling. Their reading has now become Robbie Burns's *Tam O'Shanter* (1790–1791), Sir Walter Scott's *Rob Roy* (1817), *The Lord of the Isles* (1815) and their other Highland historical romances and ballads. If they were curious about how those wonderful mountain vistas came about, they might read Dr James Hutton's *A Theory of the Earth* (1795) with all its grand volcanic geology, edging up the mountains 'by causes now in operation' across aeons of time. Then, coming south after Inverness, and all the romance of Bonnie Prince Charlie, they would naturally desire to sample the delights of the cultural metropolis of Edinburgh and climb Arthur's Seat and the once volcanic Salisbury Crags, once again pondering the vast aeons of time that had elapsed since those now docile basalt and dolerite plugs had been parts of a blazing natural inferno. They might even have met that breathing icon of Scottish legends and geology: Hugh Miller.

As our travellers cross the border back into England, the early autumnal mists are settling in the North Yorkshire Dales, which only serves to add atmosphere to the medieval ruins of Fountains and Rievaulx Abbeys. Why not make a detour into the beautiful Vale of Pickering on the way, and see Buckland's Kirkdale Cave and hyenas' lair? At least, as much as was left of it after the quarrymen had carved fine limestone out of the hillside over the past decade.

After Kirkdale, our travellers would head southwest to see the historic streets and alleyways of medieval York. They would next visit the famous Museum of the Yorkshire Philosophical Society, which exactly a year before had hosted the inaugural meeting of the British Association for the Advancement of Science. In the York Museum, they might meet John Phillips, the leading authority on Yorkshire geology, and examine the Museum's great collection of fossils and minerals. They might then crown their visit by admiring the soaring glories and delicately carved stone traceries of York Minster, before attending choral evensong, seated in the richly carved stalls of the medieval chancel, the service culminating with an inspiring rendition of Handel's 'Hallelujah Chorus' as the anthem.

From now on, as they travel south back to London, they pass through those rich, well-tilled fields and bountiful meadows on the easterly side of the country, which would soon be mentioned as Buckland's third section on England in his Bridgewater Treatise *Geology and Mineralogy* – a landscape of rich sheep pastures, and, by mid-September, well-stocked barns and granaries. For their reading on this final stage of their journey, our tourists might perhaps be perusing Arthur Young's late-eighteenth-century agricultural tours and Thomas Gray's *Elegy Written in a Country Churchyard* (1751), and revelling in the late-summer nostalgia of Keats' *Ode to Autumn* (1819–20). On their summer journey they would have seen industrial ingenuity, machinery, museums, a variety of glorious landscapes and rich farmlands, witnessed at first hand the diverse and breathtaking geology of the British mainland and been reminded of God's bounty at every turn – the very stuff of Romantic awe and wonder.

Geology: a polite and popular pursuit

We saw in Chapter 7 how geology figured prominently at the annual meetings of the British Association after its formation in York in 1831 and how Buckland had mesmerized the Association's Oxford meeting in 1832. In addition to those with a more formal connection to geology, the science was capturing the popular imagination, and on their round Britain itinerary of 1832, our imaginary tourists would almost certainly have collected shells, crystals, minerals and fossils to display in their cabinets of curiosities back at home. Such cabinets, along with albums, watercolours and sketches, were *de rigueur* for all folks aspiring to 'culture', and the geological exhibits would have been joined by other curiosities such as Roman coins and historical artefacts. John Tradescant's seventeenth-century collection, later acquired by Elias Ashmole and now preserved in the University of Oxford's Ashmolean Museum, contained a pair of Queen Elizabeth I's gloves and the lantern allegedly used by Guy Fawkes in his mercifully failed attempt to blow up Parliament in 1605. Depending on one's tastes, such a collection might also contain preserved anatomical and botanical specimens, books and pictures of objects of interest.

By 1830, most major provincial cities had Literary and Philosophical Societies for the middle classes, while the Yorkshire Philosophical Society had given rise to the British Association in the first place. These 'Lit. and Phil.' Societies ('philosophical', of course, meaning 'scientific') held social events, put on lectures and established their own libraries and museums for the use of members and subscribers. Then from the 1820s onwards Mechanics' Institutes began to spring up all round Britain, providing similar services for the less well-off, such as self-improving artisans, office clerks and even their spouses. Likewise, popular self-education journals, such as the reforming Lord Henry Brougham's *The Penny Magazine*, carried geological and mineralogical articles, often commissioned from acknowledged experts in their fields. All of this activity was on the strength of private subscription initiatives and entirely self- and commercially funded.

William Buckland's role in the advancement of geological science and informing an increasingly large public is beyond question, but by the 1830s others were also becoming prominent in the field, one of whom would become his opposite number in Cambridge.

The Revd Professor Adam Sedgwick: an accidental geologist?

If one visits the village of Dent, near Sedbergh in Cumbria, now part of the beautiful Yorkshire Dales National Park, one cannot miss seeing a large piece of rough-hewn rock set up in the street. It is the memorial to Adam Sedgwick (1785–1873), son of Richard, the vicar of Dent, and his second wife, Margaret. Coming from an old family of clergy and modest independent farmers, Adam was educated first by his father before attending the Sedbergh Grammar School.[2] At the age of 19, he entered Trinity College, Cambridge: an institution which would become his permanent home for the remaining 69 years of his long life, interspersed later with periods of residence in Norwich Cathedral Close on becoming a Prebend of Norwich. In Trinity, Sedgwick was elected to a mathematical fellowship in 1810. He showed no especial interest in geology, except when relevant to wider scientific and biblical culture, attending the lectures of the naturalist and mineralogist Edward Daniel Clarke and geologizing with the young John Stevens Henslow who later became Professor of Botany. That was until 1817–1818, when the University Electors set about finding a new occupant for the Woodwardian Chair of Geology. Wishing to widen his horizons and escape the grind of routine mathematical tutoring, and perhaps increase his income, Sedgwick put himself forward as a candidate – and was duly elected. He later admitted that he did not know a great deal about geology in 1818, yet while his rival candidate knew more, much of it was wrong.

All of this was happening at a time when Buckland, already a geologist of international standing, would have been preparing his own Inaugural Lecture, *Vindiciae Geologicae* (1820). It is hardly surprising, therefore, that while in 1818 the University of Cambridge, still basking in her glowing post-Newtonian reputation, was superior to the University of Oxford in higher mathematics, Oxford undisputedly had the edge as far as geology and mineralogy were concerned. One might find it strange that an effective beginner in an academic discipline could suddenly be elected to a prestigious chair. However, his initial ignorance notwithstanding, I suspect that it was Adam Sedgwick's social gifts and wider character that won him the Woodwardian Professorship, for he was famously congenial, a good Trinity College man and, like Buckland, a fine and charismatic communicator. How perceptive the Electors would soon show themselves to have been!

As soon as the Revd Professor Sedgwick was in his post, he threw himself wholeheartedly into his new discipline, spending his first long vacation undertaking an extensive field geological study. Reading widely, and delivering his first course of geological lectures in 1819, he began a tradition that he would continue pretty well down to the end of his life, dying in his Trinity College rooms in 1873 at age 88. Sedgwick, like most geologists, was fit, strong and vigorous, with an iron constitution, though like Buckland he had once damaged an eye from flying fragments from a rock he was hammering. As we have seen, field geology was tough work, involving endless tramping across meadow, moor and mountain, climbing dangerous cliff faces and creeping on all fours into narrow caves. It is hardly surprising that it attracted retired soldiers and hard-riding hunting gentlemen, such as Murchison and De la Beche. While we today might regard clergymen and university dons as 'gentler types', this was not the case around 1830, when prodigious walking itineraries might take a reverend gentleman from France to Italy and across the Alps on foot for a summer adventure, or he might even rough it exploring bandit-infested Sinai and Palestine, as did the Revd Arthur Penrhyn Stanley, who in 1863 would follow Buckland (after Dean Richard C. Trench) to the Deanery of Westminster.

All the evidence tells us that, far from being rivals, the two clerical professors of geology, Sedgwick and Buckland, became good friends. Sedgwick came to enjoy field geology and was a great natural teacher. As a pioneer of Welsh geology and the elucidation of the Old Red Sandstone, he helped to educate the student Charles Darwin, taking him on a walking tour of north Wales and Snowdonia and teaching him how to interpret landscapes and fossils. He also paid a visit to the equally congenial Dr Robert Darwin in Shrewsbury, Charles's medical father, who had serious interests and investments in the economic geology of pottery clays, canals and mines. Like Buckland, Adam Sedgwick was an instinctive performer, and the two men's dramatic lectures could be the high points of British Association meetings. Nothing could better have shown Buckland's regard for Sedgwick than the fact that he and Mary named one of their sons Adam Conybeare Sedgwick Buckland, (Conybeare being after Buckland's old clergyman geologist friend William Daniel Conybeare).[3] Sadly, Adam died at the age of six years and eight months, joining his siblings Willie and Eva in their vault in Christ Church Cathedral.

Adam Sedgwick never married, though his and other writings reveal he loved feminine company; ladies found him captivating and, whenever the conventions permitted, attended his lectures. His letters contain many references to such ladies, and while he considered the prospect of marrying when a young man, one suspects that he became increasingly attached to the freedom of his bachelor lifestyle in Trinity, while also enjoying a degree of female adulation. Might he have thought differently had he met someone like Miss Mary Morland?

Geology's wide appeal did not encompass only clergymen, soldiers, professors and hunting gentlemen. Dr Gideon Algernon Mantell FRS's professional reputation lay in his skill as a Brighton and Lewes surgeon and obstetrician, though his wider fame as 'The Wizard of the Weald' and friend of Sir Charles Lyell lay in his discovery of the iguanodon in the Tilgate quarries and surrounding terrain; he became the foremost authority on the geology of the Sussex Weald. Geology also had a following – as did astronomy, botany and most of the other sciences – among working people, and one of the most remarkable of these was the Scotsman Hugh Miller, referred to above.

Hugh Miller: stonemason, evangelist, author and geologist

Georgian and Victorian Britain were richly endowed with self-made men and women, as we have seen above: people whose talents and determination had brought them up from obscurity to success in a variety of fields of endeavour, from music to astronomy to business to engineering. In addition to William Smith, geology possessed two such noteworthy individuals whose achievements would do the rounds of Europe and the United States. One was Hugh Miller and the other Miss Mary Anning, whom we shall meet below.

Hugh Miller was born in Cromarty, Scotland, in 1802, the son of Hugh and Harriet. Hugh senior, who commanded a local trading vessel, was lost at sea when his son was six years old. From his earliest years, Hugh junior had a passion for books and read anything he could lay hands on. He was also strong and good with his hands, leading him to be apprenticed to a stonecutter and stonemason when he was 17. In his subsequent autobiographical writings, however, Miller brings out the squalid, uncertain nature of the life of an itinerant stone worker – he and his fellow workmen sometimes being forced to sleep in bothies, or shacks that on other occasions would accommodate pigs.[4] After enduring such conditions for several years, Miller, with his passion for self-education and self-improvement, got a much better job working in a bank, and then, at the age of 28, published a volume of poems. He had now crossed the great divide from being an itinerant workman to becoming a rising literary star in the Edinburgh firmament. Over the next quarter century, he would move in Scottish intellectual and ecclesiastical circles and win fame and admiration. Scottish politics, the state of the Church of Scotland, especially around the Great Disruption of 1843, Christian evangelism and geology would now become the driving forces in his life.

One of the things that makes Miller's geological writings so easy to read today was his gift for storytelling: a skill perfected through conversation and the learning and writing down of Scottish legends and tales, some of which he published in 1835. Central to all his writings was his stonemason's eye for rocks, minerals and fossils. At first, his opportunity to meet working field geologists was inevitably limited, although his studies of fossil fish found in the beds of the local Old Red Sandstone of Cromarty won him European recognition, especially from the Swiss Louis Agassiz, whom we shall meet below when dealing with Buckland and the Ice Ages. Miller's first major geological work, of 1840–1841, was entitled *The Old Red Sandstone*, published originally in instalments in *The Witness* evangelical magazine, and then in book form.

Other major geological works soon followed, notably *Footprints of the Creator* (1849–1850) and *Testimony of the Rocks* (1857), which appeared the year after his death. In them, he developed a view of geology which was empirical, while also deeply providential, possessing a clear affinity with the style of long-term Natural Theology seen in Buckland's works. Miller saw the earth as extremely ancient and living species as special creations intended and designed by God, becoming extinct, and then replaced by later ones. He firmly repudiated the proto-evolutionary arguments of Jean-Baptiste Lamarck and Robert Chambers, which we will examine in Chapter 12, though rejecting the idea that the world and the universe had been formed over six natural days. Miller fully accepted the importance of floods in forming parts of the globe, although he came to reject the idea of the Noachian Deluge as a universal agent, seeing it instead as a relatively local Middle Eastern phenomenon. Judging from his failure to emphasize the universal power of Noah's Flood in his *Geology and Mineralogy* (1836), it is clear that Buckland and other geologists were now, in the 1840s, thinking along similar lines.

It is hard to think of Hugh Miller's life, circumstances and career without seeing him as an integral part of Scottish romanticism. Here was the humble orphan lad whose genius and determination enabled him to rise from heavy manual work to fame and not inconsiderable wealth, leaving £7,788–9s–10d when he died. Yet in the grand romantic style, his life was one of constant tension: with his genius, success, acclaim and deep Christian devotion on the one hand, and what a modern psychiatrist might diagnose as psychosis and recurrent bouts of severe depression on the other.

One detects a clear sense of theatre in Miller as well, for with his heavy thatch of tousled, curly red hair, whiskers and powerful facial features – winning him the nickname 'Old Red' – he epitomized the romantic Scotsman. One only needs to glance at the undated but *c*.1843 daguerreotype photograph by the Edinburgh photographers Hill and Adamson to catch a sense of that romantic theatricality: the powerfully built geologist, standing in good tweeds, but with his waistcoat unbuttoned, sleeves rolled up, mason's chisel and mallet in hand, weighing up what looks rather like a fossil-rich slab of stone. One senses Miller knew how to play up this theatricality, which helped to smooth his passage from the squalid bothies of the itinerant labourer to the polite drawing rooms of early Victorian Edinburgh – as it had for his poetic forebear, Robert Burns.

Perhaps following a bout of depression or another psychotic episode, Hugh Miller shot himself with a revolver at his house in Portobello, Edinburgh, on Christmas Eve, 1856. He did not blow his brains out, as was normal in suicide by shooting, but fired the bullet through the chest and heart. Was he thinking about how he might look in his coffin to family members and those admirers who came to see him before the lid was nailed down?

Mary Anning: first lady of the fossils

If Hugh Miller represented what might be called the high romanticism of geology, so, in many respects, Miss Mary Anning epitomized a difference of emphasis, and yet her life, achievement and acknowledged reputation were not without romance. Born in 1799 and living at the opposite end of the British Isles from Miller, Mary Anning spent the whole of her relatively short life in the popular seaside town and resort of Lyme Regis, in Dorset: familiar to William Buckland from his earliest years, being only a few miles away from his native Axminster, just over the Devon-Dorset border.

The Annings belonged, however, to a very different social station from that of the Bucklands and on his mother's side, the Okes. Richard Anning was a carpenter who often found it hard to make ends meet amid the rising food prices of the Napoleonic Wars. As a result, Mary, her mother Mary and her brother Joseph (the only other surviving Anning child) supplemented the family income by setting up a table outside their cottage from which they sold fossils and other curios, as they were styled, to the wealthy ladies and gentlemen who came on holiday to the town, curios destined to join chipped flints and Roman coins in the curiosity cabinets of gentry drawing rooms. When Richard, the breadwinner, died in 1810, Mary Anning senior and her two young children had to fend for themselves.

Fortunately, the rich Liassic cliffs along this Jurassic Coast were rich in fossils, and especially following landslides during the winter storms, the beach could be strewn with the remains of strange ancient creatures, which the Annings would do their best to collect, clean up and sell from their cottage. Then in 1811, Joseph found a strange, elongated skull, some four feet long with enormous eyes. Soon after, sister Mary, then 12 years old, located the rest of the skeleton still in the cliffs and carefully excavated as much of it as had survived. Consequently, British palaeontology made a significant leap forward at the hands of the two children when circumstances forced them to work for a living instead of obtaining a regular schooling.

Mary Anning would soon reveal herself to be an exceptionally intelligent and talented child and a born fossil geologist. She was also locally famous for having survived a lightning strike, which killed three other women.[5] She seemed to share several traits with Buckland's future wife, Miss Mary Morland, to whom she was two years junior. Not only did the young girls, one in Devon, the other in Oxfordshire, share intelligence and a fine manual dexterity, but also both had a fascination with fossils and their anatomical structures. But Miss Mary Morland, no doubt under the tutelage of the family friend and Regius Professor of Medicine Sir Christopher Pegge, grew up to be a well-to-do lady of science, whereas Miss Mary Anning spent her life as a self-taught working girl, who recognized the economic as well as the intellectual value of her finds. They probably first met when both were adult women, either when the Bucklands were visiting Lyme, or perhaps when, in her early twenties, Mary Morland was on one of her geological trips to Dorset.

The crocodile-like lizard, ichthyosaurus (fish lizard), discovered by Mary and her brother, being over 20 feet long, snout to tail, became a source of fascination to William Buckland and his fellow palaeontologists. Buckland subsequently excavated specimens of ichthyosauri, and would describe and discuss the creature, most notably in his *Geology and Mineralogy*. The original fossil bones excavated by Mary and Joseph Anning

would be purchased for the British Museum for £23: a sum
with any commission or agent's fees deducted, must have r
huge boost to the Anning family budget, being roughly equiv
or six months' wages for a working carpenter. Mary Anning w
to discover and excavate plesiosauri and pterodactyls, often b
perils of landslips on the fossil-rich Liassic cliffs. On one occ.
was lucky to escape with her life, though the sudden landslip b
pet dog Troy.

By her adult years, Mary Anning's fame had spread across Brit
Continental Europe, and she and her elderly mother acquired a
shop with a glass window, in which her finds were exhibited fo
In 1844, the King of Saxony, when visiting England, went to Lyme
upon entering her shop, saw on display 'a perfect ichthyosaurus
least six-feet' embedded in its enfolding fossilized matrix. His Maj
regarded the £15 asking price for the ichthyosaurus 'very moderate', a
reckoned that it would have been a major acquisition for 'many of t
cabinets of Natural History on the Continent'.[6]

By her mid-thirties, Mary Anning was making a reasonable living fror
her curio shop, especially as her fame as a fossil geologist in her own righ
spread across Europe and America. Her financial circumstances were at
last stabilized after 1838 when William Buckland, the British Association
and the Prime Minister Lord Melbourne succeeded in obtaining a Civil
List Pension for her, along with subscriptions and gifts from the Geological Society. Several auctions of her finds, organized by her scientific
admirers, also brought in a few hundreds of pounds: sums that would
have been very substantial for a working family at that period. The proceeds from the sale of Sir Henry De la Beche's imaginative drawing *Duria
Antiquior* ('a more ancient, i.e. prehistoric, Dorset') would also go to her.
It showed a prehistoric scene of living ichthyosauri, pterodactyls, plesiosauri, and other creatures discovered and excavated by Anning, in and
hovering above a primordial Dorset swamp.

Mary Anning's life and career partook of the romantic in so far as she,
like Hugh Miller, exemplified the triumph of personal energy, acumen
and innate genius in rising above poverty and social limitation. Yet like
Miller, she suffered a relatively early death. In her mid-forties, she developed breast cancer: a condition for which there was no cure in her day,

lthough the first surgical use of sulphuric ether anaesthesia in Britain
n December 1846 might have made a painless mastectomy viable. She
died on 9 March 1847, having outlived her 78-year-old mother by only
five years.

Throughout her life, Mary Anning and her family had been devout
members of the Congregationalist Dissenting church, though the departure of a popular local minister had led some local Congregationalists,
including her, to start worshipping at Lyme Regis's Anglican parish
church. In death, however, both the local community and the wider
nation did Mary proud in 1850 with the commissioning of a fine stained-
glass memorial window containing six lights in the parish church. The
panels represented the six Christian Acts of Mercy, and commemorated
Mary's own acts of charity and kindness to the poor of Lyme Regis and
district. The local working girl, who had risen above primary poverty to a
certain level of comfort, never forgot her Christian duty to those less fortunate than herself. Sir Henry De la Beche, as President of the Geological Society, wrote and delivered a eulogy for her – the first such eulogy
for a woman.

'Ice Ages' transform Buckland's geological thinking

Always open to new ideas and discoveries as he was, William Buckland's
original 'diluvialism' had been undergoing gradual modifications since
the late 1820s. As we saw in Chapter 8 and will do again in Chapter 12,
Sir Charles Lyell's 1830–1833 'gradualist' as opposed to 'catastrophe-
based' geology was leading Buckland to rethink some of his earlier ideas,
and by the time of his writing *Geology and Mineralogy* in 1836, one
looks in vain for any full-scale treatment of Noah's Flood. It is certainly
there, but no longer accorded its old primacy as a universal world- and
landscape-changing agent.

By 1840, a new transformative agent was being given serious consider-
ation by both British and European geologists, one that provided a better explanation for the great rocky moraines holding in great lakes, from
Scotland and the English Lake District down to Switzerland, as well as
long-puzzling landscape features such as the Parallel Roads of Glen Roy

in the Scottish Highlands. These Roads consisted of sets of long, parallel scars cut into the mountainsides on either side of the Loch of Glen Roy.[7] Earlier explanations for them had focused upon their having been cut by detritus from Noah's Flood, or being ancient beach levels as the waters in the Loch rose and fell as a result of Noah's Flood and other catastrophes. Similarly, the Flood had been used to explain the erratic deposition of large boulders in what seemed like incongruous geological locations. But by 1840, a more plausible and more geologically versatile agent was under discussion: ice.

As early as 1824, the Danish–Norwegian Jens Esmark had suggested ancient Norway had once been covered with ice, and the movement of great and now largely melted glaciers had carved out the Norwegian fjords. By the early and mid-nineteenth century, with rapidly improving transport, quite a number of daring gentlemen were becoming enthusiastic mountaineers (yet another expression of the romantic passion for heroic adventures in pursuit of spectacular landscapes), and were discovering the joy of climbing the mountains of Scotland, Scandinavia, the Pyrenees and most of all, the Swiss Alps. And they were becoming increasingly aware of modern-day glaciers. Professor James D. Forbes, the Edinburgh physicist, became fascinated by the physics of glaciers, Alpine and other, and how their seeming flexible nature allowed them to cut into the landscape. During the 1830s, as new data poured in from around Europe and beyond, geologists were becoming increasingly aware of the limitations of the Deluge theory to explain new finds, such as the elevation of land and sea levels and the other phenomena mentioned above, especially in the light of Lyell's slow-change, non-catastrophic 'uniformitarian' geology after 1830.

First of all, during the 1830s Jean de Charpentier, then Louis Agassiz began to study the glaciers still present in Switzerland, noting how they seemed to carve out valleys and carry erratic blocks, and probably produce a moraine. It was suggested in 1837 that much of the northern hemisphere had once been blanketed by immensely thick ice sheets, our present-day glaciers being all that survived. Fascinated by these ideas, Buckland visited Agassiz in October 1838, and having inspected glaciers in the Jura and noted how they carved through the landscape, soon saw parallels to the now glacier-free mountains of Scotland, such as those around Glen Roy. By 1840, Buckland showed he had the intellectual flexibility to become a convert to the new glacial theory, and back in England he began to advance that theory in scientific circles. One former diluvial feature after another began to yield to a more encompassing glacial interpretation, and Lyell especially was delighted, as he came to realize that geological features only a stone's throw away from his ancestral property in Scotland accorded with it. In 1840, Buckland's friend, the mining engineer Thomas Sopwith, produced an amusing sketch of Buckland, dressed in the 'Costume of a Glacier' with heavy coat, snow boots, and an array of maps and charts, off to a glacier hunt in Scotland, the stagecoach receding behind him.

The speed with which the glacial theory was adopted in scientific circles was crucial. It accounted for many of the geological features that did not fit very well into the older diluvial perspective, and the theory received a huge boost from the overt advocacy of a figure of Buckland's status. What could be more romantic than the idea that the sites of the great cultural centres of Western civilization, such as London, Paris or Heidelberg, had once lain under hundreds of feet of snow and ice, and the oceans had been smaller and shallower, as so much water was locked up in ice sheets?

Romantic glory for all

We saw in this chapter how the Romantic Movement embraced technological advancement and scientific discovery in a way that we do not generally think of today. Along with astronomy, chemistry and industrial engineering, geology exerted an especially profound impact when it came to bursting the bounds of the human imagination. After the now elderly 'Strata' Smith had first shown how to read a landscape, it would be hard to over-estimate the role played by Buckland in the promotion and teaching of geology to the rising generation. We saw in Chapter 7 how he led crowds of British Association members and associated ladies on geological field trips around Oxford to Stonesfield quarries and elsewhere, transfixing them with his open-air discourses on strata and the exotic extinct beasts entombed within the rocks. Romantic science in all its glory! This passion for outdoor, hands-on lecturing also formed an integral part of his regular University of Oxford teaching, and students sometimes received notice that 'The next lecture will take place in the fields above the quarry at Stonesfield.'[8] Always aware of the power of the new technologies to inspire the mind and make life easier, he would later use the railways to lead geological groups further afield. On at least one occasion, notice was given that 'The class will meet at the G. W. R. [Great Western Railway] station at nine o' clock, when, in the train between Oxford and Bristol, I shall be able to point out and explain the several different formations we shall cross.'[9]

This undated notice must have been between June 1841, when Brunel's railway between London (Paddington) and Bristol was completed, and the summer of 1845 when Buckland left Oxford to become Dean of Westminster. Although the complete London (Paddington) to Bristol line opened in June 1841, with trains passing between the two cities in a mere four hours, it was not until 1844 that a new north-bound line from Didcot to Oxford – some 12 miles – was opened. One presumes that Buckland's geology class met at the new Oxford station, and like today, changed trains at Didcot for Bristol and the West. Or else they took stagecoaches to Didcot station. This would have been a geologically fascinating trip, as the westbound train first crossed the rich, flat farmlands of north Wiltshire, before plunging through the hillside at Box via Brunel's spectacular tunnel and travelling through the Avon valley leading to Bath and then on to Bristol. No other figure epitomized that creative geological energy, nor did more to promote and popularize the science, than the Revd Canon William Buckland. What with throwing his hat to stop stagecoaches, spellbinding lectures on windswept hillsides, articulated giant megatheria and ichthyosauri, dangerous caverns and, by the 1840s, lectures on steam trains hurtling through the landscape and the Box Hill Tunnel at 60 miles an hour, William Buckland was Romantic science incarnate.

Chapter 10
A Gift for Friendship: Buckland's Character, Friends and Influences

We have already been given some insights into Buckland's character and temperament in the previous chapters. We have seen his natural sociability, his instinctive gift for making friends and not enemies and his willingness to openly acknowledge the discoveries and achievements of others, even if they went beyond his own prior discoveries. Very conspicuous were his love of fun, his gift for mimicry, and the often humorous theatricality of his lectures. Inextricably intertwined with these traits were his deep Christian faith and the practical expression of that faith in his concerns with alleviating poverty and disease. For him, science, humour and love of God coalesced into one coherent whole. He was, in short, the very antithesis of the stiff, solemn, rather puritanical Victorian churchman of myth. Yet not everyone was carried along by his bonhomie. As we have seen, the young layman Charles Darwin regarded Buckland as a bit 'over the top', and lacking in that seriousness which Darwin believed should be displayed by an intellectual leader. But Buckland's personality and style attracted far more people than it repelled. Let us now look at his friends and companions.

The Very Revd William Daniel Conybeare: geologist and Dean of Llandaff

When writing *The Life and Correspondence* of her late father, William Buckland, Elizabeth Oke Gordon described William Daniel Conybeare as 'one of William Buckland's earliest and most intimate companions'.[1] Presumably shortly after Buckland's death on 14 August 1856, the now elderly Conybeare, Dean of Llandaff, sent a long and detailed letter and memoir to Frank Buckland, the eldest son, recollecting the eminent geologist. Conybeare's admiration for his old friend and geological companion shines through this narrative, and emphasizes how the very environment in which Buckland grew up – around Axminster and Lyme Regis in south Devon and the Dorset border area – helped to make him the man he would become. Conybeare was born in the city of London, where his father was the wealthy Rector of St Botolph's Church, but the family had Devonshire connections and owned the advowson, or right to select the incumbent, of Axminster parish church: a preferment which William Daniel would bestow upon himself in 1836, before later becoming Dean of Llandaff.

Conybeare, who was three years younger than Buckland, came up to Christ Church from Westminster at the time when Buckland was at Corpus Christi, the college next door to Christ Church. The two men could, perhaps, have met at the mineralogical or chemical lectures of Dr John Kidd – another old Westminster and Christ Church man. Their friendship quickly flourished, and before long they were travelling together on university vacation geological tours to various parts of the British Isles. In 1813, for example, they travelled to Northern Ireland where they were fascinated by the geological features of the Giants' Causeway, leading them to conclude that the basaltic rocks of Northern Ireland, and probably those elsewhere, were volcanic in origin. It was on this expedition to Northern Ireland that Buckland recognized a curious type of flint in the chalk pit geology between Larne and Moira. This was the paramoudra, or a lump of flint around 12 to 15 inches across and a couple or so feet long, with a central aperture running through the centre. These were fully familiar to the locals, and the word was probably of old Irish or Gaelic derivation, although its true meaning was obscure. Buckland even mentions seeing some in use as stepping stones across a stream. Dr Bruce of Belfast kindly obtained a fine paramoudra specimen for Buckland's Oxford museum. Buckland had initially speculated that these paramoudras were ancient sponges, a view which subsequent geologists would confirm.[2]

Buckland's and Conybeare's Irish geological tour brings home the degree to which geologists working in the field had to rough it as far as finding food and shelter was concerned. Upon their turning up wet and muddy at the cottage of an old Irish woman, an incident was recorded that shows the level of social presumption that even a pair of devoutly Christian gentlemen like Buckland and Conybeare could display towards local country folk. It seems that upon entering her cottage, they 'demanded refreshment', leading to a meal of eggs and bacon being cooked and laid before them. They thought it amusing when she said, 'Well, I never! Fancy two real gentlemen picking up stones. What won't one do for money?'[3] Picking up stones from the fields to clear ground for agricultural planting was, of course, a back-breaking activity of the poor, and a way of making a bit of extra cash from farmers. But this was a world in which peasants, servants and working people, with their doings and turns of phrase, were often seen as figures of fun by the gentry – especially when Anglican English gentlemen were commenting upon the doings of the Irish – perhaps Roman Catholic – poor. One only hopes that the old Irish woman upon whom the wet, muddy and hungry Buckland and Conybeare deposited themselves uninvited was well paid for her refreshments. Judging by Buckland's genuine concern for the poor and the help that he gave them, I suspect that she was.

Buckland and Conybeare undertook several other geological expeditions together, including one to France in 1820 where, in addition to their field researches, the savants in Paris entertained them splendidly. Besides their passion for geology and other intellectual topics, one suspects that their friendship was invigorated by a sense of humour. It would be hard to imagine anyone having a long and mutually enriching friendship with Buckland otherwise. When he was causing a sensation with the Kirkdale Cave finds around 1822, for example, Conybeare, who possessed considerable skill as an artist, produced what we today would call a cartoon, but which then would have been called a caricature. It shows Buckland on all fours crawling through a narrow tunnel into the hyena den, candle in hand. To his horror, he finds the hyenas very much alive, tucking into a hearty feast of hunted animal fragments. Bones litter the cave floor, and the hyenas are drawn in great anatomical detail, with their hairy spines and spotted coats. It is a beautiful fine-art drawing of cave geology and of beasts, but the real comedy derives from the look of sheer terror on Buckland's face, and the then thick head of hair standing on end, as he surveys the supper party. Is he destined to be the next course?

One suspects that jokes and laughter were never far away when the two men were together, whether in College or on a fossil-hunting expedition.

One might also speculate what jokes and innuendos might have passed between these reverend gentlemen when examining coprolites, the fossilized faeces of long-dead animals, and what they could tell us about the dietary habits of their eaters. Buckland discusses and illustrates coprolites in his *Geology and Mineralogy* (1836), though some people regarded it improper that such things should warrant the attention of ecclesiastical and academic dignitaries. We will return to coprolites in more detail below.

Humour and intellectual curiosity apart, the death of his elder brother John, who shared his and Buckland's geological interests, greatly disturbed Conybeare. So affected by this death (in 1824) was he that he published nothing on geology for the next five years. His standing as a field geologist in his own right is beyond doubt. He did fundamental original work on the ichthyosaurus and his own newly recognized giant reptile, the plesiosaurus, publishing extensively, while his artistic skills also had a serious dimension, as he both illustrated his finds and worked as a geological cartographer, with Buckland, William Phillips and others. While resident in his Axminster Rectory, Conybeare was ideally placed to witness the landslip of the cliffs at Lyme Regis, which he excavated and illustrated with the visiting William and Mary Buckland – and, no doubt, Mary Anning – in 1839–1840. In 1848, he left Axminster to take up residence in Llandaff Deanery. His geological knowledge would have come in useful when work began on restoring the decayed stone of Llandaff Cathedral. He survived Buckland by only 363 days, dying on 12 August 1857, aged 70, and it is clear from his letter to Frank that their warm friendship survived to the end.

Friends in high places, riots and rural unrest

Buckland's openness and instinct for friendship never ceased to win him friends and admirers in all places, from the Oxford poor and the quarrymen on the one hand to the Prime Minister and other ministers of state on the other. His good standing with Prime Minister Lord Liverpool and, by extension, with HM King George IV (formerly the Prince Regent) led, as we have seen, to his preferment to what was effectively an *ad hominem*

Regius Chair in Geology and Christ Church Canonry, with its mouth-watering £1,000 per annum stipend, in 1825.

By 1830, one aspect of Buckland's geology was of some political importance and won him the regard of reforming politicians such as the young Sir Robert Peel – and that was scientific agriculture. Looking back from our present-day viewpoint it is all too easy to see late Georgian and early Victorian England in a roseate light. The novels of Jane Austen, Anthony Trollope, George Eliot and, retrospectively, Thomas Hardy suggest a world of elegant drawing rooms, village church bands and choirs, a largely contented peasantry and an easy industrial progress, in which coal mines, factories and thriving overseas trade provided abundant coal, textiles, tea and coffee for all. Scratch the surface, and a much more sinister circumstance is revealed: where food shortages, starvation, unemployment and woefully inadequate wages threatened to capsize the ship of state. At the heart of it was the high price of bread.

During the Napoleonic Wars, which ended in the triumph of Waterloo in 1815, the Corn Laws had effectively fixed the price of wheat, and by extension, the size and weight of the standard penny loaf. British governments had bent over backwards during the wars, fiscally speaking, to encourage British farmers to produce more and more wheat, as European Continental supplies had been cut off by Bonaparte's 'Continental System', which prevented French-occupied, generally pro-British, European countries from selling wheat to Britain. Bonaparte's strategy was to starve Britain into submitting to his rule and occupying forces; Britain's response was to become self-sufficient in bread. It was economic warfare. Further exacerbating the food problem was the rapid growth of population. Various political economists from Thomas Malthus onwards feared that mouths to feed were increasing faster than food production, and foresaw disaster ahead. The cause of the population increase was, and still is, a topic of much debate. Was it immigration from Ireland and Scotland, or had first inoculation, then after Edward Jenner's discovery in 1796, vaccination caused the population to surge as a result of effective control of that terrifying disease, smallpox, which enabled more people to survive and reproduce?

Swings in the trade cycle of Britain's increasingly complex global economy also occasioned much urban distress, especially in the new industrial towns, as Elizabeth Gaskell made clear in her *Mary Barton: A Tale of Manchester Life* (1848), where starving folk might choose to spend their spare pennies on a bottle of laudanum which would put them out for a day, rather than on some scraps of food which were in themselves insufficient to assuage their constant hunger. Buckland's England was not a tranquil place, but one of stark social divides, especially between those who had the money to gorge themselves whenever they chose and those who could not afford a basic meal: a world brought vividly to life by Charles Dickens in *Oliver Twist* (1837–1839), *A Christmas Carol* (1843), and *Hard Times* (1854). It was a world often tottering on the brink of riot, revolution and political chaos at regular intervals between 1815 and the 1840s, before Victorian prosperity began to click in during the 1850s.

William Buckland lived his entire life in that comfortable world familiar to the readers of Jane Austen, although his – and Mary's – social consciences alerted them of the plight of the poor. As country folks, they were aware of periods of exceptionally acute suffering, such as might follow a couple of consecutive years of bad harvest when the poor were becoming unbearably hungry, and hayricks, isolated vicarages and country houses might be attacked and set on fire by desperate mobs. 'Captain Swing' was the generic name given to a real or imaginary character who incited many rural riots, while there were also the Tolpuddle Martyrs in Dorset, the Rebekah riots in rural Wales and others, which invariably arose from agricultural distress, high food prices and inadequate wages. These dangerous circumstances struck to the very heart of the Buckland and Morland families. In November 1830, Buckland wrote to his friend Sir Roderick Murchison saying that while he hoped to get up to London to vote for Sir John Herschel as President of the Royal Society, he felt very concerned about leaving Oxford at the time 'for my wife's father and mother [stepmother, more correctly], six miles from here, are in hourly expectation of a mob from Abingdon to set fire to their premises, and there are threats of a mob coming into Oxford from the neighbourhood of Benson' bent on causing havoc in the city. In 1830, there was no police force, and no soldiers had been sent to help keep law and order: 'my brother-in-law [Morland] is fighting with a party of fox-hunters, turned into special constables, and galloping 60 or 70 miles a day during all the past week'.[4]

In addition to legal changes, such as repealing the Corn Laws, other long-term measures were being considered by public figures – including Buckland – such as using science, chemistry and new technologies to increase food production from the land. His gift for friendship and winning support for his ideas led him and his friends Dr Thomas Acland and Mr Philip Pusey to convene a grand event in Oxford. Held in the temporarily roofed-over quadrangle of The Queen's College, this led after 1839 to the founding of the Agricultural Society, the aim of which was to establish a science of agriculture, and to apply science – most notably geology, mineralogy and chemistry – to that end. Buckland's friend Dr Ashurst Gilbert, Vice-Chancellor of the University of Oxford and later Bishop of Chichester, was firmly behind the idea, and the agricultural nobleman Lord Spencer became founding President. Using his influence and connections with landowners, political and ecclesiastical figures – all of whom had land-based incomes – Buckland was to play a significant role in finding medium-term solutions to the agricultural and food crises. Putting down riots and burnings might be a short-term solution for maintaining law and order, but if the ordinary folk of Britain were to be made happy, peaceful and productive, they had to have full bellies, and that involved using 'earth science' to improve food production. This is where the coprolites became important.[5]

The eruption of the volcano Mt Tambora in 1815

While Buckland and others were searching for a way in which science, particularly geology, might help to reduce the chronic food shortages between 1815 and 1850, their very cause, in one significant respect, derived from geology. In 1815, the Indonesian volcano Tambora erupted with stupendous force, blasting away part of its own cone. Along with pulverized rock belching up from below, this delivered many millions of tons of dust and fine particles into the earth's atmosphere. The explosive force was such that most of this matter was blown high into the upper atmosphere, and as Tambora is close to the equator, it was inevitably discharged into the globe's main wind systems. This atmospheric dust began to act as a giant global filter, cutting out much of the sunlight coming to the earth from space. Across the northern hemisphere, 1816 became immortalized as 'the year without a summer'. Domestic fires were kept blazing and overcoats worn in June, and the weather went peculiar, with cold, rain and damp everywhere. Brown snow (coloured by the atmospheric dust) fell in Hungary, while American East Coast farmers suffered. Everywhere, harvests failed as crop yields – for what they were worth – rotted in the wet summer fields. Nor were things much better for several years to come, for such a prodigious amount of volcanic dust and debris took many years to settle down on earth or scatter into space, and allow the atmosphere to gradually rebuild its normal transparency. Earth science and tectonic forces played a major part in creating the sudden climate change that produced the starvation crises that Buckland and others would try to alleviate through improved soil chemistry.

Coprolites: a key to ancient diets and physiology

Some people may be puzzled, as were many of their late Georgian forebears, as to why coprolites assumed such a significance in Buckland's thinking and writing. As was mentioned in the Preface, they were rather embarrassing objects: fossilized lumps of dung from ichthyosauri and other giant long-extinct reptiles. They were generally found in beds of Lias rocks, such as those of the cliffs of Lyme Regis. Sometimes they were found *inside* the fossilized skeletons, indicating quite precisely where the long-decomposed guts of the great creatures had once been, although they were more abundantly found in dense layers of rock strata. When found inside a skeleton, they enabled Buckland to establish what percentage of an ichthyosaurus's body had housed the guts, thereby making it possible to compare the internal anatomy of prehistoric reptiles with that of modern carnivorous, large-mouthed reptiles, such as crocodiles. He further identified the dense, stratified beds of coprolites as once forming the floors of ancient seas upon which the reptilian droppings – often in lumps some two to four inches long and an inch or more in diameter – had fallen over millions of years between the great, world-reshaping geological catastrophes.

The coprolites possessed a further value scientifically speaking, for they enabled the present-day palaeontologist and anatomist to learn much about the insides of the great reptiles that had once produced them. Inside some coprolites, for example, were found semi-digested food fragments such as teeth, bones and scales of those now extinct aquatic beasts upon which the ichthyosauri and plesiosauri had preyed. The ichthyosaurus probably did not chew its prey, but swallowed it whole: a fact made plain by the creature's teeth, for while the ichthyosaurus's jaws, sometimes three feet long, were well supplied with biting and tearing teeth, it appeared to have nothing that resembled molars. Swallowing food whole, or in bitten-off chunks, predicated a long gut with which to digest the unmasticated raw food.

The exterior appearance of the coprolites could provide vital clues to the intestinal actions of the living creature. Some coprolites, for example, were striated, while, yet more fascinating, some were twisted into convolutions like barley sugar, allowing the palaeontologist to recognize the peristaltic action of the gut, the intestine expanding and contracting rhythmically down its length to impart a screw motion to the food passing through it. Coprolites were a gift to the comparative anatomist and zoologist, who could use them to learn something about the action of the soft internal organs and the diets of ancient creatures.

Coprolites, chemistry and new fertilizers

By the 1830s, chemistry was advancing at a prodigious rate, as the new post-Lavoisier, post-Dalton science of atoms and reactive relationships was making it feasible to undertake precise, quantitative analyses of all manner of substances. Coprolites were discovered to be rich in phosphates, as were farmyard and other excrements. Would it be possible, therefore, for these lumps of organic-based stone, discovered in Lias beds across the country, in which Buckland became seriously interested in 1829, to be quarried, ground to powder by steam-powered machines, and then spread on the fields as fertilizer? He had many chemist friends, such as Dr Charles Daubeny of Magdalen College, Oxford, Dr John Kidd of Christ Church, Sir Humphry Davy before his early death in 1829, William Prout and many more – all of whom had agricultural chemistry interests and a concern for the hungry poor.

Without doubt, however, the founder of organic, agricultural and nutritional chemistry was Baron Justus von Liebig of Giessen, Germany, who was active between the 1820s and 1870s. Among other things, he would discover the major part played by the newly discovered atmospheric gas, nitrogen, in plant growth, along with the central role of phosphate of lime (calcium phosphate) in soil chemistry. In his chemical thinking, plant growth did not take place due to some vague vital force implicit within living things, but in precise and quantifiable reactive relationships between atmospheric gases, such as nitrogen and oxygen, and non-gaseous elements such as phosphorus compounds in the soil. Even water, which Davy and others had discovered was made up of two gases that could be separated electrically, had no implicit magic within itself: it was water's ability to react chemically that helped make plants live. Far from these physical, material discoveries undermining the Christian faith of Buckland and his friends, they only enhanced their admiration for the Creator. He was not working by veiled mystery, but by the logical use of complex basic components of nature – the chemical elements, which he had formed at the creation – the knowledge of which he was now sharing with the sons and daughters of Adam and Eve.

Liebig recognized and acknowledged Buckland as an agricultural chemical pioneer in his *Familiar Letters on Chemistry* (1843). Among other things, this came from the attention Buckland had drawn to coprolites. Natural manure from living animals was relatively scarce (despite this still being a horse-drawn age), and the droppings of sheep, cows and pigs were necessary to help reinvigorate the earth to produce fresh grass in their local grazing areas. But as Liebig made clear, there was not enough of the stuff available to reinvigorate many acres of ploughed land producing cereal crops as well, for 'England requires an enormous supply of animal excrements' to keep its farming going. This is where the agricultural value of coprolites came in.[6]

William Buckland, however, had drawn attention to the abundant geological availability of 'fossil "guano", strata of animal excrements in a state which will probably allow for their being employed as manure at a very small expense'[7] Land no longer needed to stand fallow so that it could gradually recover from a combination of grazing beasts and atmospheric interaction (the nitrogen cycle), but might now produce rich yields year after year. Relatively local supplies of coprolites were available across the country, as geologists discovered rich beds in the River Severn estuary, Cambridgeshire and so on. Academic geology proved its worth yet again when it came to providing answers to practical problems. Coprolites truly were a gift from God, not only in making the soil more fertile and helping to feed the poor by making foodstuffs more abundant, but in providing landowners with a new financial bounty on their estates by mining and selling them. Coprolites brought together some of the key things that were close to Buckland's heart: geological science, God's providence and financial viability. Facilitating all his early work on coprolites and agricultural chemistry was his genius for friendship and power of persuasion, as he was able to get fellow scientists, politicians, social reformers and great landowners together to help advance the scheme.

Peat bogs and land drainage

As a star lecturer and a lucid, engaging writer, it is hard to over-estimate the impact of Buckland's teaching on the influential, landowning and opinion-forming classes of Britain between around 1812 and 1845. As we have seen, many of the men who packed out his geological lectures in Oxford year in, year out were either landowners or would soon become so, be they destined to become county landed proprietors or parish clergy whose incomes derived at least in part from well-managed glebe lands and related endowments. As many would have felt a duty of care to their tenants and rural dependants, the improvement of their estates would have had a high priority. A rebellious peasantry made the countryside physically unsafe; it also reduced its economic viability, to say nothing of that sense of duty, which, in the Christian Britain of 200 years ago, was felt by many men and women of conscience. In addition to academic audiences, one must also weigh in the thousands of people Buckland touched after 1832 at British Association and related wider public lectures; and the same applied to his friend and Cambridge colleague Adam Sedgwick, with whom he shared many interests.

As all reforming politicians and humane and progressive landlords knew, however, the problem of how to obtain mass, cheap food production was also exacerbated by the enormous acreage of bog and wetland, both in mainland Britain and especially in Ireland, which yielded no crop apart from a low-energy peat fuel. Improved drainage could help, especially as mass-produced rolled-iron and early ceramic pipes offered a better option than simple, old-fashioned ditch digging. Yet even if a bog could be drained, at least in part, its peaty texture still remained sterile. On the other hand, in this still pre-bacterial age, Buckland was struck by the healthiness of people who lived in or near bog-lands. The Irish were renowned for their hearty constitutions and overall health (at least, when well-fed). At a time when it was still assumed by the medical profession that infectious diseases were generated by miasmas or foul airs, it seemed to Buckland that the inert and sterile airs rising above peat bogs somehow cleansed the surrounding atmosphere, thereby contributing to the rude health of those who breathed them. But as he was all too aware, while the Irish bogs might have been healthy, the wetland marshes, such as those of East Anglia, were *not*. Marshes bred fevers and agues, and he noted with pleasure that the drainage and cultivation of some fenlands around Cambridge had seen a marked diminution of fevers. No one in Buckland's time was aware of mosquito-borne diseases, be they carried by a tropical or temperate climate swamp-dwelling mosquito: that would have to await the recognition of microscopic pathogens after around 1865, and Sir Ronald Ross's 1897 work on malaria.

Buckland drew substantiation for the sterility of peat bogs from the already familiar cases of ancient, perfectly preserved human remains found in them, citing instances going back to one in the *Philosophical Transactions* of 1747. To convert such bogs into useful agricultural land, he emphasized, knowledge of geology was required. Two mineral substances could be used to help in this transformation: lime, obtained from the limestone occurring in shales in many regions, and marls, especially red marls. Lord Kames in Scotland and some landowners in Ireland had already begun to reclaim peat bogs by coating them with limes and marls to initiate a chemically reactive process with the carbons in the bog.

Marshland reclamations, however, were brought about through drainage, for unlike peat bogs they were potentially fertile once the waterlogging had been removed and the earth became solid. Always willing to put his money where his mouth was, Buckland bought a farm at Marsh Gibbon, only a few miles outside Oxford, on which to put his scientific ideas into practice, followed by another at Torrington on the Dartmoor slopes of Devon.[8] He was successful in both cases and improved the value of the properties as well. Buckland's friend and colleague Dr Charles Daubeny, physician, chemist and passionate agriculturalist, also bought a plot of land for agricultural experimental purposes between Oxford city and nearby Iffley village. Though long since covered with smart late Victorian and Edwardian houses, the street name 'Daubeny Road' immortalizes his association with the area.

William Buckland, Sir Robert Peel and the scientific house party

Buckland's ease of manner enabled him to make friends on every social level. His work in agricultural science made him popular with the farmers and farm workers, with whom he had mutually fruitful exchanges. He admitted that he learned from them a great deal about agricultural practicalities, while he freely imparted his scientific ideas to them; for he was always ready to learn and picked up practical tips from the farmer, labourer, quarryman and chemist. His love of fun and both telling and hearing stories would play a vital role in this process, for Buckland was no snob.

One of his warmest admirers in high places, as we have seen, was the reforming Prime Minister Sir Robert Peel, who later admitted how delighted he had been to be able to offer the Deanery of Westminster to Buckland in 1845.[9] Sir Robert, whose background and wealth derived from the Lancashire cotton trade, shared Buckland's passion for making the world a better place and using science and technology in this process. He was also an agriculturalist, committed to improving both the quantity and the quality of food production, and making it more abundant for the poor. Perhaps his most controversial political action in this respect had been repealing the 1815 Corn Laws in 1846, ending the legal protectionism of the farmers, allowing the importation of foreign grain and greatly reducing the price of bread.

Buckland was a regular attender at the sociable yet serious thinking gatherings at Drayton Manor, South Staffordshire, which was Sir Robert's country seat. At Drayton Manor, one might have politicians, social reformers, scientists, engineers, lawyers and entrepreneurs coming together, joined, when he was in England, by Justus von Liebig, on equal and friendly terms. At one of these gatherings, George Stephenson, the Northumberland railway engineer and entrepreneur, was in conversation with Buckland about the origin and power of coal. Seeing a train shooting past, Stephenson said that what powered the large steam engine was the sun: the sun, yes, agreed Buckland, but with a 'canny Newcastle driver' in charge of the locomotive. The sun powered the engine through its coal fuel, which came from ancient sun-ripened trees and plants that had lived millions of years before, and which, through long-term geological agencies, had slowly been metamorphosed into coal.[10] Stephenson, like many other highly influential figures mentioned in this book, was a 'poor boy made good' who began his working life as a labourer, learned to read at night school, and through genius, enterprise and learning how to behave at Prime Ministerial house parties, rose to mix on equal terms with the great and the good of the age.

Cartoons, comic poems, laughter and good fellowship

As will be obvious to the reader by now, William Buckland was a highly convivial, deeply sociable man, who loved jolly gatherings. And like any experienced lecturer or popular entertainer, he was a master of the art of establishing a good rapport with or captivating his listeners from the start. The occasion could be an Oxford lecture, a field address to the British Association, a gathering of farmers or quarrymen, a country house weekend or a dinner table at one of the fashionable West End mansions. To him, humour was the key to capturing an audience, though as his friend Caroline Fox recorded in 1836, 'he feels very nervous in addressing large assemblies till he has made them laugh, and then he is entirely at his ease'.[11] Being the intellectual entertainer that he was, he knew the value of props when it came to exciting an audience's curiosity; his most famous was his legendary blue bag that accompanied him everywhere and was included in the 1843 formal full-length portrait by Richard Ansdell, RA. The blue bag was Buckland's mobile museum, containing curious fossils, minerals and such, and in the right social environment, he

157

would rummage inside it and take out specimens upon which to talk 'with infinite drollery', and pass around. Just imagine a fashionable drawing room or dinner table where Buckland is a guest. He makes people's ears tingle as he speaks of ancient times; floods, catastrophes – or even coprolites. Then he opens the bag and hands round ancient bones, and even suggests resemblances between the bones of extinct animals and those sitting on the dinner plates.[12]

Conybeare and others sketched Buckland, and several sketches survive of him on his horse, lecturing to a crowd on a hilltop and using a large fossil bone as a pointer. Others show mock-academic processions on excavation sites, and geologists dancing merrily, while two servants carry an excavated elephant-like skeleton back to Oxford!

'Buffoonery by an Oxford Don'

Perhaps because of his sharp eye for irony, and his old soldier's love of fun, one excellent Buckland chronicler was his old friend Sir Roderick Murchison, who acknowledged Buckland as his geological 'preceptor' after he had left the Army. It was he whom we saw in Chapter 2 likening the younger Buckland in his Corpus Christi College rooms to an ancient necromancer, and in his letters and journals Murchison records many entertaining occasions, which they shared. He described Buckland as 'cheery, humorous, bustling, full of eloquence with which he blended much true wit', especially when in company with Conybeare, Leonard Horner, Sedgwick and other chums. Murchison's account of Buckland's lecture on fossil footprints to the Bristol meeting of the British Association in 1836 set the seal on the man and his impact. His account is worth quoting in full:

> At that meeting . . . the fun of one of the evenings was a lecture of Buckland's. In that part of his discourse which treated of Ichnolites, or fossil footprints, the Doctor exhibited himself as a cock or a hen on the edge of a muddy pond, making impressions by lifting one leg after another. Many of the grave people thought our science was altered to buffoonery by an Oxford Don.[13]

'Mourn, Ammonites, mourn'

Buckland's Oxford friend Richard Whately, Principal of St Alban Hall and later Anglican Archbishop of Dublin, wrote a classic mock elegy on his then still young friend, dated 1 December 1820. Can we bury Buckland, Whately asks? For surely, he is most at home underground, and as soon as he is laid to rest, will start digging for fossils?

> Mourn, Ammonites, mourn o'er his funeral urn,
>   Whose neck ye must grace no more . . .
>
> If with mattock and spade his body we lay
>   In the common alluvial soil,
> He'll start up and snatch those tools away
>   Of his own geological toil;
> In a stratum so young the Professor disdains
> That embedded should lie his organic remains.
>
> Then exposed to the drip of some case-hardening spring
>   His carcase let stalactite cover,
> And to Oxford the petrified sage let us bring
>   When he is encrusted all over;
> There, 'mid mammoths and crocodiles, high on a shelf,
> Let him stand as a monument raised to himself.[14]

All of this captures the love of fun and sociability of the man, and the deep affection in which he was held by so many. For Buckland never lost a sort of childhood innocence and love of simple things. We search hard to find any evidence of spite or angst, and he and Mary appear to have seen the deaths of four of their beloved children in a Christian providential context, in the full assurance that all would one day be reunited in heaven.

Central to his appeal was his commitment to serving his fellow human beings, through education, encouraging social reforms, and perhaps most of all, in using the power of geology, chemistry and contemporary science to alleviate the sufferings of the poor at a time of national distress. As we shall see in Chapter 13, he carried this reforming zeal into new aspects of public life after becoming Dean of Westminster in 1845, by his castigation of exploitative slum landlords and assaults upon squalor and depredation – and here he did make opponents. Yet through the seeming incongruity of coprolites, peat bogs, muck and drainage, his gift for friendship and love of fun gives us a rounded vision of his character. But we must now look at those people – including many of high education or social connection – who remained unconvinced by his ancient earth ideas, and the interpretation of the Holy Scriptures which accommodated them. And no, they were not simplistic 'fundamentalists'.

Chapter 11
The Scriptural Geologists

In the present day and age, it is all too easy to conflate scriptural geology with fundamentalism. In the time of William Buckland, this was *not* the case. Modern twentieth- and twenty-first-century fundamentalism is, at source, an American phenomenon, most commonly encountered in the American southern states, the mid-west and California. It was originally advanced by a body of men, both pastors and lay, in reaction against not just scientific but also liberal academic interpretations of Holy Scripture. While the 'ancient earth' and Darwinian evolution became especial *bêtes noires* for these people, other, literary, factors were involved as well.

Twentieth-century fundamentalism and nineteenth-century scriptural geology

From 1910 onwards, Amzi Clarence Dixon, Louis Meyer, Reuben Archer Torrey and others issued a series of booklets with the title *The Fundamentals*. They called for a reversion to what might be styled the 'old-fashioned' virtues, supposedly embraced by the Christian (or more specifically, *Protestant*) world in days of yore, when everyone lived by the Bible: before geology, modern science and literary criticism had begun to muddy the pure waters of Genesis and other early Old Testament books. One *bête noire* of the fundamentalists had nothing to do with geology, but was the 'higher criticism' that had grown up in certain nineteenth-century European universities such as Tübingen. Unlike 'lower criticism', which was concerned with elucidating biblical texts and early Christian manuscripts, 'higher criticism' was heavily influenced by German metaphysical philosophy and was often highly speculative. One of its tenets had to do with the idea that human cultures build up identities on folk traditions or myths. Like the ancient Greek myths, with their gods and goddesses, or the north European folktales collected by the Brothers Grimm and Hans Christian Andersen, could not the Old and – heaven forbid – the New Testament derive from similar mythical traditions? David Friedrich Strauss's *Das Leben Jesu* (*The Life of Jesus*, 1835) presented Christ and his miracles in such a way. In this way of thinking, the Judeo-Christian faith stood not on facts and evidence, but on what were really folk tales. This concept of the biblical texts, in which they were not so much firm spiritual anchor points as speculative sociological springboards, had a major effect upon the rise of what would come to be called 'liberal theology'. Buckland and his contemporaries had been familiar with the early aspects of this Germanic tradition, and Buckland's fellow Canon of Christ Church, neighbour and spiritual comforter Edward Bouverie Pusey had become a leading critic and opponent of much higher criticism in British theological circles.

Twentieth-century American fundamentalism, therefore, was a reaction not only against nineteenth-century science, but also against several currents in contemporary theology as well. Christian fundamentalism was, and still is, what might be called a 'back to basics' movement, in which the letter of Holy Scripture was pre-eminent and would suffer no reinterpretation. This letter of Scripture was, and often still is, construed as the language of the Authorized or King James Version of 1611. Twentieth-century fundamentalism has always been radically evangelical in its agenda, catering for mass audiences, first in the USA and then worldwide. In many ways it is a simple, reassuring, anti-sophisticated Christianity that can give spiritual direction to persons possessing little education or academic aspiration. It is what I have described as confirming the values of 'Grandpa's simple old-fashioned Christianity' in a fast-changing and complex world. In that respect it served, and still serves, a very different purpose than did the arguments and debates among the Victorian scriptural geologists.

Scriptural geology and 'orthodox' geology

Between 1815 and 1850, geological discoveries were being made at such a rate, and posing so many problems and paradoxes as far as Holy Scripture was concerned, that it was inevitable that a variety of interpretative schemes would be proposed, in addition to those of Buckland and Sedgwick. Central to the whole debate was the authority and inviolable sacredness of the biblical text. What soon becomes evident from the 'scripturalist' writers, Anglican, Free Church, ordained and lay, however, was the range and sophistication of the discussion. This was *not* simplistic fundamentalism, but embraced a range of interpretation and expression which ran from the writings of deeply Christian geologists, such as Buckland, Sedgwick and Hugh Miller, to the angry, indeed *fuming*, responses of the Very Revd Sir William Cockburn, Dean of York Minster, in 1844. Several issues were clearly at stake, and one of the most obvious, to those serious, educated, learned men, was the nature of intellectual authority itself. Several issues resonate through the debates between around 1820 and 1850, which also resonated in the debates about the status of experimental instrument-based discovery two centuries earlier, but not in a geological context. Where did truth lie: in the intellect and in text-based, logic-related sources, or in facts and causes found in nature?

Since 1640, the experimental method had proved its validity in the physical sciences where measurements and carefully cross-checked experiments had produced data from which the mathematical laws of physics had emerged. But, as indicated above, there were no such hard standards and measurements in geology, which, by its very nature, was rooted in comparative techniques. These could include the anatomical parallels drawn by Cuvier between the vertebrae, teeth and joints of extinct and living species, or the occurrence of particular fossilized shells between strata in both Somerset and Gloucestershire, to which William Smith had drawn attention. Yet while these inductive facts were deeply impressive, it could be argued that unlike chemistry, physics or astronomy, geology lacked an experimental or a demonstrative foundation. The earth-history models elucidated by Buckland, Lyell, Sedgwick, Murchison – and even Werner and Hutton – were still models, or theories, incapable of experimental proof. One could not rerun the Ice Ages, or devise an experiment to discover whether Noah's Flood also engulfed China or Australia. In 1830, British science was deeply committed to the Baconian experimental and Newtonian and inductive methods of establishing scientific truth, and on these grounds, geology and all the natural history sciences fell short. The same problem would resurface 30 years later, when Bishop

Samuel Wilberforce FRS, Adam Sedgwick FRS and others pointed out the 'philosophical' or scientific shortcoming of Darwin's theory of natural selection (*philosophical*, I emphasize, not religious, for contrary to popular mythology, Wilberforce criticized Darwin's masterpiece entirely on scientific grounds).[1]

To the scriptural geologists, the very nature and integrity of scientific and wider intellectual authority was of the highest importance, for none of these men were ignoramuses. The very opposite was the case, for many were educated at Oxford, Cambridge, and the Scottish universities. Many were in the Holy Orders of the Anglican or Dissenting churches, held academic appointments or were respected members of the learned professions. To see them as simple-minded 'Bible Thumpers' is a huge mistake: they were middle-class gentlemen, the social equals of Buckland and his friends.

As far as intellectual authority was concerned, much hinged upon one's approach to scriptural authority, and in this respect, it is necessary to put things into perspective. In the 1830s and 1840s, deeply Protestant England was in a state of spiritual turmoil. The passing of the Roman Catholic Emancipation Act of 1829, which removed all legal disqualifications – such as inability to hold public office – caused uproar in many circles. To most Protestants, Rome was the enemy: superstitious, foreign, ruled by the Pope and carrying connotations going back to the Spanish Armada and other mercifully foiled invasion attempts. Roman Catholics, it was often believed, played fast and loose with Holy Scripture, twisting its meaning – interpreting it – to suit their own ends. They were perceived as the antithesis of those good Protestants who understood their Authorized Version of the Bible in a plain, straightforward way. It was the Word of God, and Genesis had been delivered to Moses at first hand on Mount Sinai and must therefore be true: a point upon which they were quite in agreement with twentieth-century fundamentalists. Herein lay the problem of spiritual and intellectual authority: for how could a theory built upon fossil strata and rock-faulting remotely compare with the ancient and established truths of Scripture? This was not simple fundamentalism, but a symptom of a style of thinking facing what seemed like a conflict of authorities: the authority of God and the authority of science.

The 'Oxford Movement': Oxford becomes an ecclesiastical battleground

In addition to the fear of 'letting in Popery by the back door', which surrounded Catholic emancipation, other aspects of spiritual and intellectual turmoil were bubbling up in the world of the middle-aged William Buckland. The Oxford Movement, which took its origin in many respects from Buckland's Christ Church neighbour Canon Professor Edward Bouverie Pusey and John Henry Newman, a Fellow of nearby Oriel College, was dividing the Church of England in an alarming way, as we have seen. Here, evangelical Anglicans found themselves at odds with the Newmanites and Puseyites who believed that Anglicanism needed enrichment from aspects of Roman Catholic tradition and worship, such as the practice of priestly confession and spiritual disciplines based upon those of the saints and the monasteries. In addition to Roman Catholic worship styles and customs, the Newmanites and Puseyites emphasized the need for Anglicans to study the early church fathers in addition to the Bible, for here, they argued, lay a profound treasury of Christian spiritual insight, largely overlooked since the Protestant Reformation. There were also, of course, the more visible indicators of division, such as the introduction of high church Anglo-Catholic vestments, liturgies and the burning of incense.

Likewise, there was the Tractarian Movement, where deeply learned Catholic-inclined clergy, such as John Keble and Richard Hurrell Froude, emphasized the need for the Church of England to arouse itself from its comfortable formality and become more spiritual (or as its opponents would have said, 'superstitious'), which made many traditional Anglicans see red. Some Oxford colleges, including my own Wadham, even altered compulsory undergraduate prayer times to coincide with the times when Newman, Pusey and their 'crypto-papist' friends were likely to be preaching in St Mary the Virgin, the University Church. The purpose of this strategy was to make it impossible for undergraduates from such colleges to ever fall under the spell of their beguiling preaching. For no matter what a given head of college or tutor might have thought about the value of science-related Natural Theology, at least it was English and uncontaminated by 'Popery'. But the leaders of the Oxford Movement, in their emphasis upon the cultivation of a deep inner personal spirituality, generally placed little value on Natural Theology and the role of science in bringing people to God.

Added to this heady mix, there were the more moderate 'Broad Church' men, who felt that the University's insistence on sworn, legally-binding oaths of allegiance to the sixteenth-century, explicitly Catholic-hating Thirty-Nine Articles of the Church of England, printed in every copy of the Book of Common Prayer, should be waived or removed altogether. Theological storms were also raging in the wake of the Roman Catholic Relief Act of 1829, which removed old political (though not educational) limitations on Catholics in public life, allowing them to sit in Parliament, but not to send their sons to Oxbridge.

Whenever Buckland set foot outside the front door of his Canonry, where he inevitably met clerical colleagues, or attended churches and college chapels within Oxford, he would have been all too familiar with this ecclesiastical maelstrom raging around him. As his deep Christian commitment sprang from roots other than those feeding the current holy war during the 1840s, he did his best to keep out of it. But as Mary Buckland was all too aware, it tended to sideline science, and this was one reason why William was glad to escape to the Westminster Deanery in 1845, as we shall see in Chapter 13.[2]

Resonances of this movement would also rattle around Anglican Cambridge, though never with the same fury as in Oxford. In 1840, the overwhelming majority of Anglican clergymen were Oxbridge educated, so the allegiances and sectarian fights were inevitably carried across the land (and the wider British Empire), thereby making the Oxford Movement both a national and an international one. Ructions were also going on in the Scottish Kirk, leading to the Secession or 'Disruption' of 1843, a movement in which Hugh Miller was actively involved. Further internal disputes were occurring within the Anglican Church of Ireland about Protestant assistance towards Irish Roman Catholic education and relief, and conflicts between the established, Anglican, Church of Wales and the Welsh Dissenting churches. All these often furious disputes taking place within various branches of British Protestantism, especially during the 1830s and 1840s, help to put the scriptural geologists into context. The points of scientific, biblical and cultural authority about which they were disputing seem almost mild compared with what was going on in wider non-geological Christendom.

What was a 'professional geologist' in 1830?

Many modern-day academic science historians tend to dismiss the scriptural geologists as non-professional amateurs: glorified dabblers, who simply lacked the understanding of the professionals, and hence made untenable assertions. Yet even in 1840, the official academic or other post-holding geologists, such as Buckland, Sedgwick and even Cuvier, had all picked up their geology as they went along, and had never passed an examination in the subject. As we have seen, Buckland learned his geology from youth upwards largely by keeping his eyes and ears open, combined with some mineralogical training from John Kidd at Oxford, though Kidd was a doctor by profession, and had in turn picked up much of his geology as he went along. Sir Roderick Murchison and Sir Henry De la Beche were former military men, while most members of the Geological Society would have acquired their geology in passing rather than have received any formal training. Even Cuvier came to the subject, in many respects, via comparative anatomy, while James Hutton was an Edinburgh physician, chemical manufacturer and successful entrepreneur. As we saw in Chapter 9, Adam Sedgwick was confessedly ignorant of geology upon his appointment to the Woodwardian Chair in Cambridge, and set about learning 'on the hoof' so as to enable him to deliver his first lecture course only a few weeks later.

Perhaps the nearest we can get to professionals in our modern sense were Abraham Gottlob Werner, a Professor of Mining at Freiburg, and William Smith, who had come to geology from reading the lie of the land as a working canal surveyor. Nor was this amateur mode of operation unique to geology, for as I have shown elsewhere, most British astronomers (and chemists, botanists and microscopists) had entered their field by a similar non-professional, partly self-taught route.[3] With the exception of the Cambridge Mathematical Tripos course, and formal medical courses in the English and Scottish universities, there were no formal qualifying examinations in science in Britain in 1830.

Who were the scriptural geologists and what was their concern?

Excluding the professorial Buckland, Sedgwick, John Playfair and a few men in Scotland, what was a professional geologist, and how did he differ from a supposedly ignorant amateur, such as, we are told, filled the ranks of the scriptural geologists? Much would have hinged upon individual circumstances: did one do geology on a sustained, year in year out basis, and publish one's findings, or did one make only occasional sallies into the field, read books, and discuss the science at second-hand? It is true that most of the scriptural geologists fell into the latter category, but they were far from ignorant, especially in their wider culture.

What all the scriptural geologists had in common was a fear of undermining the message of Holy Scripture: a fear shared by the ordained Buckland and Sedgwick. No one wanted to be accused of sliding down the slippery slope into the perceived fantasies of higher criticism and relativism. But how did you interpret the straightforward words of the Mosaic creation in Genesis, in the wake of modern geological discoveries?

All those scriptural geologists of the early nineteenth century whose works and ideas have come down to us were men of education and culture. Most were ministers of the Christian religion, ranging from figures such as the Very Revd Dr Sir William Cockburn, Bt, Dean of York Minster, to individuals who ministered to large Congregationalist, Baptist and other Dissenting chapel congregations, when not doing geology. One key issue for all Christian geologists, however, was how far it was admissible to interpret the literal Genesis narrative if one were not to risk damaging its spiritual integrity. Could one interpret at all, and if so, how might one do so in a way that remained true to its ancient meaning? Which passages could be seen as conveying particular facts about the act of creation, and which might be interpreted as poetic expressions of God's plan?

Several key matters occupied their attention: some concerning some individuals more than others. First, how did one interpret the act of divine creation in Genesis 1.1? Did this verse, the very opening words of the Holy Bible, signify the creation *ex nihilo*, or did the original Hebrew rather suggest *made*: presumably from already existing materials? The Genesis creation seemed to relate to the preparation of the globe for man in God's own image, rather than, perhaps, to God's previous *ex nihilo* creation. Second, and potentially more problematic, what was the precise biblical meaning of a 'day', in the six days of creation? Should one read 'day' as an era, or age of great length? Or was it, as Granville Penn argued in 1822, the period between two natural sunsets?[4] If this were indeed the case, then it would indicate a very young earth, although some theological geologists had suggested that they might have been 'long days', perhaps, after sufficient number-juggling, making the earth 42,000 years old. Penn seemed to be of the view, however, guided as he was by his knowledge of Hebrew, that God had accomplished his work in six natural days, from separating the waters, light and darkness, down to Adam and Eve in the Garden of Eden. Granville Penn, the great-grandson of Admiral Sir William Penn, was descended from a landowning family, and had attended Magdalen College, Oxford. He was not a clergyman, but a learned philologist and classical and biblical scholar who had been stimulated by Buckland's Kirkdale Cave discoveries. Penn, however, desired to apply a corrective to Buckland's long-time scale catastrophist geology, and reaffirm the truth of the Mosaic creation narrative; however, there is no evidence that he ever did any geological fieldwork of his own. He recognized the value of geology in indicating the glory and power of God in nature, but his *A Comparative Estimate of the Mineral and Mosaical Geologies* (1822) was written primarily to claim the primacy of the Genesis story.

Third, what was the period of time elapsing between the first (*ex nihilo* and six-day Edenic) creation and the second creation, which reshaped the world after Noah's Flood? Most scripturalists reckoned it to be 1,656 years, as might be calculated from the genealogies of the Patriarchs in Genesis. Granville Penn, like many of his scripturalist colleagues, reckoned that after the first creation, great hollows were impressed into the land, and they formed the beds of the seas, all the strata being laid down quite quickly. Then came the second revolution of Noah's Flood, where the earth became topsy-turvy, the seabeds and strata rising up to form entirely new continents and land masses, with the old ones sinking beneath the waves to become new seabeds. This model of earth history was at odds in key respects with Buckland's diluvialism and interpretation of the Kirkdale Cave finds, for if the Deluge wiped out *all* life except Noah, his family, and the animals contained in the Ark, and wholly reordered the continents, how could Kirkdale Cave and its hyena bones have survived the grand transition from ante-diluvian to post-diluvian times?

Buckland's post-Kirkdale-Cave work, and especially his Bridgewater Treatise *Geology and Mineralogy* of 1836, came under attack from the scripturalists, for between 1819 and 1836 he had gradually played down the importance of Noah's Flood in the light of new geological discoveries. Lyell's *Principles of Geology* (1831–1833) posed an even greater threat to a purely literal reading of Genesis, for Lyell replaced floods and catastrophes with a long-time gradual modelling and remodelling of the earth, as we shall see in Chapter 12. Then in 1844, the cat descended most dramatically among the pigeons when Robert Chambers' anonymously published *Vestiges of the Natural History of Creation* appeared. Not only did the still active scripturalists see red, but so did most orthodox and professional geologists, for *Vestiges* used a long-term Lyellian uniformitarian format for its scheme of global history, and mixed in evolution and other horrors as well. There were no references to Genesis, Moses, or the Flood in Chambers' entirely naturalistic scheme. We shall look at *Vestiges* in more detail in the next chapter.

Many individuals weighed into the scripturalist defence of Genesis geology with varying degrees of rancour. The Glasgow minister, theologian and Bridgewater Treatise author Thomas Chalmers was one of the more moderate, although he was far from happy with his fellow Scotsman James Hutton's 'no sign of a beginning or an end' timeless volcanic geology. An early scripturalist to respond to Lyell's uniformitarian scheme was George Fairholme. He was neither an academic theologian nor a scientist, but a wealthy merchant and financier. He rejected Lyell's model, but in his *General View of the Geology of Scripture* (1833) and *The Mosaic Deluge* (1837), he presented a response that was more moderate than that of many of his fellow scripturalists. Fairholme admitted that Genesis did not provide a total geology in itself. But what it did provide was what might be called the big picture of God's actions and intentions for our planet and the human race. It was the geologist's job to flesh out the details of this big picture, using the scientific method, yet working within the broader events contained in the scriptural narrative. Fairholme seems to have seen Scripture as essentially beyond fault, for it was God's word.

Faults and contradictions could only arise, therefore, through incorrect thinking and methods of interpretation, though this did not necessarily exclude the use of our intelligence.

Scientific eminence in the non-geological sciences did not in any way guarantee that a confirmed scriptural geologist was willing to follow Cuvier, Buckland and Sedgwick, and their friends. Professor Andrew Ure of the Andersonian Institution, Glasgow (now Strathclyde University) was a distinguished chemist and chemical analyst as well as being a renowned anatomist and medical man. It had been Ure who in 1818 had won notoriety by passing powerful bolts of electricity through the still warm corpse of the hanged Clydesdale murderer, making the dead man grimace and jerk, yet not come back to life.[5] Ure was also a technological progressive, and wrote with passion on the wonder of the steam engine and the power of engineering to change the world for the better. When it came to geology and Scripture, he remained firmly grounded in the book of Genesis, and his *New System of Geology* (1829) was attacked fiercely by Sedgwick and other academic geologists.

The Revd George Bugg, a graduate of St John's College, Cambridge, disagreed with the statements of the modern-day geologists such as Buckland and Sedgwick, on grounds that were neither bigoted nor naïve, in the light of what was known when he published his hefty *Scriptural Geology* in two volumes in 1826 and 1827. He argued, for example, that while Copernicus's heliocentric cosmology could be harmonized with Scripture, modern geology could not. While not everyone might have agreed with this statement, what could not be denied was that astronomy was an ancient and mature science, as was biblical theology, and connections could be made between them. Geology, on the other hand, was an infant science in the 1820s, yet geology was making claims about global history and the origins of living things, quite out of proportion to its scientific maturity. Furthermore, this infant science was demanding biblical reinterpretations that ran against the plain meaning of the word of God, and against the accumulated theological wisdom of the centuries.

As we have noted above, many modern-day science historians prefer to characterize these scripturalists as a backward, simplistic, lunatic fringe, like the early academic geologists and especially Adam Sedgwick who, unlike Buckland, enjoyed controversy. Yet as things stood in 1830, their conservatism and defence of the letter of Holy Scripture were quite understandable. These invariably learned men stood by the wisdom of the centuries against what seemed to them a speculative avant-garde, who seemed to be giving more credibility to scattered fossil bones and strata than they gave to the creation story passed on by God to Moses on Mount Sinai. The two centuries that have rolled by since Buckland dug up his hyenas in a Yorkshire cave have shown that he, with his long geological ages, was indeed glimpsing the truth about the very ancient history of our planet, but this was far from obvious to the more conservative scholars of late Georgian and early Victorian Britain in 1822.

The clerical dignitary, theologian and amateur geologist the Very Revd Dr Sir William Cockburn, Dean of York Minster, founding Vice-President of the Yorkshire Philosophical Society, found it impossible to reconcile the numerous submergings, elevations and changes supposedly undergone by our planet with what he read in the Bible. He claimed to have visited many quarries and inspected many rock strata, and had read Buckland's *Geology and Mineralogy*, Sir Roderick Murchison's *The Silurian System* (1839), Adam Sedgwick's publications and those of other geologists, yet he still could not square their sense of 'deep time' with Scripture. As far as Cockburn was concerned, Scripture was the ultimate authority on such matters. This clearly scientifically minded senior clergyman may have felt he had been cheated by bodies that he once supported. These included the Yorkshire Philosophical Society, and its national offshoot the British Association for the Advancement of Science, founded in York in 1831. He became increasingly distressed by what he saw as the unbiblical tendencies developing in both, as more and more gentlemen and ladies of science came to accept the new ancient earth, as opposed to the Mosaic timescales. All of this culminated in his blistering attack on the British Association at its next York meeting in 1844, encapsulated in his 23-page essay *The Bible Defended Against the British Association* (1844). His argument, quite simply, was that divine miracles had been the key agents in the formation of the earth, rather than vast, slow-moving naturalistic changes extending across countless ages.

I specifically mention *ladies* of science above, for Cockburn seems to have singled out Mrs Mary Somerville as one of the figures for condemnation. As Mary subsequently told her daughters, who recorded the incident, she 'was preached against by name in York Cathedral'.[6] Sir George Biddell Airy had also sent an account of Adam Sedgwick's 'hammering down' of Cockburn in a letter to his wife, Richarda: an 'execution' which, according to Airy, numerous ladies (who, it would appear, could attend the meetings by 1844) had gone along to witness.[7] Only a few weeks after the British Association's York meeting, in October 1844, however, the publication of Robert Chambers' *Vestiges of the Natural History of Creation* would act as a red rag to a whole field of both geological and theological bulls. Ironically, Cockburn and Sedgwick would now be on the same side in 'hammering' *Vestiges*, along with the rest of the scientific and theological 'establishment', both lay and academic.

One academic theologian and minister who would do much to pour oil upon the troubled waters of the scripturalist versus modern geology controversy was the Congregationalist Revd Dr John Pye-Smith. In 1840, he published *On the Relation between the Holy Scriptures and Some Parts of Geological Science*, which praised Buckland and Sedgwick in their recognition of the divine source and nature of scientific knowledge, while accusing many of the scripturalists of being unscientific, dogmatic and ignoring the fact that geology amplified and broadened our knowledge of the glory of creation, rather than challenging it. This truly learned and devout clergyman, one of many distinguished Dissenting ministers and intellectuals, prepared a series of interpretations aimed at putting both geology and biblical understanding into context. He argued, for example, that Genesis and the other Mosaic books in the Old Testament were primarily concerned with rehearsing purely *human* genealogies, from Adam and Eve onwards, and *not* with providing a detailed history of the earth as a planet. He was willing to admit that a period of unspecified duration had elapsed between the creation *ex nihilo* and the Genesis creation, followed as it was by purely human genealogies. In consequence, he proposed the biblical narrative referred only to a relatively small part of the earth's surface, such as somewhere in Asia, what we today call the Middle East. Similarly, Noah's Flood as described in Genesis 6–8 probably referred to a relatively local inundation: 'the whole world', as it would have seemed to someone in northern Syria or Mesopotamia, but not global as we now understand it. He also suggested that Mount Ararat in Armenia was too high for Noah's Ark to have come to rest upon, considering the amount of water ascribed to the Flood. In his considered opinion, the Mosaic narrative was intended by God for people with only a very limited geographical knowledge, and was a human or moral narrative rather than a textbook of science. It was erroneous, therefore, to attempt to read Genesis and the Holy Scriptures as a treatise on science and geology.

By 1850, it is probably true to say that scriptural geology had passed its zenith in terms of wider credibility, as an increasing succession of new geological and other scientific discoveries made the scripturalist arguments appear increasingly contrived. Yet scripturalism was to have its dramatic swan-song in 1857, at the hands of a south Devon lay minister of the Plymouth Brethren community (the Brethren had no formal ordained ministry), who was a renowned marine biologist and inventor of the aquarium: the Revd Philip Henry Gosse, FRS, of Ellacombe, near Torquay. Gosse hoped not to advance a simplistic scripturalism, but to offer a reconciliation between the geologies of Buckland, Lyell and Sedgwick, and Scripture. He did this through a peculiar route: accepting all the lay findings of modern geology, (as had most of the scripturalists over the past half-century, though the crunch came for them in the *interpretation* of these scientific facts). Gosse's interpretation hinged upon what he saw as circularity, or what some contemporary physiologists in Germany (whom we shall meet in Chapter 12) styled 'recapitulation'. For did not everything contain within it its own ancestry? Trees, flowers, animals, humans and all living things carried their past within themselves – almost what we today might call a genetic trace. So why should not the earth itself? If the earth had passed through cycles since the Genesis creation, and become turbulently overthrown at the Flood, could not God have built a sort of ancestry or 'identity' into the rocks themselves, as the cycles rolled on? Could not the young, biblical, earth have been made by God with ancient traces of what might have been, complete with ancient-looking but new fossils, which had never been alive – God's creative thoughts, or ancestral prototypes, almost?

It was this line of thinking that gave rise to the title of his book, *Omphalos: An Attempt to Untie the Geological Knot*, for *omphalos* is the Greek word for 'navel'. So could Adam, made directly by the hand of God, and not born of a woman in the course of nature, ever have had a navel? (One could apply the same argument to Eve – but not to Cain, Abel and their descendants, who were born by natural processes.) In this way of thinking, Adam (and Eve) *must* have had navels if they were to be fully human ancestors. In other words, God had created them looking as if they were born naturally, even if they were not. Ergo, could not the divinely created earth have been born with the geological equivalent of a navel – namely, fossils, strata and other marks of antiquity and ancestry?

Gosse styled his idea of cycles 'prochronism', and published the year following Buckland's death in 1856, only two years before Darwin's *The Origin of Species*. It is hardly surprising that the scientific world in particular regarded *Omphalos* as bizarre. The book was a publishing disaster and failed to sell, with piles of unsold copies being pulped. Yet here was an otherwise impeccably respectable marine biologist, microscopist, pioneer of the aquarium for the scientific study of marine life and Fellow of the Royal Society, shooting off at an eccentric scripturalist tangent, which did no good to his future scientific standing.

The scripturalist sunset

The death knell of scriptural geology came in the 1850s, culminating in Gosse's *Omphalos*, although, as I suggested above, I believe that it possessed a greater credibility in 1835 than American fundamentalism does today. Scriptural geology drew no especial social or political agendas in its wake as fundamentalism did, and still does. It was not especially concerned with the banning and demonizing of alcohol, though some scripturalists might have had their own objections to drink. Neither did it ever have a political dimension; it did not lobby Members of Parliament as fundamentalists lobbied Congress and state legislatures in the USA, nor did it establish its own churches, let alone cult followings. Scriptural geology, therefore, must be seen in the context of its own time. Its effective dying away after around 1850 reflected an intelligent response to new scientific discoveries, along with an acknowledgement that sincere and prayerful fresh understanding of Holy Scripture in the light of deeper insights across the board did not of itself lead to scepticism or unbelief.

Chapter 12
Stability, Progress or Evolution?

To understand William Buckland in his true historical context, and perhaps to understand the scriptural geologists, it is essential to appreciate the sheer speed at which geological science had changed over the period of just a few years. Since what appeared to be the obvious diluvialism of 1819, the discoveries of Lyell, Sedgwick and Murchison, Buckland's *Geology and Mineralogy* and even the young Darwin's observations on Andean mountain-building and the slow, gentle growth of coral reefs, had all given rise to a veritable *deluge* of new scientific facts which compelled a fundamental rethink of earth-forming processes and time-scales. This is saying nothing about the Ice Age discoveries of Louis Agassiz and other European Continental and American geologists. By 1845 geological surveys were also being conducted in parts of Africa, India, Australasia, the Andes, the Caribbean and Indonesia, as the science spread beyond Europe and became global – which, after all, was the only way to fully understand the physical history of our planet. Nor was it just in geology that science was advancing by leaps and bounds. Similar great leaps forward were being made with the organic chemical discoveries of Liebig, Michael Faraday's electromagnetic physics, the deep-space observational cosmology of Lord Rosse and the Herschels, and anatomical and physiological discoveries, plus anaesthetic surgery and the transformative world-changing power of engineering science. It is hardly surprising that some people found it hard to keep pace as long-standing, traditional frameworks of understanding were being challenged. So, what was happening in geology and the ancient life sciences?

Sir Charles Lyell: the transformative power of small changes over time

Like most geologists of his generation, Sir Charles Lyell, a legally trained, Scottish-born landowner and baronet who had grown up in southern England, was a Buckland disciple. In 1819, while a student at Exeter College, Oxford, he started to attend Buckland's lectures, at the outset of what was probably the most influential period of Buckland's international career. For a time in the 1830s, Lyell held the Geology Chair at the newly founded King's College, London, although he belonged to that class of independent gentleman scientist which abounded in Georgian and early Victorian Britain. In addition to field geologizing, he read widely and diversely, and while never really accepting the ideas of the proto-evolutionary Jean-Baptiste Lamarck, he became increasingly convinced that earth history had come about not by violent, world-changing catastrophes, but by constant, accumulative small changes which, given enough time, could change the world many times over.

In this respect, Lyell had been interested by the ideas of Dr James Hutton in the 1790s and his 'spokesman' John Playfair. As we saw in Chapter 3, Hutton's *Theory of the Earth* (1795) had argued for a globe shaped by gradual small changes, brought about primarily by volcanic and tectonic as opposed to aquatic causes. This had given rise to the two rival schools of geology, the Plutonist (fire) and Neptunian (water) schools of geology, which had been active especially in early nineteenth-century Edinburgh.

Lyell's inclination to view the geological landscape in 'gradualist' terms had been confirmed over 1828–1829, when he and his geological friend Sir Roderick Murchison had geologized in southern France and Italy, both regions possessing clear and dramatic marks of ancient volcanic activity. By examining strata layers in these volcanic regions, such as around the Bay of Naples, dominated as it was by Mount Vesuvius, Lyell was struck by the sedimentary strata sandwiched between strata of volcanic rock. This layering suggested that marine deposition, with its shells and shell-fish forms, was periodically interrupted by volcanic eruptions, some of them extending back into the deep past, long before the famous eruption of AD 79 which destroyed Roman Pompeii and Herculaneum, long familiar to classically-trained gentlemen through the writings of Pliny the

177

Younger. Yet all of this was clearly *local* activity, with no direct parallels to the volcanic mountains of Scotland, or the Auvergne, Peru and Indonesia.

Likewise, travelling deeper into the volcanically unstable south of Italy, Lyell was struck by the remains of the classical temple of Serapis, near Naples in southern Italy. This temple had clearly been built well within the period of advanced classical civilization. Yet while in ruins, several of its great columns were still standing erect, although the pavement of the temple was now under water. Clearly, the classical builders had not built it so, opening up the possibility that there had been a long, gradual subsidence of the whole site over a couple of millennia. But the still-standing columns suggested that the subsidence must have been gradual, given the odd local earthquake in this unstable region, as opposed to a global catastrophe. And while the age of the great catastrophes would have long since passed by 1827, it was clear that successions of small shakings and the gentle subsidence of the underlying bedrock had been, and probably still were, at work.

Lyell suggested other pieces of evidence for a world that might have been formed by innumerable small changes, as opposed to great catastrophes punctuated by long periods of stability. Scandinavia also suggested a case for gradualism, for in the area of the Gulf of Bothnia at the northern end of the Baltic, there were man-made features such as rings set into the rock for the tying up of boats which were now too high, given the sea level. Had the sea level fallen in the Baltic, or had some of the rocks at the northern end of that sea been raised up within a remarkably brief human period? The sea levels in the lower Baltic, around Poland and Denmark, did not appear significantly changed in a thousand years, so had parts of the Gulf of Bothnia been elevated? If they had, however, the elevation had been gentle and imperceptible, with no accompanying catastrophes or earthquakes. Once again, it appeared that slow, gentle, non-dramatic, yet genuine and accumulative changes were taking place.

Lyell presented these and plenty of other evidences for gradual change by 'causes now in operation' in Volume I of his profoundly influential *Principles of Geology* (1830). In the *Principles*, he presented what he saw as a body of observed empirical evidence for slow changes, although some of his critics (but *not* Buckland) tried to sidestep it as being too theoretical. Yet one very big problem faced Lyell if his slow change model for the earth was true: why did the fossil record show particular species, such as ichthyosauri, existing at specific times but not around later? In addition to the extinction of ancient species, where had modern ones – monkeys, bears, cats and dogs – come from, for their remains were never found in the fossil record? Cuvier's and Buckland's catastrophic geology supplied a sound explanation: they were *new* creations from the hand of God.

After leaving Oxford, Lyell had trained as a barrister, and in his late twenties had been impressed and fascinated by the ideas of the French anatomist and zoologist Jean-Baptiste Lamarck. Lamarck – of whom more will be said below – had developed an early 'transmutationalist', or *evolutionary*, theory of species origin. This was roundly condemned in many circles, however, especially in England, where it was deemed to savour of French Revolutionary scepticism and anti-Christianity. Writing to his friend the physician and geologist Dr Gideon Mantell on 2 March 1827, while on the legal circuit, Lyell said that he had been impressed by his reading of Lamarck's *Philosophie Zoologique* (1809). On the other hand, he remained unconvinced, comparing his reading of Lamarck with listening to the arguments of the rival counsel in a law case ('an advocate on the wrong side, to know what can be made of the case in good hands'), and assessing how best he might counter them.[1] Yet if one were not to have catastrophes and wholesale new divine creations of fresh, more advanced species, then one had to find a way of explaining the appearance of new forms that possessed no anatomical equivalents in the earlier fossil record. Lyell also remained unconvinced (though not theologically repelled) by the idea that mankind had gradually developed from lower creatures. In *Principles of Geology* Vol. II (January 1832), Lyell writes as an ingenious barrister advancing an argument about which he was not entirely clear. For if one were *not* to have constant 'special creations' of new species, and at the same time were *not* to have evolution, what could one do to explain speciation?

Here Lyell becomes somewhat slippery. Could it be that at the creation, God had made particular types of species in particular places, such as horses, cats and dogs on some parts of the earth's surface, and the great lizards, fish and similar aquatic creatures on others? All may once have been on the earth at the same time, though not in the same place, but as slow changes over many millennia caused swamps and seas to dry up and continents to gradually rise and fall, with new seas and swamps coming into being, some types of creatures could cope better than others. Could it be that as particular swamps dried up, some creatures inevitably became extinct, for there were no new accessible habitats for them, in consequence of which these less adaptive and less versatile creatures perished and ended up as fossils in the strata? Whereas the more versatile animals, like horses and dogs, which did not reside in swamps and could always migrate to more accommodating environments such as new pasture lands or new hunting grounds, would have survived.

Moreover, as dogs, cats and horses did not live in swamps, when they perished, they did so on hard ground. Here, they probably got torn to pieces and eaten by fellow solid land dwellers, rather than sinking to the bottom of a swamp alongside dead saurians. Could this explain why modern palaeontologists did not generally find the fossils of modern mammals in the strata? There were clear caveats to this line of thinking, for what about the fossilized hyenas found by Buckland in the Kirkdale Cave, which he had shown to be anatomically identical to modern African and Abyssinian hyenas, along with fossilized bears, Siberian mammoths and similar creatures found in German and other caves? One might, however, try to explain these instances in terms of purely local conditions, such as a sudden local flood, sudden volcanic or earthquake activity or a sudden freeze. Yet on 3 January 1825, Lyell passed on to Mantell an amusing story. Buckland had just received a letter from India informing him about local hyenas. So similar were the Indian to the Kirkdale hyenas, commented Lyell, that one might have assumed they had 'attended regularly three courses of his [Buckland's] lectures'.[2]

Lyell's real problem, though, was how to explain the origin of the human race. If one could not use some sort of evolutionary process to explain the appearance of humanity, then one had no real alternative to postulating some kind of special creation. On this point, especially in the *Principles*, he uses rather obscure language, for men and women suddenly come out of what seems like nowhere. One is left to assume they had been there all the time; or alternatively, was Lyell willing to acknowledge special creation in his otherwise naturalistic, long-term uniformitarian terrestrial cosmogony?

The three volumes of Lyell's *Principles*, and the facts and theories they contained, would exert a profound effect upon the future of geology as well as the future of the wider life sciences. Adam Sedgwick could not accept Lyell's steady, uniformitarian model of earth and life history, though it clearly fascinated him; for before his old pupil, the 22-year-old Charles Darwin, boarded HMS *Beagle* in December 1831, Sedgwick presented him with a copy of Lyell's *Principles* to read on the voyage, suggesting that, though he might be intrigued by the theory it proposed, he should *not* believe it. But from first seeing St Jago in the Cape Verde Islands, only three weeks out from Devonport, and during the rest of his almost five-year *Beagle* voyage, Darwin was coming to see the world through Lyell's eyes. Volcanic islands, the grandeur of the Andes rising from the Argentinian Pampas, and in particular the aftermath of the devastating earthquake at Concepción, Chile, which had destroyed towns and villages, caused tidal waves and cracked and fissured rocks in that part of the Andes: all were evidences of relatively local geological activity. Given sufficiently long stretches of time, could not countless local quakes and shudderings of the earth bring about fundamental changes to the mountains, continents and seas, *without* the need for Buckland's great global catastrophes? Darwin soon became a convinced uniformitarian, and that worldview would later be the stage upon which the gradualist drama of non-Lamarckian organic evolution would be played out. But more of Darwin in Chapter 14.

Volcanoes, vulcanism and their causes

One subject under discussion by several geologists and chemists during the 1820s was the nature of vulcanism. In particular, this pertained to Hutton's uniformitarian earth-shaping processes, along with Lyell's and Murchison's researches in the Auvergne and southern Italy. No one doubted the effects of intense geothermal energy: where the dispute lay was in the source of that energy. Did planet earth possess an intensely hot interior, congruent with Laplace's model of the origins of the solar system, where the earth and other planets were the cooling, condensing, fragments of a filament thrown out by a white-hot spinning sun? This deep internal heat model was advocated, among others, by that widely travelled explorer and 'universal scientist' Alexander von Humboldt. In this model, volcanoes were cracks in the thin terrestrial crust through which the scalding internal magma occasionally poured to produce volcanic eruptions, earthquakes and related phenomena. Alternatively, there was the chemical theory of volcanoes, first put forward by Sir Humphry Davy but developed by Buckland's chemist and botanist friend and colleague in nearby Magdalen College, Professor Charles Daubeny, whom we met in the context of Liebig and early soil and agricultural chemistry in Chapter 10. In this model of vulcanism, volcanic heat, pressure and energy were generated relatively close to the earth's surface by water penetrating cracks in the crust and falling upon unoxidized minerals and other subterranean chemicals. This would be similar to what happens when one pours water on to slaked lime or baking soda: it effervesces, expands and can generate heat.

Daubeny developed this model on the strength of laboratory experiments and his own travels to see volcanoes, geothermal springs and related phenomena across Europe and the eastern seaboard of the United States. In his *A Description of Active and Extinct Volcanoes* (1826), he pointed out that most volcanoes (at least the ones known in 1826) were near the sea or large lakes. The Italian, Caribbean, Indonesian and central American continent volcanoes were all near the sea. Once the sea had started to pour through a crack in the earth's crust, a violent chemical reaction would take place, and intense pressure and heat would be generated; the whole powerful panoply of a volcanic eruption and accompanying rock slips would follow. On the whole, the Davy–Daubeny chemical model of vulcanism did not really have a very great impact upon geological thinking, ingenious and to some extent chemically demonstrable as it might have been. The internal heat model, fitting in with the Laplacian idea of the earth being a gradually cooling ball flung out of the sun, would win the day on increasing evidential grounds.

Evolutionary thinking
before Charles Darwin

It is popularly believed that Charles Darwin invented evolution in 1859, and that his *Origin of Species* took a simple, literalist Bible-reading world by storm. As we have seen in previous chapters, the Genesis creation story had been subject to critical analysis and interpretation well before 1859, and we must also remember that early evolutionary ideas were doing the rounds long before Darwin was born in 1809. In his 'Lectures and Discourses of Earthquakes', Robert Hooke had pondered whether species might mutate, while the eccentric Scottish nobleman James Burnett, Lord Monboddo (whom Dr Johnson and James Boswell had met in their tour of the Highlands in 1775), had believed that orangutans were close enough to man to be trained to do menial tasks. Darwin's brilliant and insightful physician grandfather, Erasmus, had speculated about plant species blending together to form new types in his botanical poem, *The Botanic Garden* (1791). To the educated mind, species mutation was by no means a novel idea at the time, at least on an imaginative or speculative level. Every boy who had done Latin at school, which meant all who would go on to the universities or enter the learned professions, would have been acquainted with the Roman poet Ovid's *Metamorphoses*. In these stories things mysteriously change into other things, such as the huntsman Actaeon being turned into a deer only to be devoured by his own dogs when pursuing the chaste Artemis. While this was clearly no more than myth, the idea of metamorphosis was there, familiar to any classically trained man.

The great Swedish Professor of Medicine at Uppsala University and the founder of taxonomic botany, Carl Linnaeus (1707–1778), made one of the strongest cases against botanical and animal change in the real world. The inventor of that double-name system of taxonomic botany, which we still use today, Linnaeus had conducted the most exhaustive study to date on the nature of speciation. He had elucidated a massive, complex connectedness in nature, especially in plants, and had studied and classified the kinds and extent of variation. He concluded there were clear, empirical barriers which individual living creatures could not transcend. Living things were capable of enormous variation, yet that variation was strictly contained within each species or genus boundary. And when two related but separate species did mate, the offspring, if there were any, were sterile. So, while a horse might well be able to mate with a donkey, the resulting mule was sterile. Species were fixed on what seemed to be firm, scientific rather than biblical grounds.

Yet what was the mechanism that lay at the heart of biological inheritance? Why did certain traits seem to run in human families, such as blue eyes or red hair, yet sometimes the trait would fail, and a child with dark hair and eyes might be born? This fascinated many medical men, such as Dr Erasmus Darwin, who was interested in the passing on of what were thought to be hereditary diseases, such as tuberculosis, cancer or mental illness within families. The importance of nurture, as well as nature, was a subject of much interest at this time, and what caused traits and tendencies to be passed on. It appeared, for example, that the offspring of working animals, such as performing circus dogs walking on their hind legs, learned their curious tasks more quickly than did animals unfamiliar with such activities. Were the performing skills of the parents passed to the puppies through something in the blood, or was it simply a matter of youngsters imitating the behaviour of their parents? All of this was in the air long before *The Origin of Species* appeared, for there was a large contemporary body of scientific literature pertaining to these things, all of which fed into the debate about stability or change in nature. And one of the most influential, discussed and vilified contributors to this debate was a French comparative anatomist who was no friend of Cuvier.

Jean-Baptiste Lamarck

After a youthful career as a daring and decorated soldier, Jean-Baptiste Pierre Antoine de Monet, later Chevalier de Lamarck, underwent a medical training. Though born in Picardy in 1744 to an old, aristocratic family, they were broke, and Jean-Baptiste was obliged to fund his own way through medical school by working in a bank. Yet like many young men who trained as doctors in the past, Lamarck was less interested in clinical work with the sick than in anatomy, chemistry and the problems of physiology: most notably inheritance, growth and development. His wider ideas may now strike us as displaying some stark contrasts. On the one hand, while his early evolutionary ideas might seem very advanced, his chemistry was intensely conservative. Rejecting Lavoisier's new, post-1780 chemistry based upon primary chemical elements, such as oxygen and the metals (the basis of modern chemistry), Lamarck held to an earlier chemistry, closer in spirit to alchemy. He appeared to believe that the four elemental forces of earth, water, air and fire had a place in scientific understanding, while he also gave some credence to the spontaneous generation of life forms.

In popular scientific understanding, Lamarck is remembered for his ideas on the inheritance of acquired characteristics, such as successive generations of giraffes developing longer and longer necks to gain access to the highest and juiciest leaves on the eucalyptus tree. But this was only a part of Lamarckianism. Fitting in with his ideas of spontaneous generation was his view that specific animals came into being as a result of environmental, perhaps even local, factors. While not as concerned with teeth, eating and anatomy as his contemporary and deadly rival Georges Cuvier (who inspired both William and Mary Buckland), Lamarck was nonetheless aware of how diet, lifestyle and location were reflected in anatomy, most obviously in the fact that mammals possessed teeth but birds did not. He also pointed out that moles were very largely blind, as a result of their living underground in burrowed holes and not needing to see. He went on to develop perhaps the first integrated and coherent model for evolution. One of the driving forces was a tendency towards complexification, as living structures became forever more functionally intricate. A second was adaptation to local environmental conditions, for all populations gradually moulded themselves to suit prevailing conditions. This was *not* a 'natural selection' process, as later presented by Charles Darwin, so much as an indicator of the natural adaptability of living things. In Lamarck's model, therefore, all living forms adapted, diversified and became more and more complex. Organs developed strength in relationship to how much they were used. This might explain why largely subterranean creatures such as moles lost their eyesight, and why predatory birds, such as hawks and eagles, developed extremely acute vision. This is where Lamarck's famous 'inheritance of acquired characteristics' comes in, for he argued that these useful traits could get passed on to a creature's offspring.

It is clear that Lamarck's model of speciation was directly at odds with the fixed, divinely and individually created species of Cuvier and Buckland. Lamarckianism transcended the purely biological, especially in England, where it took on alarming political and theological implications. It was seen as carrying more than just a whiff of French Revolutionary radicalism, although this is hard to justify, considering his background and royal appointment as Keeper of the Paris Royal Herbarium before the Revolution. He diplomatically changed its title to the Jardin des Plantes after 1790 to avoid any now dangerous royalist connotations.

More problematic in many ways, certainly for British readers, were the religious implications of his ideas. One was that his thoroughgoing axiomatic uniformitarianism seemed to give no openings for divine action. Lamarck's own religious beliefs were a disconcerting grey area. From his writings, it is clear that he was *not* a theist, and was not of the opinion that a Creator God continued to lend a guiding hand to his ongoing creation. Though Lamarck did make passing references to God, it would appear that he was a deist. That is, he acknowledged that God had made everything, and had furnished nature with beautiful, self-regulating laws, such as those of Newtonian gravitation, but believed that he had then stood back and let the great machine of Nature run on its course through the ages. Lamarck's earth history was a world removed from that of Buckland, with its catastrophes and re-stockings of the earth with new species, superior to what had gone before, with new oceans and new continents for them to live upon, and all care of a loving, providential Deity.

One of the most distressing aspects of Lamarckianism for English readers, furthermore, was its implications for the status of the human race. Plainly, there were no Adam and Eve in Lamarck's scheme of things, and one faced the clear implication that we humans were just a product of the wider scheme of complexification and inheritance. Were we, as Sir Roderick Murchison and Dr Gideon Mantell mentioned in their correspondence, no more than 'pithecoids', orangutans or other ape-like ancestors – an idea which both men found repellent? To most British people, scientific and otherwise, Lamarckianism was axiomatically unacceptable.[3] It was all the more fascinating, therefore, when in 1844 a book was published which seemed to make Lamarckianism look almost tame. It would be seductively written by an accomplished journalist, who was, no doubt, aiming for a bestseller, which in the event probably even transcended his expectations. This was the notorious *Vestiges of the Natural History of Creation*.

Vestiges of the Natural History of Creation: a Victorian literary time bomb

We saw in Chapter 11 how, when the British Association for the Advancement of Science met in York in 1844, its geology was castigated by the scriptural geologist the Very Revd Dr Sir William Cockburn, Bt, for having deserted the truths of Genesis and Holy Scripture. It was at that York meeting that Mrs Mary Somerville, who was not a 'formal geologist' yet whose scientific ideas were at one with it, was 'preached against by name' from the pulpit of the Minster Church, no doubt by Dean Cockburn himself. But when *Vestiges of the Natural History of Creation* appeared soon after, in October 1844, the ecclesiastical and scientific communities, which united scripturalists and orthodox geologists, released a scream of anguish. Who was the author of the anonymously published *Vestiges*, and what was its message? No matter how much one might criticize and attack the science, the sheer reasonableness of the text could not be denied. The author knew how to explain complex matters in an engaging way, as well as how to captivate and retain the attention of his readers. For many academic scientists, this only added to the sheer mischief of the book.

The author of *Vestiges* was Robert Chambers, who along with his brother William, headed the eminently respectable publishing house of W. & R. Chambers. Acting through intermediaries, such as Alexander Ireland of Manchester, he brought out *Vestiges* under the imprimatur of the medical publisher John Churchill of Soho, London. One might speculate about these elaborate subterfuges to conceal Chambers' authorship. Was it a stratagem to conceal the book's connection with the Edinburgh firm that produced works on Scotland and Scottish culture, as well as their famous *Cyclopaedia*? On the other hand, Robert Chambers, a canny Scot, no doubt realized that such a potentially provocative book as *Vestiges*, if published anonymously, would sell even more copies, unleashing something of a 'find the author' literary manhunt, as indeed it did. In the wake of its publication, numerous public figures, including Prince Albert, would be suggested as the author. Provocative anonymity is always good for business.

Vestiges and its message

Robert Chambers, like many gentlemen, was not only an amateur geologist and a member of the Geological Society, but perhaps even more importantly, he was very widely read across much of the scientific literature of the day. This breadth of reading and acquaintance with a great diversity of scientific ideas shines through the book. And this is what it said. Familiar as Chambers was with the cosmological researches of Sir William Herschel and his son Sir John, and the famous 'nebula hypothesis' of Pierre-Simon Laplace, *Vestiges* saw everything as beginning in deep primordial space. Nebulae no doubt condensed under gravitational attraction, thus producing the sun, earth and solar system deep in the mists of time past.[4] This was not, however a Genesis-style divine creation, but one occurring as a result of the laws of physics and chemistry, although somehow the work of a creator-principle.

So how did life itself come about? While in no way denying the divine nature of creation, Chambers proposed naturalistic as opposed to miraculous mechanisms, and here he selected some discoveries, which had been largely discounted by 1844, yet which, after all, might contain a grain of truth. For one thing, some French scientists had claimed to have generated 'globules' in albumen by electrifying it with an electric battery.[5] Most compelling of all had been the researches of the gentleman scientist Andrew Crosse, and then of Mr W. H. Weekes. Crosse, nicknamed the 'Wizard of the Quantock Hills' in Somerset, where he owned land, had been experimenting with powerful electric batteries and lightning bolts some 20 years before. And wonder of wonders, he had apparently generated a naturalistic electro-chemical model for the appearance of life, and was said to have produced living spiders. This was, however, a claim he roundly denied, when it was realized that his apparatus was contaminated by the eggs of a known spider species which had probably hatched out during the experiment. But the possible creation of spiders from an electrolytic solution was too good a sensation to miss for a wily journalist and publisher like Chambers, and in Chapter 12, he kept the door of possibility slightly ajar.[6] Chambers's was in no way a godless cosmos, for in many places in his text he spoke of 'Providence', the 'Creator', the 'Divine Author', 'Gt. Architect', and so on. Yet his scheme was essentially deistic, for the coming into being of the globe, he says, 'was the result, not of any immediate or personal exertion on the part of the Deity, but of natural laws which are expressions of his will'.[7]

Chambers' *cosmogony* – for that is what it was, potentially extending from nebulae to the origins of human intelligence – was also thoroughly uniformitarian. He did not speak of Buckland-style global catastrophes, but rather of gradual changes and tweaks over long periods of time. On the other hand, he distanced himself from Lamarckianism, which he saw as inadequate to explain the sheer diversity of life forms. But his mechanisms for both geological and biological change were naturalistic and not natural theological. Once living forms appeared, according to him, they began to modify slightly under favourable conditions. Biologically, he was not only sympathetic to spontaneous generation, but even to what is generally styled 'recapitulation biology', in which the developing foetus 'recapitulates' earlier and more primitive forms – such as a frog passing in its foetal stage through a fish-stage, as a result of natural laws and environmental conditions.[8] One was left wondering whether a foetus might somehow 'overcook' and be born one step further up the ladder than its parents, an idea that was then being discussed by some recapitulation biologists. Nor, in Chapter 16 of *Vestiges*, entitled 'Early History of Mankind', were humans an exception to these natural laws; while humans were more advanced than the beasts, Chambers saw the white Caucasian part of the human family as the most advanced.

Fury breaks loose against *Vestiges*

The *Vestiges* taught,
That all came from naught,
By 'development', so called, 'progressive';
That insects and worms
Assume higher forms
By modification excessive.

'Monkeyana', a poem by 'Gorilla'[9]

The runaway popular success of *Vestiges* notwithstanding, the scientific community soon began to pour fire and brimstone on *Vestiges*, especially in the influential review journals of the age. One can, to some extent, understand why. For while the learned reviewers lambasted *Vestiges* as 'shallow', 'trash' and even 'foul', it was true that the germs of so many ideas which it contained were borrowed from scientific gentlemen of the highest repute – and all mixed up to produce an intellectual pudding that to some was delicious and to others poison. Uniformitarianism and geological gradualism, which underpinned the entire rationale of *Vestiges*, came from Sir Charles Lyell's *Principles of Geology* (1831–1833) and from James Hutton's geology. Likewise, the cosmologies of Sir William and Sir John Herschel, along with that of Laplace, were of the highest academic repute. Murchison's Silurian System geology, the Old Red Sandstone, the Oolites and much else besides, discussed in the earlier chapters of *Vestiges*, came from the pens of gentlemen of impeccable standing.

But what caused the fire and brimstone to descend upon *Vestiges* was the ingenious 'speculative' and 'hypothetical' way in which Chambers mixed and matched, while also stirring into his ingenious pudding both shaky and disproved theories: ideas such as Mr Crosse's and Mr Weekes's electrically-generated spiders, along with largely German 'recapitulation' biology. One can understand how scientists of the calibre of Buckland, Sedgwick, Murchison and William Whewell must have hit the roof upon seeing research upon which their academic reputations rested being cleverly twisted to produce the *Vestiges* vision. It was, however, Adam Sedgwick who won the prize for both length and vituperation in his review of *Vestiges*. His response was published in the July 1845 edition of the prestigious *Edinburgh Review*, and covered no fewer than 85 printed pages: about a quarter of the entire page length of *Vestiges* itself (390 pages). Sedgwick savaged more or less everything about *Vestiges*: its geology, addled biology, electro-chemistry, cosmology, philosophy and theology. There was only one thing its anonymous author did well: being a clear, engaging and seductive writer, an attribute commented upon by many reviewers. Yet that skill in itself told against it, for it made the book deceptively easy to read, and hence added to its capacity to lead the uninformed reader astray with its blandishments.

At first, Sedgwick admitted, he even suspected that the author was a woman, the book being intellectually shallow and lightweight! (One wonders what Mary Buckland, Mary Somerville, Ada Lovelace and many other intellectually powerful women of the period would have made of that supposition.) But he soon abandoned that idea, for upon reflection, there was something too immodest about parts of the book for it to have been the work of a lady, such as those chapters dealing with the biology of reproduction and foetal development, which could not avoid 'raising a blush upon a modest cheek'. Did not part of the dangerous seductive power of *Vestiges* lie in the danger of its exposing our 'glorious maidens and matrons' to the 'dirty knife of the anatomist',[10] and presenting them with grisly material (much of it incorrect anyway) that would destroy the 'joyous thought and modest feeling' of such sweet, pure innocents? (Incidentally, Sedgwick's concern with feminine purity mirrors similar fears expressed by some contemporaries about the dangers of teaching girls Latin and Greek, after which they might read the same rollicking classical tales of debauchery and perversion, and dirty jokes, that so delighted their brothers.) Perhaps most horrific of all, what would happen to the pure morals of those innocent females when they learned 'that their Bible is a fable'?[11] Not only were innocent women in danger from *Vestiges*, for its deistic naturalism could be disruptive to the social order, but also Jack might now get the idea that he was as good as his master. In these hungry decades of the nineteenth century (1830s and 1840s), high food prices, industrial unrest and Chartist riots were posing a serious problem to the stability of the nation, as we have seen in earlier chapters.

From our own perspective, some 180 years after the event, we might feel that the responses to *Vestiges*, and especially that of Adam Sedgwick, were unfounded, hysterical and even slightly laughable. But in the 1840s geology was taking on the appearance of an intellectual avalanche, so fast was it progressing. In little more than a quarter century from Buckland's *Reliquiae Diluvianae*, Noah's Flood, after millennia of acceptance as orthodoxy, had been discounted as a global geological event, and divinely sent catastrophes replaced by a gradual uniformitarian 'naturalism'. Slow-moving ice ages that had no place whatsoever in Holy Scripture had supplanted deluges as the shapers of the landscape, while – horror of horrors – Lamarckianism had supplied a cogent, albeit heretical, blueprint for the origins of life itself. Add to that heady mix the sheer, captivating mischief of *Vestiges*, seemingly stirring up all the 'dangerous' ideas into one intoxicating and seductive brew, and one might get some sense of why the scientific establishment greeted *Vestiges* as it did. Yet as will be recalled from what has been said above, in spite of its rapid progress since around 1800, geology had an important limiting factor as a science: it lacked experimental, mathematical criteria. In 1845, it had nothing equivalent to gravitation mathematics, the laws of chemical combination or electromagnetic induction to give it a firm and unchallengeable foundation. And with the possible exception of the new post-1825 high-powered microscopes and simple chemical tests with which to examine mineral and fossil structures, geology possessed no instrumental armoury with which to measure, calibrate and substantiate its claims. All this, however, was set to change in the decades to come, with the laws of thermodynamics, photography, spectroscopy, sophisticated thermometry and chemical analytical techniques. Then in the twentieth century, aerial, and later satellite, photography and digital imaging would help create geology's sister science of geophysics. But more will be said of these twenty- and twenty-first-century advances in Chapter 14.

As things stood in 1845, however, the geologist's only aids were an iron constitution, physical agility and an ability to draw, sketch and remember what he saw; his tools were nothing more sophisticated than a geological hammer and a pocket magnifier. Considering these factors, it is hardly surprising that all the leading geologists were countrymen born and bred, adventurous ex-soldiers or independent-minded risk-takers who loved adventure and did not mind roughing it. Many were serious in their Christian faith, be they ordained or lay, who felt inspired to trace the finger of God in the creation. This would be a decisive year for William Buckland, which is perhaps why he did not play an especially prominent role in the condemnation of *Vestiges*. He would make a decisive career change, as he and Mary left their beloved Oxford, and William became something of a national figure on the wider public stage. For in the summer of 1845, his admirer and friend, Prime Minister Sir Robert Peel, offered him the prestigious Deanery of Westminster: an offer and a career move that the 61-year-old Buckland could hardly refuse.

Chapter 13
The Dean of Westminster

One wonders how happy the Bucklands were with the state of Oxford by the summer of 1845. As we have seen, the Oxford Movement was dividing the Church of England into several warring factions, as Puseyites, Anglo-Catholics, Tractarians, converts to Catholicism who were following Newman from Oxford to Rome, fiery Protestants, 'low-church' Evangelicals, reformers and traditionalists battled it out amongst themselves. The genial Buckland had no taste for such ecclesiastical partisanship, especially as his approach to Natural Theology did not seem to figure among the new ecclesiastical priorities.

This theological partisanship even seems to have had its influence upon science, when the devout lay ex-soldier-astronomer and friend of John Henry Newman, Manuel Johnson, was appointed to the Directorship of Oxford's Radcliffe Observatory, in 1839. For the low-church Protestant professorial appointers failed to elect Johnson to the Savilian Professorship of Astronomy, although the Observatory Directorship and the Professorship had been held by the same man since the 1770s. The Devonshire Commission, which initiated the strongly resisted reform of the University of Oxford in the 1850s, took the step of creating whole new disciplinary schools, such as natural sciences and modern languages, in the hope, among other things, of breaking the theological warfare impasse. This Commission made it possible for the first time for undergraduates to take science degrees at Oxford, and not do science just as a voluntary addition to a classical and theological degree. But it lay a decade into the future when, in November 1845, Mary Buckland wrote to their friend Sir Philip Egerton about how much she lamented the official and academic neglect of science in 1840s Oxford. Though the University had a set of long-established scientific institutions, such as the Botanic Garden, the Ashmolean Science Museum and Laboratory, Christ Church's

Anatomy School and the Radcliffe Observatory, along with endowed chairs in chemistry, botany, medicine, astronomy and William Buckland's in geology, they lacked the resources and prestige of these same subjects in Continental Europe's great universities. Mary also drew attention to the paradox of how a man who studied God's creation in deeply Christian England might, in some quarters, be regarded with suspicion, whereas on the Continent – 'where there is far less religion than in England' – men such as Cuvier and von Humboldt were held in the highest renown and given public honours.[1]

No doubt she and William, after 20 years in Christ Church and with the theological wars raging around them, felt that it might be time for a move. It would be a wrench, as Mary had lived in or near Oxford for most of her 48 years by 1845, and William had been there since his undergraduate days, or 44 years, and they had many friends and connections in the city, the University, and the surrounding counties; but the Westminster Deanery offered the prospect of exciting new things. Not that leaving Oxford was a matter of urgency, as Mary told Egerton that William had already turned down the offer of the Deanery of Lincoln, received while on holiday in France. She did, however, think that Prime Minister Sir Robert Peel, a family friend, had 'shown much moral courage in making choice of a person of science' to the Westminster Deanery.[2] This may have been not just because of his science, but the kind of person Buckland was. As we have seen, Georgian and Victorian churchmen, especially those appointed to high ecclesiastical office, invariably cultivated a persona of deep gravitas. They did not entertain lecture audiences by doing silly walks in imitation of a fossilized turtle; they did not do comic impersonations; they did not go around with a legendary blue bag of fossils and geological curiosities and use its contents to captivate West End dinner-party audiences; they did not, at a society dinner-table, take a curious-looking fish from the butler, carve out its skeleton at table, wrap it in a napkin and put it in the said blue bag. And they absolutely did not laugh out loud, tell jokes and partake in schoolboy pranks. But William Buckland did all of these things – and more!

The Westminster Deanery

As Buckland's daughter Elizabeth recorded in her father's *Life and Correspondence*, however, Prime Minister Sir Robert Peel said 'I never advised an appointment of which I was more proud, or the result of which was in my opinion more satisfactory, than the nomination of Dr Buckland to the Deanery of Westminster'.[3] Westminster was no ordinary Anglican cathedral and deanery. Like St George's Chapel, Windsor, with its Order of the Knights of the Garter, and all manner of state and royal functions, it was a Royal Church and national shrine, and Peel no doubt knew instinctively that the genial Buckland was the ideal man for the appointment, especially in that politically turbulent time in history. Peel was wholly correct in his judgement.

Buckland's Westminster appointment, however, inevitably brought about a quite new mode of living. The inspired geology professor persona which went back to his bachelor years as a Fellow of Corpus Christi College was no longer to the fore, although he did return to Oxford to deliver geological lectures occasionally. But in his new post, Buckland became a figure in wider public life. This involved state, ecclesiastical and even informal connections with the Royal family, although Prince Albert and Queen Victoria would have met him previously. It is unlikely that a man who was not on good terms with the Royal family would ever have been appointed to the Westminster Deanery, quite apart from his unusual background for such an office.

Although the Buckland's canon's house in Christ Church's Tom Quad, Oxford, had been large and spacious (as I know, for since the late nineteenth century it has been the residence of the Archdeacon of the Diocese of Oxford), it was modest compared to the Westminster Deanery. This vast house, standing to the west of the Abbey, was said by Mary to be the size of *four* normal (i.e. large and elegant) houses, and had no fewer than 16 staircases. It also contained the famous Jerusalem Chamber in which King Henry IV had died in 1413 – enabling him to achieve his proclaimed ambition of dying in Jerusalem.[4] In addition to the 16 staircases, the Deanery was a veritable rabbit warren of ancient wainscoted passages, and inevitably such an ancient and venerable fabric was said to have ghosts. Following a violent windstorm, however, one of these hauntings received a rational explanation. A loose piece of wainscoting was blown away, exposing a shaft. At the bottom was a bed and other pieces of furniture, all rotting away, which turned out to be the hiding place of Dean Francis Atterbury, a strong Roman Catholic sympathizer and supporter of The Old Pretender, who might have used the refuge when the prospects for the Catholic House of Stuart were dashed by the Hanoverian King George I in 1714–1715.

Science was by no means off the agenda after the Bucklands came to reside in the Westminster Deanery. With his fascination with the lie of the land and all kinds of stone, Buckland took an early interest in the site and surroundings of the vast medieval church. It stood upon the ancient 'Thorney Island', a bed of solid ground in what had once been a wet and marshy area. The geology of Thorney Island was found to consist of ancient gravel beds topped with a thick layer of sand. This geology, with its natural purifying properties, made the water from the pump in Dean's Yard sweet and pure. As we shall see, clean water and public health were always close to Buckland's heart, both as a scientist and as a social improver.

There were other scientific delights in the Deanery as well as the surrounding geology. On 13 June 1849, Buckland wrote to Professor Michael Faraday of the Royal Institution, inviting him to the Deanery, where William Harcourt would perform the experiment of attempting to administer chloroform to several fish, reptiles and other creatures. In June 1849 chloroform was a new wonder drug, first produced by Liebig in 1832, and, more significantly, used as a surgical anaesthetic by Sir James Simpson in Edinburgh in November 1847, where it was found to be superior to sulphuric ether, the surgical properties of which had only been discovered in Boston, USA, in October 1846. Anaesthesiology was an entirely new branch of medical and chemical science in 1849, and was already transforming surgery. Yet how did ether and chloroform actually work in bringing about a whole new physiological state: namely, a sleep so deep that one was unaware of a limb being amputated? And how might it work upon birds, reptiles and especially fish, with their different respiratory mechanisms?

One opportunity which the vast and rambling Westminster Deanery provided was for something which no previous Dean had ever required of it: namely, to house a museum and a zoo.

Tiglath-Pileser the bear goes to church

The Buckland move from Christ Church to Westminster fell at an opportune time for Frank Buckland in particular. A Christ Church undergraduate in 1845, Frank's eccentricities and hilarious madcap stunts have often been merged with those of his father, in their retellings. As William had imported the young hyena, Billy, from South Africa in the early 1820s in the wake of his Kirkdale Cave researches (see Chapter 4), so Frank acquired a bear cub. Whether it lived in the Buckland Canon's house or in Frank's undergraduate rooms in a different part of College is not clear, but on one occasion the bear somehow slipped his leash and wandered around Christ Church. Frank's undergraduate and Buckland family friend, the subsequent Revd William Tuckwell, tells us what happened next.

Seemingly unnamed up to this point, Frank's bear wandered into Christ Church Cathedral, which also served as the College Chapel, just as the officiating canon was about to read the Old Testament lesson, which Tuckwell says was 2 Kings 16, where Ahaz, the wicked king of Judah, gives the gold and treasures of the Jerusalem Temple as a bribe to Tiglath-Pileser, the mighty king of Assyria, for military assistance in his war against the king of Syria. As soon as the reverend gentleman saw Frank's bear (which was a very friendly animal) walking down the cathedral, he gave a shriek and bolted, just as he had uttered the name 'Tiglath-Pileser', accompanied, no doubt, by sniggers of amusement on the part of the undergraduates. Thereafter the bear would be known by the king's name – abbreviated to Tiggy or Tig.

Not everyone saw the joke, however, including the formidable Very Revd Dr Thomas Gaisford, Dean of Christ Church, who told Frank that Tiggy had to go: 'You or that animal, Mr Buckland, must quit the College.'[5] He was to take up residence, with Frank's eagle and the Buckland family's collection of exotic pets (including a cobra) in the Westminster Deanery – until he became too big and needed to be rehoused in the Zoo. One wonders how much growling, barking, hissing and shrieking reverberated through the ancient and venerable passages of the Deanery during Buckland's time at Westminster. (I suspect, however, that Dean Gaisford's bark was worse than his bite, for William and Mary enjoyed dining in the Deanery, sometimes, when the weather was bad, having a sedan chair sent for Mary to convey her the couple of hundred feet between their two front doors. The Dean was very fond of the Buckland children as well.)

Renovating the fabric and reforming the School

Nowadays, we are accustomed to seeing our ancient churches, cathedrals and other venerable buildings in a state of manicured perfection. Scaffolding is rarely absent from at least some part of one of our English cathedrals as ancient stonework, worn and degraded by time, weather and atmospheric pollution is replaced by a pristine, meticulously detailed copy, or reconstruction of the original. Buckland's own twelfth-century Christ Church Cathedral is a case in point, as now degraded Victorian restoration work is replaced by new. But in Buckland's time this was not the case. Our ancient buildings, including Westminster Abbey, were blackened by centuries of sulphur-rich coal smoke, while medieval statues, pinnacles, traceries and fine details had often been reduced to shapeless lumps. Medieval stained-glass windows fared no better, as the lead traceries oxidized away, and pieces of beautiful painted glass simply fell out. Even worse, there are records from some cathedrals of boy choristers (a thoroughly mischievous part of the human race) throwing stones at the windows without rebuke from seniors and clergy – who had probably done the same in their own day.

When Buckland entered into the Westminster Deanery in 1845, he found parts of the medieval monastic cloisters so broken down that some arches were held up by semi-permanent wooden supports (as recalled by the Revd William H. Turle many years later), while some traceries and even small walls had simply fallen down. The Green or Cloister Garth in the middle of the cloister, the former burial ground of the monks of St Peter's Abbey prior to the Reformation, was the acknowledged fighting ground, where prize-fight-like boxing contests were held between Westminster schoolboys who angered and challenged each other. Far from treating even the semi-sacred monuments in the Abbey with respect, schoolboys, visitors and memento-collectors were not above breaking fingers and other bits off statues, and, on one occasion, using a pen-knife to carve a large splinter from the Coronation Throne.[6] These crimes were attested by packages sent to the Dean and Chapter, decades after the offences were committed: packages containing the stolen fragments which the person, on reaching riper, wiser years, or even on their death-beds, had returned with full penitential apologies.

Buckland was anxious to restore the Abbey to its true form, and another of his concerns was the reinstitution of devout conduct within the sacred space and during Divine Office. It may seem strange to us today that, during the early Victorian era, public worship was sometimes quite bad and often irreverent. Worshippers, especially those of high social status, might take snuff or a nip of brandy, or chat during Divine Service, and in some country parish churches the squire might have a meal brought in to him and his family in their private pew during the long sermon. Even the choirboys were not concentrating. Some of William Hogarth's prints and engravings from a century earlier, the 1730s and 1740s, capture this laxity, as parish clerks look bored, fat men openly snooze and young couples paw each other suggestively during service.[7] One of the goals of the Oxford Movement, with which Buckland agreed, was to restore reverence to church services, and he did his best to do this in the Abbey.

During his first three or four years in the Deanery, in addition to anaes-thetizing fish and finding a home for Tiglath-Pileser, Buckland devoted an enormous amount of energy to the restoration and improvement of the Abbey fabric, including the Church's interior, the pinnacles, towers and cloisters. Here he was in his element, bringing his massive practical geological knowledge to bear on the properties of different types of stone used for restoration work. On several occasions, as he had in Christ Church when Tom Tower was being repaired, he surprised the masons and contractors with his intimate knowledge of stone. When he detected that an untrustworthy craftsman had slipped in inferior stone, he sternly told him to replace it with better.

Buckland's strongly technical cast of mind was always on the lookout for ways in which recent technological innovations might make life better for people. In an age still dependent upon those ancestral biblical illuminants, candles and oil lamps, the Third Collect (or Prayer) of Evensong, 'Lighten our darkness, we beseech thee, O Lord' and 'Defend us from all perils and

dangers of this night', from the Book of Common Prayer, possessed a reso-
nance quite lost upon our own light-polluted age. Night-time could be Sty-
gian in its darkness, replete with physical 'perils and dangers': holes in the
road to fall down, being lost in an unfamiliar place on a moonless night,
being easy prey for footpads, or worried about alleged ghostly hauntings.

Buckland loved the new, dazzling form of illumination: coal gas. Back
in Oxford, he had promoted the use of gas lighting, especially in the street
and public places, even sitting on the board of the Oxford Gas Company.
In the late 1840s, he brought the first pipes and gas burners into the Abbey
precincts and Westminster School. Crude coal gas might stink and occasionally lead to accidental explosions, but by its means, the dark ages of past
millennia were finally brought to an end. Light, clean water, fresh air, whole-
some food and efficient drains were all part of Buckland's wider reforming agenda, all helped along by his technical mastery of practical geology,
chemistry and physics. Sand-filtered water, deep artesian wells, and, in this
pre-bacterial age, the perceived inherent toxicity of dirty water and food all
came together for him, the sanitarian and practical social reformer.

In his new office of Dean of Westminster, a new aspect of Buckland
came to the fore: less the geologist and more the Christian gentleman,
out to make war upon dirt, squalor and the exploitation of slum dwellers by unscrupulous landlords, and, by means of gaslight, to make the
night brighter. Both these traits had been present in the Oxford Buckland,
but now, with the high prestige of his new and venerable office, his very
practical concern with making the world a better place came to prominence. It would appear to Revd Henry Thompson (author of Westminster
School's Head Master Henry Liddell's *Memoir*), however, that 'Buckland
had no aesthetic sensibilities, and was fond of corrugated iron' as a cheap
and efficient building material, and even used it for some of the new addi-
tions to the School buildings.[8]

The distinctive Buckland eccentricities were still there. He loved
conducting groups of visitors around Westminster Abbey, pointing out
its history, associations, monuments and statues of the great and good.
On these occasions, he would often carry a very long feather duster with
which to brush away cobwebs and similar blemishes that had recently
accumulated. And of course, the Deanery itself was a repository of state,
a social centre for friends and distinguished visitors, and a zoo!

What especially shocked Buckland on becoming Dean was the appalling state of the School. Not academically, but physically, being in a poor state of repair, with some glass-less windows and leaking roofs, squalor in the dormitories, filthy floors and an ancestral sewerage problem deriving from a long-blocked drain, which led to recurrent local epidemics of 'Westminster fever', or typhoid. As the newly installed Dean of Westminster told the Revd Professor Arthur Penrhyn Stanley, probably on a train journey in January 1846, 'the counterpanes in the dormitories [were] not washed for 11 years, [and the] School not cleaned since Queen Elizabeth died' (1603).[9] It sounded rather like Charles Dickens's fictional Dotheboy's Hall, but with the addition of good Latin and Greek.

In 1846, Buckland was delighted to join forces with the new reforming Head Master of the School, the young Revd Dr Henry Liddell, later Dean of Christ Church. Liddell shared many of Buckland's views about health, dirt and reform, and the two men began to wage war against the filth of what was in 1846, and still is, one of the great English public schools. Such radical changes to ancestral ways –including having sewers that actually worked – aroused opposition from an old guard of Westminster masters, pupils and alumni, who regarded coping with squalor as a toughening process equipping the young gentlemen for public life. Particularly offensive to Buckland and Liddell was the brick-lined sewer that had been choked with filth for so long that the tidal Thames could no longer get inside to flush it out. It was dug out and rendered serviceable once more. Buckland's interest in and knowledge of new iron technologies also saw the introduction of mass-produced iron pipes into the School and Abbey precincts – some to bring in fresh water, others to take away sewage – although only to dump it in the Thames. These inventions would lead to a significant fall in outbreaks of Westminster fever. Tragically, the digging-up of the School and Abbey precincts to lay modern sewerage and water pipes appears to have released some ill-understood malignancy – styled a 'miasma' (or bad air) – that attacked Buckland and two family members. They were lucky to survive, but two promising schoolboys and two of the Abbey Canon's daughters died, while Mrs Liddell's life hung in the balance for several days before she pulled through.[10] (Henry and Lorina Hanna Liddell would later become the parents of the real-life Alice, of *Alice in Wonderland* fame.)

'Wash and Be Clean': the sermon that let all hell loose

In addition to typhoid, typhus, scarlet fever and several other infections that routinely plagued Europe and America, in 1832 a new and terrifying disease had arrived in Britain from India, by way of Russia and Europe: Asiatic cholera. William and Mary had battled against the disease in Oxford, and they did so now in Westminster when it returned in 1848. In both epidemics, it clearly hit the poor in their squalid slums far harder than those people in more salubrious districts. Various theories were put forward to explain this circumstance: was it because the poor, with their assumed tendency to idleness, drunkenness, sexual promiscuity and violence, were weaker and somehow more susceptible to the deadly infection? Yet some people of impeccable morals and lifestyle, such as slum priests, charity doctors and well-meaning visiting gentlefolks, also developed the terrifying symptoms of abdominal muscular cramps, violent diarrhoea, dehydration and exhaustion, and died. Was cholera somehow carried on the wind, as medieval bubonic plague and a host of other infections were believed to be? Was it occasioned by curious meteorological circumstances, such as changes in humidity, barometric pressure and temperature? James Glaisher FRS of the Royal Observatory, Greenwich, whom Buckland must have known through the Fellowship of the Royal Society, collected and analysed meteorological and environmental records to see if specific atmospheric conditions or Thames river temperature could be linked to cholera outbreaks.

Another theory proposed that cholera was associated with dirt: which might explain why the well-scrubbed middle classes suffered far less severely than the great unwashed in the slums. This was the line of thinking that the Bucklands were pursuing by the time of the 1848 epidemic. But how could dirt cause disease, as opposed to alcohol, idleness or promiscuity? This was a good two decades before Louis Pasteur in Paris and Robert Koch in Berlin provided evidence that infections were caused by an 'animalcule', a micro-organism or a germ (which was not universally accepted). If one took a swab from the mouth of a cholera patient and another from a healthy individual and examined them beneath the microscope, both swabs were found to be full of a variety of creepy-crawlies.

Sadly, Filippo Pacini's discovery, in 1854, of the *Vibrio cholerae* bacillus seems only to have been reported within the Florentine medical community and ignored by the rest of the European medical profession. It would take the experimental insight of Robert Koch in 1880 to realize that specific bacilli caused specific diseases, and that many of the teeming germs in our bodies were harmless or even beneficial. The correct identification and eradication of the cholera 'villain' would lay the foundation for much of the subsequent science of microbiology.

Was dirt especially malignant? Generally speaking, the dirt associated with cholera came to be seen by Buckland and others as connected with human excrement, and with foul matter somehow finding its way into the drinking water. This was a much greater threat for slum-dwellers using primitive privies shared by a dozen families, along with water taken from a nearby smelly well or even out of the filthy river Thames. One needs only to think back to the abovementioned Westminster fever and the clogged main drain to see this circumstance occurring even in an ancient and venerable public school, let alone in a slum. Typhoid, like cholera, is a water-borne, dirt-related disease, though occasioned by a different bacterial strain from the *Vibrio cholerae* that caused cholera.

In 1848, when Buckland was involved in his Westminster reforms, the river Thames was often little more than an open sewer, with over two million people living on or not far from its banks. Human waste, slaughterhouse offal, dead cats and dogs, and toxic chemicals used in a variety of riverside industries were routinely dumped into it, and before the sinking of large numbers of artesian wells and the use of iron pipes to bring in clean drinking water by the mid-1860s, much drinking water came from this very same river. In the summer of 1858, the stench of the river Thames, even upstream in Westminster, had become so bad that the air in Parliament actually stank, obliging MPs to hold handkerchiefs to their noses. Three years earlier, on 7 July 1855, Professor Michael Faraday had already written an alarming letter to *The Times* about the stinking river, and on 21 July there followed a cartoon in *Punch*.[11] He is shown standing in a boat on the Thames, holding his nose. With his other hand, he presents his card to a filthy, weed- and offal-strewn 'Old Father Thames', as he emerges from a river in which dead dogs and other putrefying objects are floating. Faraday's offering of a card was the way by which one gentleman challenged another to a duel. The message of the picture was that Professor Faraday and his sanitarian reforming friends (including William Buckland, living in the recent battle zone of Westminster) were about to use science as a weapon of war against filth, disease and want.

This war was already being fought on two further fronts in addition to the offensives in Westminster in the late 1840s. One new weapon, for which Buckland had a high regard, was statistics. On the basis of statistical studies of cholera in different locations, the groundbreaking Public Health Act of 1848 was passed, creating public doctors, or Medical Officers of Health, and official administrative structures for dealing with epidemic outbursts and preventing the malady from spreading. The other statistical weapon in the war against cholera, during the epidemic of 1854, was Dr John Snow's inspired study of contiguous households that were cholera-infected and cholera-free in the Broad Street area of Soho, London (only a couple of miles from Westminster Abbey). Clearly, a windblown miasma could not cause a disease that ravaged one family while leaving a neighbouring family untouched. Although Snow, like Buckland and Edwin Chadwick, the civil servant largely behind the 1848 Public Health Act, had concluded filth, squalor and polluted water were the culprits, his Broad Street study of 1854 supplied a dramatic confirmation. Households with access to good artesian or other wells, such as one at a nearby brewery, his investigation discovered, never developed cholera. Those who drew their water from the popular Broad Street pump, however, which supplied poorly treated Thames water, developed cholera. The solution was simple but dramatic. After chemical analyses of the pump water, Snow advised the local magistrates to immobilize the Broad Street pump by simply removing the handle. There were hardly any new cases thereafter, and efforts were made to make well water generally available.

All of this was a good two decades before Pasteur and Koch identified specific water-borne bacteria. The control and eventual elimination of cholera from London was a triumph of careful observation, statistics and experiment, and could be summed up in one simple rule: keep sewage and drinking water apart! Dean Buckland would be a major early player in this drama of discovery.

It is hard to estimate the effect that the artesian water-table studies of the Thames Valley by Buckland and his friend William Daniel Conybeare had upon the eventual supply of good, sweet water to the people of London. Their work was certainly well known, and was depicted in Plates 68 and 69 of Volume II of Buckland's *Geology and Mineralogy* and accompanying text. The water was there and ready: all that was needed was the engineering technology to utilize it. First, a massively complex system of iron pipes was needed to bring the sweet water up, or in from outside, and to supply it abundantly to tens of thousands of households. Second, a parallel yet wholly separate system of main sewers and local feeder sewers would be required to drain away faecal matter and keep it out of the Thames; and then powerful steam engines on the north and south banks of the lower Thames estuary to pump the sewage into the sea, way downstream at Erith on the outgoing tide, after which it would rapidly biodegrade in the North Sea.

This miracle for the health and happiness of Londoners would be brought about by Sir Joseph Bazalgette during the 1860s, in a coming together of practical geology, civil engineering and meticulous organization. None of Bazalgette's great life-saving engineering projects would have been possible, however, without an intimate knowledge of the lie of the land, the subterranean water systems, soil and clay of London and the Thames Valley.

An official day of thanksgiving to God for delivery from the cholera epidemic of 1848–1849 was to be held on 15 November 1849, and Buckland marked it by preaching a sermon in the Abbey. He chose 2 Kings 5.10 for his text, where the prophet Elisha sends a messenger to the leper Naaman the Syrian, telling him to go and wash himself in the river Jordan and 'be clean'. This was Buckland's highly controversial 'Wash and Be Clean' sermon. Confident by this time that dirt, escaped sewage and polluted drinking water were major and quite likely the chief causes of cholera and Westminster fever, Buckland openly attacked 'the avarice and neglect of small landlords and owners of the filthy, ill-ventilated habitations in which the poorest and most ill-fed and helpless are compelled to dwell'.[12] He fulminated against the way the negligent owners of the dwellings of the poor 'by the jealousy of interference by public officers or public Boards of Health with parochial or with city authorities' starved them of adequate supplies of water. If these 'crying evils' are not 'instantly' remedied in the next 'two or three years' and 'our city is not duly supplied with water', he affirmed, the next epidemics would be ascribable only to 'the fault of man', selfishness and negligent public bodies. In short, if cholera and Westminster fever returned, do not blame God, misfortune or the assumed lax lifestyle of the poor: blame instead the negligence, greed and failure of public duty of those people who had it within their power to prevent such a tragedy. He then thundered on to his peroration, with an adaptation of Elisha's advice to Naaman the Syrian, and to the neglectful elders of Israel, 'Above all things, cleanse your hearts, and not your garments only, and turn unto the Lord your God.'

Considering his sustained fulminations against bad landlords, negligent public bodies and even Parliament, it is hardly surprising that this sermon, delivered from the pulpit of Westminster Abbey on a public occasion, ruffled feathers across the board. Here was the charismatic geology lecturer turned fiery preacher, using new scientific knowledge about the importance of clean drinking water and general cleanliness to defend the poor and downtrodden and castigate the rich and neglectful. It must have been quite an occasion. But the Bucklands were not just concerned with the bodies of the poor of Westminster and further afield, but also their minds and souls. The burgeoning population of Britain, and of London in particular, meant that the old system of parish churches was creaking, and more churches and Christian facilities were needed. The 1840s and 1850s heralded a nationwide project to build more Anglican churches, as old, big parishes were carved up to form new, smaller ones, especially in the great urban centres. William and Mary Buckland were active in this movement, particularly on their own doorstep, and were instrumental in establishing the new parish of St Matthew in Westminster.

Like many other practical social reforming Christians, however, they recognized that simply going to church was not enough. Churches had to provide social facilities in areas of acute deprivation, such as Westminster's notorious Devil's Acre district. Here were homelessness, prostitution, gangs of rough-living men, women and boys, and poor housing for those fortunate enough to find a home of any kind. Sanitation facilities were best left to the imagination. Schools for the poor were few and inadequate, and decent job opportunities likewise. As far as social meeting facilities were concerned, what was there beyond street corners, rough pubs, low boozing kennels and cheap brothels? So much social distress was fuelled by alcohol, and that, in turn, was fuelled by despair. It was recognized by many social reformers, however, that in such circumstances the Church could provide invaluable services of Christian charity, or practical love and care. For instance, largely on the initiative of Mary Buckland, a coffee club and social centre for the poor were set up in the new St Matthew's parish. The great and the good got on board, and HM Queen Victoria herself made a £50 donation to the project. There would be speakers and lecturers, including Frank Buckland, then a medical student. Sadly, in spite of the resources, both human and financial, that were poured in and the untiring efforts of Mary Buckland and the Revd Mr R. Malone, the first Vicar of St Matthew's, the club increasingly became a haunt for idlers and loungers. Yet even around 1850 (as is the case with social and outreach workers in our own time), it was recognized that it was not sufficient just to feed and wash the persons of the poor, but it was necessary to stimulate and nourish their minds as well.

As indicated above, William Buckland's approach to social problems and social reform stemmed from the duty of the prosperous Christian to their less fortunate brethren. In social terms, Buckland was not an egalitarian, and had no truck with the French socialistic ideas of the period. Quite simply, he recognized that many people lacked the abilities and personal resources to prosper. The models of conduct for Buckland's approach to poverty and the poor were Christ's parables of the Good Samaritan and Dives the rich man and Lazarus the beggar at his gate. This was another example of his instinctive pragmatism. Washing, feeding and helping the poor as human beings were of far greater concern to him than some fanciful scheme aimed at re-engineering the whole of society along theoretical lines. It was also of a piece with his sense of providence, God's bounty and good management. As in his providential Natural Theology, where a loving God gradually developed his creation over time, so Christian love, charity, good works and science would alleviate the sufferings of the poor.

One might wonder why William Buckland's public health assault in 'Wash and Be Clean' in November 1849 did not lead on to further action in conjunction with Faraday and others in the mid-1850s. Sadly, however, soon after, he suffered the onset of a long and debilitating illness that would last until his death in 1856. We will return to this in Chapter 14.

Yet there was a light-hearted incident that occurred during his period of office as Dean, recorded by the young Cornelia Augusta, the future second wife of Andrew Crosse, of electrified insects fame, whom we met in Chapter 12. During the politically volatile summer of 1848, when Continental Europe was being rocked by waves of revolutionary chaos, Buckland and his friends Dr Charles Daubeny, Dr (later Lord) Playfair and Baron von Liebig were visiting the Cheddar region of Somerset to study the chemical processes involved in cheese-making. They were staying at Fyne Court, Broomfield, as guests of Crosse. It seems, however, that some people at Bridgewater became suspicious when they heard Liebig's German accent, and perhaps spoken German, and informed the authorities that there were dangerous characters afoot in the area. When the story came out, Buckland and his friends were highly amused to learn that the Very Revd Dean of Westminster had been consorting with assumed anarchists and revolutionaries.[13]

But let us now look at one of the joys of the Westminster Deanery: the Rectory of Islip.

William Buckland, Rector of Islip

For a long time by 1845, the beautiful parish and rectory of Islip, just a few miles out of Oxford, had been the rural summer residence of the Dean of Westminster. Quite apart from the social and intellectual joys that the parish might offer, with its proximity to Buckland's *alma mater*, the village itself, with its parish church, was a delight. The birthplace of King Edward the Confessor, who in the eleventh century rebuilt and improved the earlier Abbey Church of St Peter in royal Westminster, the village of Islip had a long and proud history of both royalty and Westminster Abbey connections.

The rectory was a fine house, surrounded by well-cultivated terraced gardens located beside a medieval, stone-built Oxfordshire village, with its bridge across the river Ray, which further downstream flows into Oxford's river Cherwell. The Bucklands loved this summer retreat, to which they could invite guests and where they could indulge their passion for gardening, flowers and natural history. Both also acknowledged their local duties. As the rector was absent for most of the year, Islip Church was administered by a full-time curate, but when in residence Buckland served his parish as a full-time rector, officiating in church, preaching plain, common-sense sermons, doing house calls in the village and serving the poor. At a time when many a high-ranking Anglican clergyman would be reluctant to enter a peasant's cottage, Buckland, with a lifetime's social skills cultivated in speaking with Devon fishermen, smallholder farmers, quarry workers and farm labourers across the land, experienced no awkwardness when moving among ordinary country folk. His lack of stuffiness, sense of humour and playfulness would help, and he became a popular rector.

Improvement projects to help the villagers soon got under way, including the creation of small allotment plots, where villagers could grow their own vegetables, in addition to their daily work upon other people's farms. Mary was involved in various activities with the women, girls and children of the village, as well as giving practical assistance, food and small sums of money to the poor and the old. And along the lines of the failed coffee club project in Westminster, Buckland developed an adjacent property to act as a social centre for the villagers. As education and self-improvement were priorities for him, this new village centre hosted various classes and lectures to help stimulate and entertain the local folk.

The 1848–1849 cholera epidemic which had hit London and Westminster had struck Oxford by 1849 and spread to some nearby towns and villages. As Islip sent produce to Oxford market, it was feared that the epidemic would come to the village. Buckland brought his Westminster 'wash and be clean' principles to bear, however, examining the local waste disposal and water supply, and ensured that the twain never met. He tells us that while the local folks could not always see the connection between dirt, water and disease, they obediently dug out clogged ditches and observed his simple rules. These measures paid off, and Islip remained cholera-free.[14] In 1849, neither Buckland nor any other scientific men could be absolutely certain that bad smells and miasmas did not also play a part in cholera transmission. But what was increasingly clear, on an entirely empirical level, was that dirt, sewage and contaminated water (with their bad smells) went along with cholera, whereas clean water and safely removed sewage resulted in neither cholera nor stinks.

At this time, when the increasing use of machinery on farms, the growing importation of food from overseas and occasional potato blight were making life harder for poor country families, many people in public life saw emigration as a possible way forward. With the opening up of Australia and New Zealand in particular, many energetic and enterprising local agricultural working families were encouraged to go abroad, where land was cheap and fertile, and an English landless labourer could easily end up as a rich freeholder farmer under the Southern Cross. The Bucklands made arrangements for several local families to emigrate to Australia, some of whom seem to have prospered. Some emigrants even took cuttings of their local plants to begin new gardens, complete with other mementos from Islip.[15] The Bucklands appear to have been active philanthropists, contributing from their own pockets towards the various improvement schemes which they promoted.

Chapter 14
Decline, Death and
Historical Legacy

Around the time of his iconic 'Wash and Be Clean' sermon in Westminster Abbey in 1849–1850, William Buckland was struck down by a baffling illness. His lifelong driving energy and intellectual curiosity somehow dried up. He did not appear to be unhappy or especially depressed, just switched off. The affable, driven Dr Buckland suddenly became quiet, unsociable and had little to say. He no longer read anything except the Bible and some light magazines, and he dozed a good deal. This greatly distressed Mary, although it was hoped that it would prove to be a temporary condition, and would, given time and relaxation, pass over, leaving the Dean his vital self once again. But sadly, it did not, and his mental decline baffled medical opinion. The Bucklands had many high-powered medical friends, and their son Frank was now a trained surgeon. Was the distressing condition perhaps a delayed response to a carriage accident suffered earlier in Germany, when William had been knocked unconscious after his head had struck a stone?

Although Frank Buckland, with his medical knowledge, said there had been some signs of this illness before 1850, it was soon clear that William was no longer capable of fulfilling his regular duties as Dean of Westminster. There was no pressure on him to resign, however, for in 1850 an ecclesiastical benefice, like a professorship, a fellowship, a Civil Service post or even an armed forces commission, was regarded as equivalent to a piece of freehold property, to be enjoyed with all of its emoluments for life, though a wave of reform movements would sweep through the Church, universities and state over the next 20 or 30 years and fundamentally alter that situation. Buckland was as secure in his Deanery and Islip rectory when dozing in his armchair as he had been in his years of vigour and creativity. In the 1850s, long before retirement pensions came into being, a sick or exhausted clergyman simply remained in post, and appointed a deputy to do the work until he finally died. At Westminster, Lord John Thynne, the Sub-Dean, '... a real gentleman ... a most agreeable, kind, good man' carried on the daily work and ministry of the Abbey, along with helping at the School.[1] Precisely the same circumstance prevailed in Islip, especially as the Rector, as Dean of Westminster, depended on a full-time resident curate to continue the ministry to the parish. The Bucklands did move from Westminster to Islip, however, partly in the hope that the peace, calm and sweet air of an Oxfordshire country parsonage would enable William to recover his mental capacities. But sadly, he deteriorated further, much to the distress of Mary, the family and many friends and admirers.

One wonders, however, just how far back some of Buckland's occasional mental lapses may have extended, judging by an old story set down on paper by the Victorian raconteur Augustus Hare under the date 1882. He tells us that on one occasion when Buckland was staying with his friends at Nuneham Courtenay, some five miles away from Oxford, his host showed him the preserved and shrunken heart of a French king (probably Louis XIV), kept in a silver casket: a trophy rescued by English travellers after the Revolutionary mob had desecrated the royal tombs in St Denis Basilica, Paris. As Buckland had always prided himself on his quick analysis of minerals and other substances by tasting them, he placed the heart in his mouth – and promptly swallowed it, saying 'I have eaten many strange things, but I have never eaten the heart of a king before.'[2] If this piece of dinner-party gossip was indeed true, then Buckland had displayed a deeply uncharacteristic discourtesy to his host. If the heart was so valued as to be housed in a silver casket, it must have been a highly prized curiosity, not something a guest should have eaten and then joked about afterwards. As the story appears to relate to the time when Buckland was still socially active and was probably already Dean of Westminster, perhaps between 1845 and 1849, and prior to his mental failure becoming evident, it is possible that the heart-eating incident represents a sudden, transient episode in his decline.

We will return to Buckland's last illness in more detail anon, but as his creative life was over by 1850, this is a good place to take stock of his overall career and achievement, and then to examine how geological science, in its increasing intellectual and technical range, developed in the approximately half-century after his death in 1856.

William Buckland's geological achievement

As shown in the earlier chapters of this book, geology was in its infancy when Buckland began to take a serious interest in the science as an undergraduate. By the time of his death, it had moved from vigorous adolescence to early adulthood and was now an undisputed science in its own right, and not just an aspect of natural history or a handmaiden of civil engineering. So, what had Buckland achieved that was of enduring value? I would suggest that his adoption and development of Cuvier's ideas on prehistoric and modern animal anatomy would be of fundamental importance to the establishment of scientific palaeontology. In the wake of his amplification of Cuvier's model of the laws of anatomical congruence, Buckland had taught and popularized a technique by which scattered, broken fossil bones could be reconstructed into great lizards, or what Sir Richard Owen in 1840 would christen dinosaurs: creatures with parallels to modern-day elephants or crocodiles, yet differing significantly from them. Buckland, like Cuvier, would emphasize how teeth were the key to understanding an extinct animal, for teeth predicted diet, which in turn predicted key features of the creature's anatomy and lifestyle. Alongside Cuvier, Buckland was one of the first to recognize the fundamental significance of William Smith's stratigraphy, fossil-signature identification and geological mapping. He would also play a leading role, over the decades, in winning public recognition for Smith's achievement.

Buckland's work was also of great significance in so far as he drew attention to caves as a clue to the remote past. While he came increasingly to downplay the great Flood of Noah as an agent for entombing hyenas and other beasts in caves, he was in effect the founder of speleology (the scientific study of caves, their formation, geology and contents). Shortly, we shall see how cave finds would undermine Buckland's presumption of a 'young' human race, but mercifully this would not really happen until after his death. He had also played a preeminent part in establishing the science of hydrology, in his study of caves, rivers, watercourses, artesian wells and springs. This would have a major impact upon public health, via the provision of fresh drinking water, and the realization of the vital importance of keeping drinking water well removed from sewage and effluent.

Central to Buckland's enduring contribution to geological science was his firm recognition of its intimate connection with agriculture. His famous coprolites, alongside their chemical analysis by Justus von Liebig, were key in reclaiming and invigorating the soil, helping to keep down the price of bread and enable the poor to eat a more abundant and nutritious diet. For palaeontology and great lizards apart, feeding the poor was never far from William and Mary's concern.

Yet perhaps William Buckland's greatest and most lasting legacy lay in his genius for publicizing and teaching geology. His Oxford lectures, across nearly 40 years, combined with his British Association and other lecture activities, took the science of geology to thousands of people. In Oxford he was also an active promoter of what we now call field studies, where both undergraduate and senior members of the University rode out of Oxford to the quarries at Stonesfield, Headington and elsewhere, and received on-site instruction in how to read a landscape and excavate a promising rock face. Some of the surviving cartoons of Buckland depict him at these quarries, using a fossil bone as a landscape pointer. Then when Isambard Kingdom Brunel's Great Western Railway reached Didcot, some ten miles away from Oxford on the way to Bath and Bristol, Buckland would sometimes use the railway to demonstrate the geology revealed by great railway cuttings, such as that at Sonning in the Thames valley. It is hard to overestimate his significance in creating a geologically literate body of people in late Georgian and early Victorian England, including those ladies who had seen him perform on a British Association excursion or read his books and papers.

His sustained emphasis upon the compatibility of geology with Christian theology was also central to his achievement, especially with the Argument from Design in Natural Theology. It is true that Darwinism and the emergence of a form of agnosticism and evangelical atheism may appear to have sidelined Natural Theology, but it is far from being dead, even today. While we may no longer go down the line of imputing joy to schools of leaping shrimps, as William Paley did, or of regarding the dispatch by their fellows of a creature that has become too infirm to hunt or even defend itself as an indication of divine mercy, the sheer beauty and order in nature still captivate us. For anyone whose mind is inclined that way, it is so easy, when contemplating the night sky, dramatic landscapes and seascapes, flowers, birds and animals, to have one's thoughts elevated towards the Supreme Being.

It was perhaps providential that Buckland lost his cognitive powers when he did, for a body of new evidence was building up, both at home and abroad, which fundamentally challenged, then overturned, some of his most strongly held assumptions. Perhaps the most far-reaching discoveries were those that led to the conviction that the human race vastly pre-dated the accepted creation date of 6,000 years ago for Adamite man. Some of these discoveries had been made remarkably close to home, in Buckland's beloved south Devon.

The antiquity of the human race

One will recall from Chapter 8 how Buckland devoted a whole section of his *Geology and Mineralogy* Bridgewater Treatise of 1836 to demonstrating that human bones and artefacts found by various European geologists could not have predated Adam. Yet in addition to the French cave of human remains and artefacts which he dismissed in 1836, and his supposedly Roman Red Lady of Paviland mentioned in Chapter 4, a wave of fresh discoveries came to light during the 1850s and subsequent decades, which showed that the human race was indeed very ancient. Before the discovery and identification of ancient human bones began in a serious way, however, there had been a growing mass of evidence for the existence of human-manufactured flint and other stone implements. One of the pioneers in this field, along with Philippe-Charles Schmerling, was Jacques Boucher de Crèvecoeur de Perthes, a French Civil Servant and geologist who, from the 1830s onwards, had been excavating such artefacts in the valley of the River Somme, in northern France. The first explicitly humanoid bones, however, had been skull and other bone fragments discovered in a cave in the valley of the river Neander, east of Dusseldorf, Germany, in 1856. The skull dome suggested a quite large cranial, and hence brain, capacity, but the cranial vault was nonetheless much flatter than that of *Homo sapiens*. The forehead, jawbone and dentition also differed from that of modern humans, while Neanderthal Man's short legs in relation to body size, pelvis and other anatomical details seemed more simian than human. Some even speculated whether the Neander bones might be those of a Russian Cossack killed fighting with the French troops when the Russians drove Bonaparte's armies all the way back to France in 1812, for as everyone believed, Cossacks were a somewhat primitive lot! Cossacks apart, however, it was increasingly recognized that the Neanderthal bones had related somehow to the modern human race.

Then, as we saw in Chapter 4, workmen digging in Brixham, just across Torbay from Torquay, broke into a sealed, virgin cave in 1858. After its excavation by William Pengelly, a local geologist and naturalist, over 30 human-manufactured artefacts, including worked flint implements and even charred wood fragments, which were the remains of an ancient fire, were found beneath its thick stalagmite floor. The artefacts from the Brixham cave (which, like Kent's Cavern, I have visited) are now curated in the Torbay Museum, Torquay. Considering the thickness of the stalagmite deposition, which even in Buckland's time was known to form very slowly over many centuries, from the gradual limestone-enriched roof drippings within a cave, it was now hard to deny that the Brixham artefacts predated Adam and Eve.[3] Further, three years after Buckland's death, in 1859, Charles Darwin's *The Origin of Species* was published, and while in the early editions, he avoided suggesting an evolutionary connection with humans, the possibility was clear, and he would later explore it in considerable detail in *The Descent of Man* (1871).

Meanwhile, as the nineteenth century rolled on, the passion for geological digging, combined with the related passion for archaeological excavation, produced all manner of shaped, figured and polished implements. During Buckland's earlier years, and even when he dismissed Schmerling's finds in *Geology and Mineralogy*, such artefacts might safely be ascribed to Ancient Britons or the wild and primitive races of the north described by the Roman writer Tacitus. But by 1860, as the evidence built up, such explanations were no longer academically plausible. It was becoming increasingly plain that humanoids of some kind had walked the earth before the biblical Adam, and had indeed been contemporary with woolly mammoths, cave bears and European hyenas. Even the Scottish Christian Evangelical writer, Isabelle Wight Duncan, acknowledged this in her beautifully written yet anonymous *Pre-Adamite Man: Or, the Story of our Old Planet and its Inhabitants, Told by Scripture and Science* (1860). She takes up the apparent biblical paradox of Genesis 1 and 2, where there seem to be two separate and distinct human creations, and examines it in the light of modern discoveries. In Genesis 1, God forms both male and female humans, apparently from nowhere, and grants them dominion. Then in Chapter 2, he seems to do the same again, but now makes Adam specifically from the dust of the earth and Eve from Adam's rib, and breathes an immortal soul into this apparent second creation.[4] If this Adam and his wife Eve were the parents of all humankind, then what happened to the being created in Chapter 1? Could he have been the father of the pre-Edenic, prehistoric race of humanity? She cites many references from both the canonical Old Testament and the Apocrypha, and even parts of the New Testament and elsewhere, to back up her argument. Recent prehistoric discoveries could now be seen as giving scientific substantiation to the idea. *Pre-Adamite Man* deftly crafted the latest discoveries of ancient human artefacts around the biblical narrative of a creation, and won glowing reviews in many papers and journals of the period.

In the mid-1860s, less than a decade after Buckland's death, prehistory and prehistoric man came into being as fitting subjects of scientific study. The first of these studies would come in 1863, when Sir Charles Lyell, the uniformitarian geologist, published his *Geological Evidences of the Antiquity of Man with Remarks on Theories of Species by Variation* (1863). Lyell, who 30 years before had abandoned catastrophist geology in favour of a 'causes now in operation' gradualism to explain geological change, had been deeply impressed by Darwin's *Origin of Species*, in the same way that his scientific imagination had been stimulated by his reading of Lamarck some 30 years before. Although cautious in his commitment to evolution, and especially to Darwin's natural selection model, as he indicated in Chapters 21 and 22, Lyell could see a possible evolutionary connection between the bodies of humans and those of apes. Where he held back, however, was in contemplating the origins of humanity's intellectual and moral gifts and capacities. Even so, he was convinced by emerging archaeological evidence that there had been ancient primitive cultures in Europe, and that their bones and artefacts unequivocally predated 4004 BC. In the mid-nineteenth century, there were no carbon 14 or other modern methods of dating organic materials such as bone or wood fragments, but what could not be denied was the significance of very slow-forming stalagmite deposition, which sometimes buried prehistoric artefacts to a depth of several inches, suggesting the passage of many millennia.

On the other hand, Lyell's *Antiquity of Man* received something of a hammering from certain quarters. Not, it should be emphasized, from post-Edenic traditionalist supporters, so much as from other men of science. Charles Darwin criticized Lyell because of his caution about the limits of natural selection when it came to producing moral and intellectual attributes. Sir John Lubbock also criticized Lyell, more or less accusing him of plagiarism, alleging that he lifted his, Lubbock's, ideas and finds pertaining to prehistory without properly acknowledging them. Like many great scientific and cultural innovations, prehistory as a recognized historical and archaeological discipline was the child of an independent Grand Amateur, Sir John Lubbock. A wealthy banker who grew up largely in Down, the same Kent village in which Charles Darwin and his family resided, Lubbock became fascinated by natural history and was rapidly won over to Darwinian evolution by natural selection. He was also a reforming Member of Parliament, especially concerned about the long working hours of shop and office workers, and the driving force behind the Bank Holidays Act (1871) and the Shop Hours Act (1889), aimed at giving more holidays and reducing the length of the working day.

Perhaps more than any other individual, it was Sir John Lubbock who launched a developmental prehistory on to the cultural landscape, for there had not simply been primitive man, but a pre-Adamite man who was learning and getting cleverer all the time. The key indicator here was the increasing sophistication of the excavated artefacts being discovered. These individuals had learned how to generate and control fire, in a way that no other primate could, and their flint and other stone implements displayed a growing technological sophistication. Lubbock introduced the terms *Palaeolithic* and *Neolithic* for the Old and the New Stone Ages. Flint tools classed as Neolithic, such as scrapers, knives and spearheads were better shaped, polished and finished than the Palaeolithic, indicating a higher degree of social and technological sophistication. He also found evidence for the musk ox in early Britain, and used it to argue for the existence of an Ice Age within the early human period.

Once the prehistoric watershed had been crossed by the 1860s, and it became clear that human ancestors had not only existed, but had even made things and manifested creative intelligence long before 4004 BC, a whole new world of prehistoric anthropology began to emerge. Then after 1869, when the first of the painted caves was discovered and excavated at Altamira in Pyrenean Spain (the famous Bull Caves), so-called primitive man took on a new mantle of sophistication when he was acknowledged as an artist. The animal paintings found at Altamira and elsewhere gave a glimpse of prehistoric man's mental life, and posed all manner of questions. It was plain that these long-dead individuals had lively minds, could remember what they saw in graphic detail, and then took the trouble to paint them on walls in the deepest recesses of their caves. Were these paintings intended to help with the hunt, or did they possess some kind of religious significance? Or were they art for art's sake?

Within little more than 15 years of Buckland's death in 1856, pre-Adamite men had progressed from a denial of their existence to a clear demonstration of it, through developing levels of technical sophistication to becoming creative artists with minds perhaps similar to our own. What Buckland would have made of this new world of prehistoric man, had he lived with a sound mind into his early 80s, one can only guess.

Prehistoric finds galore

William Buckland was but a child of four when some strange bones were discovered in 1788 by Manuel Torres, on the bank of the river Lujan in Argentina. These first prehistoric beast remains turned out to be from a megatherium, or giant ground sloth. As Argentina was then part of the Spanish Empire, the fossilized bones were shipped to the Museum in Madrid, where they still reside. But it was Georges Cuvier who first articulated megatherium's fragments to show what this ancestral giant sloth actually looked like. As we have seen, many fresh types and species of great beasts would be found in Europe over the ensuing decades, giving birth to what Sir Charles Lyell would christen palaeontology. But as the American Continent, and in particular the great plains and the far west, came to be mapped and explored, many hundreds of dinosaur types emerged from the rocks, including what is acknowledged as the biggest of these beasts, the great four-legged brontosaurus or 'thunder lizard', discovered by Othniel Charles Marsh at Como Bluffs, Wyoming, in 1874 and described in 1879. The American continent – north, south and central – would yield not only hundreds of new dinosaur types, but also early human remains, probably of the earliest settlers and explorers of the New World, travelling from Asia via the Bering Straits or in boats across the Pacific: undisputed pre-Adamites of 10,000 BC and more. Likewise, Africa, Asia and Australasia would begin to yield dinosaur remains well before 1900, and in Africa, China and elsewhere, fossilized ancestral human bones would come to light, making it possible by the middle decades of the twentieth century to identify a biological ancestry for the human race, from our first beginnings in the African grasslands.

What would William Buckland have made of all this? The proliferation of dinosaur types would have delighted him, for much of the anatomical, diet and lifestyle aspects of these beasts would stand upon foundations which he and Cuvier had laid back in the 1810s and before. What he would have made of the human remains and the new science of anthropology, however, is a matter for conjecture. I think that in his love of evidence and new scientific facts, and in his deep sense of God's providence and design in creation, he would, like many other devout Christian life scientists, have come to accommodate an ancient humanity. But what might have made him howl with laughter is the present-day metamorphosis of the giant saurians and other fearsome prehistoric beasts into smiling soft toys in pink, green and yellow cloth. Cuddly tyrannosaurus rex and brontosaurus (neither of which had been discovered in his day), along with a grinning ichthyosaurus as companions for little children in their cots and prams would have delighted him, I am sure – as they also delight me. (And perhaps, like me, he would have had a collection of them, sitting on the mantelpieces in his Christ Church Canonry and Westminster Deanery.)

Early studies in the geology of the moon

Ever since Robert Hooke in 1665 had dropped lead pistol balls into tubs of semi-solid pipe-clay to simulate lunar craters formed by impact, astronomers and physicists had been fascinated by the complex surface of the moon.[5] But it was the large-aperture telescopes of the Victorian age which initiated a wider interest in the formation of the lunar terrain, and how it might have come into being. The Scottish–Manchester ironmaster and Grand Amateur astronomer James Nasmyth did some especially remarkable work, combining high-powered observation of lunar geological features with experiments, and even modelling these features.

What was obvious, however, is how radically different from planet earth our satellite was. All the evidence suggested that it was airless and waterless, and that its mountains and other geological features were sharp-edged and – unlike their terrestrial equivalents – entirely un-eroded. And in spite of the notorious 'Great Lunar Hoax' New York newspaper sensation of 1835,[6] it seemed to be dead and uninhabited. Clearly, the moon was unlikely to have had any sedimentary rocks or fossils, being instead the product of internal vulcanism and possible bombardment from space, combined with a computed low gravity and no erosion whatsoever. What a strange world for planet earth to be gravitationally locked in with!

Although no doubt familiar with the lunar geological experiments of Robert Hooke, reported in his *Micrographia* (1665), Buckland could never have known about the experiments of James Nasmyth. For Nasmyth's lunar work really only got under way after 1848, when he built a splendid 20-inch-aperture reflecting telescope capable of giving crystal clear images of lunar features of several hundred diameters magnification.[7] His results and conclusions, though already known through conversation and references elsewhere, were not formally published until Nasmyth and James Carpenter produced *The Moon* in 1874. In this work, Nasmyth presented a volcanic view of the moon, even suggesting that the lunar craters were formed from volcanic ejecta.

For unlike terrestrial volcanoes, the ejecta of which rapidly fall back to earth to form large cones, the weak lunar gravity meant that matter blasted out from a lunar volcano would rise high above the surface, only falling back to the moon when the moon's pull finally became greater than the original explosive force of the eruption. Hence, in their descent, the ejecta would build up the beautifully circular ramparts of a lunar crater, with the exhausted volcano itself remaining as a central mountain in the exact centre.

Indeed, the ancient lunar surface must have been remarkably fluid to cause that buckling which resulted in the pushed-up, sharply-delineated, un-eroded lunar mountains, along with the vast, flat lava plains which Galileo in 1610 had suggested might be watery seas, until more powerful telescopes had revealed them for what they were. And the much-debated question was: is the moon still geologically active? Especially at a time when astronomers occasionally claimed to see flares and bright spots of light on parts of the earth-facing side of the moon currently still in shadow. On the other hand, both manned and unmanned probes to the moon since 1969 have shown that our satellite appears to be solid, with little in the way of a lava interior, and has long since been geologically 'dead'.

What especially fascinated Nasmyth were the visual parallels between the scum or scoria and slag that formed on the surface of a pot of molten iron in the foundry and the surface features of the moon. So, could the lunar surface once have resembled the seething surface of a white-hot 'kibble' of molten iron? If this were indeed the case, then it was clear that the earth's and the moon's origins had been very different.

In Buckland's time, and for a century thereafter, big telescopes were the nearest we could get to understanding the geology of the planets. But one wonders what Buckland would have made of late-twentieth-century space probe discoveries, such as the vast Olympus Mons volcano and the Valles Marineris system of canyons on Mars. For while Mars is only half the size of the earth, it has a volcano bigger than any terrestrial one, and the Valles Marineris crack in the Martian surface makes earth's Grand Canyon look like a scratch in the paintwork. Clearly, Mars once had flowing water and a fascinating soil chemistry, and may even have fossils. And that is saying nothing about the liquid oceans beneath the frozen ice-age surface of Jupiter's satellite Europa, and the peppering with craters of Pluto, its satellite Charon and even some large asteroids. For we now know that our own earth is not the only place in creation with a complex geology – and goodness knows what future exoplanet researches will reveal.

I suspect that, from their current vantage point in the heavenly realms, William and Mary Buckland would be delighted, for the rocks of Pluto are no less a part of God's creation than are the fossils from the Stonesfield quarries.

From geology to geophysics

In the half-century after Buckland's death, geophysics, or the study of the physics and chemistry of our planet, touched upon in its proto form by figures such as James Hutton and the Edinburgh Vulcanists of the 1790s, became a true part of geology. Advanced in its early days by global travellers such as Alexander von Humboldt and portrayed in fiction by Jules Verne in *Journey to the Centre of the Earth* (1864), geophysics came to address the very moulding forces that made, and continue to re-make, our planet. The great HMS *Challenger* global survey voyage, 1872–1876, with its team of on-board scientists, collected global geophysical, oceanographic, meteorological and magnetic data. In 1868, the English astronomer and physicist Sir Joseph Norman Lockyer discovered a new line in the solar spectrum, which he believed to represent a gas unique to the incandescent sun, which he named helium. Then in 1881 Luigi Palmieri, in his chemical and spectroscopic studies of the gaseous and lava emissions from Mt Vesuvius and other volcanoes, found the same spectral signature, known as the 'D2' lines, in volcanic gas. So did helium also exist on earth? – a discovery which would be further substantiated through Palmieri's post-1881 laboratory researches. Then in the 1890s, Per Teodor Cleve and his colleagues at Uppsala, Sweden, William Hillebrand in the USA and definitively, Sir William Ramsay in Glasgow, detected the gas in Norwegian cleveite, an impure uranium compound, thus supporting Palmieri's finding and confirming that helium was indeed also a terrestrial gas. This dramatic demonstration of the presence of a solar gas on earth strongly implied a general spread of the elements of the periodic table throughout the universe.

Two other discoveries came to the fore in the half-century following Buckland's death that would add weight to the new science of geophysics. One was the thermodynamic research of William Thomson, later Lord Kelvin, regarding the earth's gradual loss of heat by radiation into space. Like Comte de Buffon with his cooling cannonball experiments in the eighteenth century, Thomson began by positing that the earth had once been in a molten state and had been losing heat at a given rate. But his calculations indicated that the earth was only somewhere between 20 and 400 million years old: a figure later narrowed down to around 100 million. When seen alongside other astronomical and physical evidence available at the time, this was simply not old enough. Among other things, the available time span was too short for Darwinian natural selection to have produced every living thing that we see about us today. It would be thermodynamics, and *not* Holy Scripture, that would prove to be a crucial early stumbling block for Darwinian evolution.

Things would not really change until the early twentieth century, when new discoveries in atomic physics indicated that in addition to radiating mechanical heat, our planet was radiating on the atomic level, which allowed the calibration of time scales, to indicate a vastly older earth going back billions of years. As a committed advocate of a very ancient, albeit undated, earth from the first decade of the nineteenth century, Buckland would probably have been delighted, even if slightly overawed, by the subsequent physics discoveries indicating that he was right after all. He might also have been fascinated by Alfred Wegener's 1912 announcement that the earth's continents were not 'fixed and stablished', but were in a state of change. Going back to the Fleming Abraham Ortelius's 1596 observation that the South American and African continents could easily dovetail into each other, various geographers and other scientists had pointed out this and similar congruences. But Wegener's 1912 paper to the German Geological Society gave a new focus to geophysical thinking. He suggested that the archaic earth had had one great land mass, Pangaea, and that this had broken up to form the continents we know today.

As the twentieth century unfolded, geophysics and physical geography diversified into specialist disciplines and sub-disciplines, to say nothing of lunar and planetary physics, chemistry and geology. But it is hard to overestimate William Buckland's influence in carrying mineralogy over into geology, and in the maturation of that science by 1850. Then from geology and physical geography, the other earth sciences flowed. But we must now return to the last six, sad years of William Buckland's creative and colourful life.

William Buckland: the final years

We have already seen how, soon after his November 1849 'Wash and Be Clean' sermon in Westminster Abbey, William Buckland suffered a strange six-year mental decline. It was immensely distressing to Mary and the family, for it is clear that he was a deeply loved and cherished husband and father. Of their surviving five children, it seems that William had a special relationship with his son Frank, who not only shared his father's intellectual brilliance, but many traits of character as well, being eccentric, charismatic, fun-loving, kind and daring. Frank's lifelong passion for all things anatomical and physiological ensured his reputation as a chip off the old block. I suspect, however, that Frank was given more to madcap capers than even his father had been, and over the ensuing decades one sees some of the eccentricities of Francis Trevelyan Buckland being ascribed to his father. Yet with Buckland and Morland genes in him, one need not be surprised to find Frank the colourful genius that he was.

In addition to his other gifts and attributes, it is clear that William Buckland had the power to engender a deep love in those around him, especially in family members, who quite simply adored him. When he died, in August 1856, it was while lying in the arms of Frank who, as a medical man, also took a detached interest in his beloved father's mysterious medical condition.

It is not clear whether Frank attended the post-mortem conducted upon William's corpse, but he left a detailed account of its findings. Both father and son, and Mary, were scientists driven by an intellectual curiosity about how nature, as God's creation, worked. While Frank never took Holy Orders, he was nonetheless a devout and committed Christian layman. The post-mortem found that five cervical vertebrae at the top of William's spinal column were in a decayed or damaged state. They were subsequently donated to the Royal College of Surgeons' Museum, in Lincoln's Inn Fields, London, bearing the label 'Occipital bone, Cervical Vertebrae, Tuberculosis, Osteoarticular, Cat. RCSPC/49a. 5',[8] where they still remain.

As we saw above, a head injury suffered in a carriage accident in Germany some years before was considered a contributory factor in Buckland's mental decline and death. The tuberculosis, however, and the post-mortem discovery of a hard vertebral tumour may indicate suspected tubercular spinal damage, such as that resulting from Pott's Disease, or tuberculosis of the spinal vertebrae. I am not aware, however, that Buckland, famously fit and healthy throughout his life, ever appeared to display tubercular symptoms. At the time of his death in 1856, however, tuberculosis, like all other infectious diseases in this pre-bacterial age, was only vaguely understood, and Robert Koch's 1882 discovery of the *mycobacterium tuberculosis* and its mode of transmission and effect upon the human body still lay in the future. From what we now know of the human brain and its ailments, it is possible that Buckland suffered a succession of mini strokes, which in his day would have been both undiagnosable and misunderstood. Small, localized strokes which were not accompanied by paralysis could have led to serious changes in cognitive awareness, which could have given the impression of his not being fully 'switched on'. Yet the overall condition, especially by 1851 or so, could also suggest the onset of some form of progressive dementia.

Many old and dear friends used to visit at the Islip rectory, including Buckland's close friend Sir Roderick Murchison. Buckland seems to have enjoyed the peace of Islip and its gardens, while Mary continued active in projects to improve the lot of the poor of the village. When time permitted, she may have pressed on with her microscopic research, for Mary and her daughter Caroline were skilled users of the new high-powered microscopes of the 1850s.

What passed through Buckland's mind during the years 1850–1856, we shall never know, but as far as one can tell, his decline, like that of many sufferers from Alzheimer's, was probably more distressing to Mary, their children, friends and those around him than it was to him, and he seems to have gently faded into a state of senility. It is likely, however, that he became harder to manage as his illness dragged on, as is often the case with dementia, because by the end he was residing in John Bush's Asylum at Clapham, south London. The word 'asylum' did not necessarily carry the subsequent connotation of being a place for lunatics; rather, it was more like what we today might call a care home. This no doubt would have relieved the exhausted Mary of some of her burden. He passed away peacefully at Clapham, on 14 August 1856, age 73, and was brought home to Islip for burial in St Nicholas's churchyard.

Mary Buckland now moved to the Sussex seaside town of St Leonards. Her own health, however, was no longer good, for in addition to the drain on her physical and emotional energies during William's slow decline, with all its accompanying stress, she too had sustained injuries in the German coach accident in which William had been knocked unconscious. At St Leonards, however, her powerful mind and undimmed scientific curiosity about God's creation led her to continue a series of researches into rare marine sponges and zoophytes with her powerful microscope. Dr James Scott Bowerbank FRS, a fellow marine microscopist, sometimes joined her in this research. Having spent the morning of 29 November 1857 with Mary Buckland on their research, he agreed to revisit the following Monday to continue their work. Then suddenly, on the evening of 30 November, Mary quietly passed away. She was just 60. Her body was brought to Islip (which now had a new rector), where she was interred with William.[9]

Mary Buckland had, in many ways, been a scientist all her life, from her girlhood fascination with natural history and comparative anatomy in the household of Sir Christopher and Lady Pegge down to her research as a serious microscopist before her sudden death. In fact, the new high-power 'achromatic' microscopes developed by Joseph Jackson Lister FRS (father of Joseph Lister, the pioneer of antiseptic surgery) after 1825 transformed the microscope, making it possible to increase magnifications from ×125 to ×500 and beyond. Microscopy would become a branch of science in which educated ladies of independent means would make serious contributions, as did Mary Buckland and her daughter Caroline.

When another Buckland daughter, Elizabeth Oke Gordon, began to write her beloved father's *Life and Correspondence* almost 40 years later, she included a Preface written by William Boyd Dawkins, Professor of Geology at Manchester University. Dawkins had never known Buckland, still being an undergraduate in 1859, some three years after Buckland's death and nine years after the onset of his strange illness, but it is clear that Buckland's reputation was still formidable. He placed Buckland in the 'heroic age' of geology, coming from a time when (at least in England) only William Smith was really doing anything in the science, with Murchison, De la Beche, Sedgwick and all the others building upon the foundation which Buckland had laid. Nor was it only Buckland's science and geological discoveries that had become legendary, but also his inspirational teaching and geniality.

It is hard to find a better way to complete a life of William Buckland than by quoting Dawkins's own peroration. He writes:

> In concluding these remarks I would remind the reader that Buckland belongs to the heroic age, when Natural Science was young, and that he belongs to a type of man now extinct. Whatever estimate may be formed of his life and works, it cannot be denied that he was one of the makers of modern Oxford, and one of the founders of the science of Geology.[10]

Postscript

When I was a doctoral student in Oxford during the 1970s, I had a research supervisor, Professor Gerard L'Estrange Turner – microscopist, science historian and sometime President of the Royal Microscopical Society – who was a profound admirer of Buckland. Gerard and his wife, Helen, went to live in Islip village, and he proudly related how he had already reserved the vacant grave plot next to that of Buckland in the churchyard. Gerard clearly felt honoured at the prospect of having the great geologist and theologian as a neighbour until Judgement Day, and looked forward to jolly conversations with him in the hereafter.

I attended Gerard's funeral in Islip's beautiful parish church (Helen having predeceased him) at the end of July 2012, and saw him laid to rest beside his hero. I have often wondered whether they have since made subterranean contact, as Gerard imagined. For as Archbishop Whately had said in his comic eulogy to his then living and vigorous friend Buckland in 1820:

> Where shall we our great Professor inter,
>   That in peace may rest his bones?
> If we hew him a rocky sepulchre,
>   He'll rise and break the stones,
> And examine each stratum that lies around,
> For he's quite in his element underground.[11]

Requiescant in pace to Judgement Day.

Appendix

Elegy. Intended for Professor Buckland. December 1st, 1820. By Richard Whately. (From Elizabeth Oke Gordon, *The Life and Correspondence of William Buckland*, pp. 41–2.)

Mourn, Ammonites, mourn, o'er his funeral urn,
　　Whose neck ye must grace no more;
Gneiss, granite, and slate, he settled your date,
　　And his ye must now deplore.
Weep, caverns, weep with unfiltering drip,
　　Your recesses he'll cease to explore;
For mineral veins and organic remains
　　No stratum again will he bore.

Oh, his wit shone like crystal; his knowledge profound
　　From gravel to granite descended,
No trap could deceive him, no slip could confound,
　　Nor specimen, true or pretended;
He knew the birth-rock of each pebble so round,
　　And how far its tour had extended.

His eloquence rolled like the Deluge retiring,
　　Where mastodon carcases floated;
To a subject obscure he gave charms so inspiring,
　　Young and old on geology doated.
He stood out like an Outlier; his hearers, admiring,
　　In pencil each anecdote noted.

Where shall we our great Professor inter,
　　That in peace may rest his bones?

If we hew him a rocky sepulchre,
    He'll rise and break the stones,
And examine each stratum that lies around,
For he's quite in his element underground.

If with mattock and spade his body we lay
    In the common alluvial soil,
He'll start up and snatch those tools away
    Of his own geological toil;
In a stratum so young the Professor disdains
That embedded should lie his organic remains.

Then exposed to the drip of some case-hardening spring
    His carcase let stalactite cover,
And to Oxford the petrified sage let us bring
    When he is encrusted all over;
There, 'mid mammoths and crocodiles, high on a shelf,
Let him stand as a monument raised to himself.

Notes

Full details of the books and articles cited in the Notes may be found in the Bibliography.

1 The British Parson-Scientist: William Buckland in Context

1. Information generously communicated to me by scholars in Corpus Christi College, Oxford, Exeter Cathedral Archives, and the Devonshire Record Office.
2. Gordon, *Life and Correspondence of William Buckland*, pp. 3–4.
3. Gordon, *Life and Correspondence of William Buckland*, pp. 4–5; Edmunds, 'Patronage and privilege in education'.
4. Sprat, *History of the Royal Society*, p. 53; Purver, *The Royal Society*, pp. 128–42.
5. Chapman, chs 4, 6, 7, 9 in Fauvel, Flood, and Wilson, *Oxford Figures*; also Chapman, *The Victorian Amateur Astronomer*, pp. 13–33.
6. Michell, 'On the means of discovering the distance . . . of the fixed stars'.
7. Roberts, *Memoirs of the Life . . . of Mrs Hannah More*, vol. 2, p. 144; Chapman, *Physicians, Plagues, and Progress*, p. 316.
8. Haas, 'The Reverend William Henry Dallinger'.
9. Gordon, *Life and Correspondence of William Buckland*, p. 5.

2 A Geologist at Oxford

1. Joyce, *History of Passenger Transport*, pp. 30–58.
2. Gordon, *Life and Correspondence of William Buckland*, pp. 1–11.
3. Gordon, *Life and Correspondence of William Buckland*, pp. 20–1.
4. Geikie, *Life of Sir Roderick Murchison*, vol. 1, p. 125.

3 Rocks and Ages

1. Chapman, *Slaying the Dragons*, ch. 8, pp. 121–30.
2. Hooke, 'Lectures and discourses of earthquakes', *Posthumous Works*, p. 395.

3 Hooke, 'Lectures and discourses of earthquakes', *Posthumous Works*, pp. 346–50.
4 Halley, 'Account of the cause of the saltness of the ocean'.
5 Halley, 'Some considerations about the cause of the universal deluge'.
6 Toulmin and Goodfield, *The Discovery of Time*, pp. 176–8.
7 Buckland, 'Notice on the megalosaurus'; Gordon, *Life and Correspondence of William Buckland*, pp. 203–6; Howlett, Kennedy, Powell and Torrens, 'New light on the history of megalosaurus'.

4 Geology Vindicated and Noah's Flood Comes to Yorkshire

1 Barlow, *Autobiography of Charles Darwin*, p. 102.
2 Dawkins, 'Preface', in Gordon, *Life and Correspondence of William Buckland*.
3 Gordon, *Life and Correspondence of William Buckland*, p. 57.
4 Buckland discusses the Paviland finds in p. 82–98 of *Reliquiae Diluvianae*: p. 85 for quotation.
5 Buckland, *Reliquiae Diluvianae*, p. 92.
6 Gordon, *Life and Correspondence of William Buckland*, p. 31.

5 Geologists in the Landscape

1 Torrens, 'William Smith', *Oxford Dictionary of National Biography*.
2 Cuvier, 'Mémoires sur les espèces d'éléphants vivants et fossiles'.
3 Wendt, *Before the Deluge*, p. 95.
4 Rudwick, *The Great Devonian Controversy*, ch. 2.
5 Morrell, 'John Phillips', *Oxford Dictionary of National Biography*.

6 The Geological Canon of Christ Church and Miss Mary Morland

1 Fox, *Memories of Old Friends*, p. 44, 8 October 1839; Gordon, *Life and Correspondence of William Buckland*, p. 91.
2 Fox, *Memories of Old Friends*, p. 44.
3 Lyell to Mantell, 20 July 1825, Lyell, *Life, Letters, and Journals*, vol. 1, pp. 160–1.
4 Woodham-Smith, *Florence Nightingale*, p. 1.
5 Gordon, *Life and Correspondence of William Buckland*, p. 93.
6 Gordon, *Life and Correspondence of William Buckland*, pp. 93–4.

7 Tuckwell, *Reminiscences of Oxford*, p. 95.

8 Tuckwell, *Reminiscences of Oxford*, p. 40.

9 Buckland, 'Observations on the bones of hyenas'.

10 Shapter, *History of the Cholera in Exeter*, pp. 74–83.

11 Airy, *Autobiography of Sir George Biddell Airy*, pp. 140–1.

12 Gordon, *Life and Correspondence of William Buckland*, p. 105.

13 Gordon, *Life and Correspondence of William Buckland*, p. 107.

14 Gordon, *Life and Correspondence of William Buckland*, p. 104 (for crocodile); Bompas, *Life of Frank Buckland*, pp. 14–15 (for turtle).

15 Bompas, *Life of Frank Buckland*, p. 12.

16 Bompas, *Life of Frank Buckland*, p. 13.

17 Gordon, *Life and Correspondence of William Buckland*, pp. 112–13.

7 'Gentlemen, Free and Unconfin'd'. Paying for Geological and Other Scientific Research in Buckland's Britain

1 Sprat, History *of the Royal Society*, p. 67.

2 Lyell to Mantell, 14 June 1832, Lyell, *Life, Letters, and Journals*, vol. 1, p. 388; Gordon, *Life and Correspondence of William Buckland*, pp. 126–34.

3 Fox, *Memories of Old Friends*, p. 4.

4 Gordon, *Life and Correspondence of William Buckland*, p. 123.

5 McMillan, *Queen of Science*, pp. 145–6.

6 McMillan, *Queen of Science*, p. 140.

7 Macdonald, *Kew Observatory and the Evolution of Victorian Science*, pp. 154–64.

8 Buckland's Bridgewater Treatise and Natural Theology

1 Buckland, *Geology and Mineralogy*, vol. 1, pp. xi –xii.

2 Gordon, *Life and Correspondence of William Buckland*, p. 193.

3 Gordon, *Life and Correspondence of William Buckland*, p. 193; Buckland, Frank, 'Memoir'.

4 Buckland, *Geology and Mineralogy*, vol. 1, p. 59.

5 Buckland, *Geology and Mineralogy*, vol. 1, p. 61.

6 Buckland, *Geology and Mineralogy*, vol. 1, p. 103.

7 Buckland, *Geology and Mineralogy*, vol. 2, p. 110, note on pl. 69, fig. 3.

8 Buckland, *Geology and Mineralogy*, vol. 1, p. 175.

9 Buckland, *Geology and Mineralogy*, vol. 1, pp. 173–5.

10 Buckland, *Geology and Mineralogy*, vol. 1, p. 175.

11 Buckland, *Geology and Mineralogy*, vol. 1, p. 263.

12 Buckland, *Geology and Mineralogy*, vol. 1, p. 14.

13 Buckland, *Geology and Mineralogy*, vol. 1, p. 23. The full footnote is printed across pp. 22–6.

14 Buckland, *Geology and Mineralogy*, vol. 1, pp. 29–30.

15 Fox, *Memories of Old Friends*, p. 45.

16 Dawkins, 'Preface', in Gordon, *Life and Correspondence of William Buckland*.

9 A Passion for Minerals and Mountains: Geology and the Romantic Movement

1 Buckland, *Geology and Mineralogy*, vol. 1, pp. 1–7.

2 Clark and Hughes, *Life and Letters of the Reverend Adam Sedgwick*, vol. 1, ch. 1.

3 Gordon, *Life and Correspondence of William Buckland*, p. 105.

4 Miller, *My Schools and Schoolmasters*, ch. 3, etc. Miller was clearly a captivating writer and storyteller.

5 Torrens, 'Mary Anning', *Oxford Dictionary of National Biography*; Cadbury, *The Dinosaur Hunters*, pp. 4–8.

6 Gordon, *Life and Correspondence of William Buckland*, p. 115.

7 Buckland, 'A memoir on evidence of glaciers'.

8 Gordon, *Life and Correspondence of William Buckland*, p. 30.

9 Gordon, *Life and Correspondence of William Buckland*, p. 30.

10 A Gift for Friendship: Buckland's Character, Friends and Influences

1 Gordon, *Life and Correspondence of William Buckland*, p. 2.

2 Buckland, 'Description of the paramoudra'.

3 Gordon, *Life and Correspondence of William Buckland*, p. 14.

4 Gordon, *Life and Correspondence of William Buckland*, pp. 151–2.

5 Gordon, *Life and Correspondence of William Buckland*, p. 157.

6 Gordon, *Life and Correspondence of William Buckland*, p. 164.
Mrs Gordon cites from Liebig's *Familiar Letters on Chemistry* (1843), Letters XI and XII, pp. 116–32 (New York edn).

7 Gordon, *Life and Correspondence of William Buckland*, p. 164.

8 Gordon, *Life and Correspondence of William Buckland*, pp. 158–9.

9 Gordon, *Life and Correspondence of William Buckland*, p. 219.

10 Gordon, *Life and Correspondence of William Buckland*, p. 167.

11 Fox, *Memories of Old Friends*, p. 5. Also cited by Gordon, *Life and Correspondence of William Buckland*, pp. 27–8.

12 Geikie, *Life of Sir Roderick Murchison*, vol. 1, p. 115.

13 Geikie, *Life of Sir Roderick Murchison*, vol. 1, p. 234.

14 Whately, 'Elegy', in Gordon, *Life and Correspondence of William Buckland*, pp. 41–2. See Appendix for full text of poem.

11 The Scriptural Geologists

1 Wilberforce, 'On the Origin of Species', pp. 256–7; Chapman, 'Monkeying about with history'; Chapman, *Slaying the Dragons*, ch. 7, pp. 113–20.

2 Gordon, *Life and Correspondence of William Buckland*, pp. 219–20.

3 Chapman, *The Victorian Amateur Astronomer*, pp. 3–13.

4 Penn, *A Comparative Estimate*, Supplement, pp. 164–70.

5 Chapman, *Physicians, Plagues, and Progress*, p. 367.

6 McMillan, *Queen of Science*, p. 300, n. 121; Somerville, *Personal Recollections . . . of Mary Somerville*, p. 375.

7 (Lady) Richarda Airy to Lady Margaret Herschel, 6 October, 1844: letter in the private possession of the Airy family, to whom I am indebted for kindly granting me access to this archive.

12 Stability, Progress or Evolution?

1 Lyell to Mantell, 2 March 1827, Geikie, *Life of Sir Roderick Murchison*, vol. 1, p. 168.

2 Lyell to Mantell, 3 January 1826, Geikie, *Life of Sir Roderick Murchison*, vol. 1, p. 164.

3 Lyell to Mantell, 2 March 1827, Geikie, *Life of Sir Robert Murchison*, vol. 1, p. 168.

4 Chambers, *Vestiges of the Natural History of Creation*, pp. 1–43.

5 Chambers, *Vestiges of the Natural History of Creation*, p. 173.

6 Chambers, *Vestiges of the Natural History of Creation*, pp. 185–6.

7 Chambers, *Vestiges of the Natural History of Creation*, pp. 153–4.

8 Chambers, *Vestiges of the Natural History of Creation*, pp. 198–9.
9 'Gorilla', 'Monkeyana', *Punch* 40 (18 May 1861), p. 206.
10 Sedgwick, 'Review' of *Vestiges*, p. 3.
11 Sedgwick, 'Review' of *Vestiges*, p. 3.

13 The Dean of Westminster

1 Gordon, *Life and Correspondence of William Buckland*, pp. 219–20
2 Gordon, *Life and Correspondence of William Buckland*, p. 220.
3 Gordon, *Life and Correspondence of William Buckland*, p. 219.
4 Gordon, *Life and Correspondence of William Buckland*, pp. 221–5.
5 Tuckwell, *Reminiscences of Oxford*, p. 106.
6 Gordon, *Life and Correspondence of William Buckland*, p. 238.
7 Uglow, *Hogarth*, 'Credulity, Superstition, and Fanaticism: A Medley' (1762), p. 653; also Hogarth's 'The Sleeping Congregation' (1762), reproduced widely and available on the Internet.
8 Thompson, *Henry George Liddell*, p. 92.
9 Thompson, *Henry George Liddell*, p. 88.
10 Thompson, *Henry George Liddell*, pp. 100–1.
11 Leech, 'Faraday giving his card to Father Thames'.
12 Gordon, *Life and Correspondence of William Buckland*, p. 249.
13 Gordon, *Life and Correspondence of William Buckland*, p. 246.
14 Gordon, *Life and Correspondence of William Buckland*, pp. 264–5.
15 Gordon, *Life and Correspondence of William Buckland*, pp. 258–9.

14 Decline, Death and Historical Legacy

1 Thompson, *Henry George Liddell*, p. 89.
2 Hare, *The Story of my Life*, vol. 5, pp. 357–8.
3 Prestwich, 'Report on the exploration of Brixham Cave'.
4 Duncan, *Pre-Adamite Man*, pp. 1–14.
5 Hooke, *Micrographia*, p. 243.
6 Locke, 'Great astronomical discoveries . . . lately made by Sir John Herschel'.
7 Nasmyth and Carpenter, *The Moon*, pp. 95–116.
8 Girling, *The Man Who Ate the Zoo*, p. 103.
9 Gordon, *Life and Correspondence of William Buckland*, pp. 272–3.

10 Dawkins, 'Preface', in Gordon, *Life and Correspondence of William Buckland*, p. xii.

11 Whately, 'Elegy', v. 4, in Gordon, *Life and Correspondence of William Buckland*, p. 42.

Bibliography

Airy, Wilfred (ed.), *The Autobiography of Sir George Biddell Airy, KCB, etc.*, (CUP, 1896).

Alexander, E. M. M., 'Father John MacEnery, scientist or charlatan?', *Report and Transactions of the Devonshire Association* 96 (1964), pp. 113–46.

Armstrong, Patrick, *The English Parson-Naturalist. A Companionship between Science and Religion* (Gracewing, Leominster, 2000).

Bailey, Sir Edward, *The Geological Survey of Great Britain* (Thomas Murby, London, 1952).

Barlow, Norah (granddaughter of Charles Darwin), *The Autobiography of Charles Darwin, 1809-1882* (Collins, London, 1958). (Restores original omissions and includes appendix and notes.)

Bate, D. G., 'Sir Henry De la Beche and the founding of the British Geological Survey', The *Mercian Geologist* 17, 3 (2010), pp. 149–65.

Bompas, George, *The Life of Frank Buckland* (1885; undated Thomas Nelson and Sons edn, London, *c.* 1909).

Borley, L. (ed.), *Hugh Miller in Context: Geologist and Naturalist, Writer and Folklorist. A collection of papers presented at two conferences: The Cromarty Years* (2000) and *The Edinburgh Years* (2001) (Cromarty Arts Trust, Cromarty, 2002).

Buckland, Francis Trevelyan (Frank), 'Memoir' to his father in the third edition of William Buckland, *Geology and Mineralogy*, ed. John Phillips (1856).

Buckland, William, 'Description of the paramoudra, a singular fossil body that is found in the chalk of Northern Ireland . . .', *Transactions of the Geological Society* 1, 4 (1817), pp. 413–23.

Buckland, William, *Vindiciae Geologicae, or, the connexion of geology with religion explained: in an inaugural lecture delivered before Oxford University, May 15, 1819, on the endowment of a Readership in Geology by His Royal Highness The Prince Regent* (Oxford, 1820).

Buckland, William, *Reliquiae Diluvianae, or, observations on the organic remains contained in caves, fissures, and diluvial gravel, and on other geological phenomena, attesting to the action of an Universal Deluge* (London, 1823).

Buckland, William, 'Notice on the megalosaurus or great fossil lizard of Stonesfield', *Transactions of the Geological Society* 2, 1 (1824), pp. 390–6.

Buckland, William, 'Observations on the bones of hyenas and other animals in the cavern of Lunel near Montpellier: and in the adjacent strata of marine formation', *Edinburgh Journal of Science* 6, 12 (1827), pp. 242–6.

Buckland, William, *Geology and Mineralogy, Considered with Reference to Natural Theology*, 2 vols (London, 1836).

Buckland, William, 'A memoir on evidence of glaciers in Scotland and the North of England', *Proceedings of the Geological Society* 3, 2, 72 (1840), pp. 332–7, 345–8; also in *The Edinburgh New Philosophical Journal*, 30 (1841).

Buckland, William, 'Anniversary Address of the [Geological Society] President', *Proceedings of the Geological Society* 3, 2, 81 (19 February 1841), pp. 469–540.

Cadbury, Deborah, *The Dinosaur Hunters. A True Story of Scientific Rivalry and the Discovery of the Prehistoric World* (Fourth Estate, London, 2000).

Chadwick, Owen, *The Victorian Church*, 2 vols (Adam and Charles Black, New York, 1966 and later editions).

Chambers, Robert, *Vestiges of the Natural History of Creation* (published anonymously) (London, 1844). (The identity of the author remained unknown for over 25 years.)

Chapman, Allan, *The Victorian Amateur Astronomer. Independent Astronomical Research in Britain, 1820-1920* (Praxis, Chichester, 1998; Gracewing, Leominster, 2017).

Chapman, Allan, *Mary Somerville and the World of Science* (Canopus, Bristol, 2004; Springer, 2014).

Chapman, Allan, 'Monkeying about with History: remembering the "Great Debate" of 1860', Oxford *Magazine* 299 (Noughth Week, Trinity Term 2010), pp. 10–12.

Chapman, Allan, *Slaying the Dragons. Destroying Myths in the History of Science and Faith* (Lion Hudson, Oxford, 2013).

Chapman, Allan, *Physicians, Plagues, and Progress. The History of Western Medicine from Antiquity to Antibiotics* (Lion Hudson, Oxford, 2016).

Clark, J. W. and Hughes, T. M. (eds), *The Life and Letters of the Reverend Adam Sedgwick*, 2 vols (CUP, 1890).

Cobbett, William, *Cobbett's England. A Selection from the Writings of William Cobbett*, ed. John Derry, illustr. James Gillray (Parkgate Books, London, 1968, 1997).

Cohn, Norman, *The Pursuit of the Millennium. Revolutionary Millenarians and Mystical Anarchists of the Middle Ages* (1957; Paladin, 1970).

Cuvier, Baron Georges Léopold Chrétien Frédéric Dagobert, 'Mémoires sur les espèces d'éléphants vivants et fossiles', *Journal of Physics, Chemistry, Natural History, and Arts* 50 (1800), 207–17.

Cuvier, Georges, *Recherches sur les ossemens fossiles de quadrupèdes*, 4 vols (Paris, 1812).

Cuvier, Georges, *Essay on the Theory of the Earth* (1813; tr. Robert Kerr (CUP, 2009)).

Dawkins, William Boyd, 'Preface', in Gordon, *The Life and Correspondence of William Buckland, D. D., F. R. S.*, pp. v–xii.

Duncan, Isabelle Wight, *Pre-Adamite Man; Or, the Story of Our Old Planet and its Inhabitants, Told by Scripture & Science*, published anonymously (Saunders, Otley, 1860).

Edmunds, J. M., 'Patronage and privilege in education: a Devon boy goes to school, 1798', Transactions *of the Devon Association* 110 (1978), pp. 95–111.

Faber, Geoffrey, *The Oxford Apostles. A Character Study of the Oxford Movement* (Faber and Faber, London, 1933).

Fauvel, John, Flood, Raymond and Wilson, Robin (eds), *Oxford Figures. Eight Centuries of the Mathematical Sciences* (2nd edn, OUP, 2013).

Fox, Caroline, *Memories of Old Friends. Being Extracts from the Journals and Letters of Caroline Fox of Penjerrick, Cornwall, from 1835 to 1871*, ed. Horace N. Pym (Smith, Elder and Co., London, 1882).

Geikie, Archibald (ed.), *Life of Sir Roderick Murchison, Based on his Journals and Letters*, 2 vols (London, 1875).

Gillispie, Charles Coulston, *Genesis and Geology. A Study of the Relations of Scientific Thought, Natural Theology, and Social Opinion in Great Britain, 1790–1850* (1951; Harvard Univ. Press, 1996).

Girling, Richard, *The Man Who Ate the Zoo. Frank Buckland, Forgotten Hero of Natural History* (Chatto and Windus, London, 2016).

Gordon, Elizabeth Oke, *The Life and Correspondence of William Buckland, D. D., F. R. S.* (John Murray, London, 1894; repr. CUP, 2010).

'Gorilla', pseudonym of the author of the comic poem 'Monkeyana', *Punch* 40 (18 May 1861), p. 206.

Haas, D. W., Jnr, 'The Reverend William Henry Dallinger FRS (1839–1909)', *Notes and Records of the Royal Society* 54, 1 (January 2000), 53–65.

Hallam, A., *Great Geological Controversies* (OUP, New York, 1983).

Halley, Edmond, 'A short account of the cause of the saltness of the ocean . . . with a proposal, by help thereof, to discover the age of the world', *Philosophical Transactions of the Royal Society* 29, 344 (1715), pp. 296–300.

Halley, Edmond, 'Some considerations about the cause of the universal deluge, laid before the Royal Society on 12th December 1694...', *Philosophical Transactions of the Royal Society* 33, 383 (1724), pp. 118–23.

Hansen, Bert, 'The early history of glacial theory in British geology', *Journal of Glaciology* 9, 55 (1970), pp. 135–41.

Hare, Augustus, *The Story of My Life*, vol. 5 for 1882 (Dodd, Mead, New York, 1896–1901).

Hendry, Archibald W., *The Age of the Earth. A Physicist's Odyssey* (World Scientific, 2020).

Hooke, Robert, *Micrographia: or Some Physiological Descriptions of Minute Bodies Made by Magnifying Glasses, with Observations and Inquiries thereupon* (London, 1665).

Hooke, Robert, 'Lectures and discourses of earthquakes and subterraneous eruptions . . . ', in Richard Waller (ed.), *The Posthumous Works of Robert Hooke, M. D., S. R. S.* (1705), pp. 279–450.

Howes, C. J., 'The Dillwyn Diaries, 1817–1852. Buckland and the caves of Gower [South Wales]', *Proceedings of the University of Bristol Speleological Society* 18, 2 (1988), pp. 298–305.

Howlett, E. A., Kennedy, W. J., Powell, H. P. and Torrens, H. S., 'New light on the history of megalosaurus, the great lizard of Stonesfield', *Archives of Natural History* 44, 1 (Edinburgh Univ. Press, 2017), pp. 82–102.

Hughes, Thomas, *Tom Brown's Schooldays* (Macmillan, London, 1857).

Jenkins, Alan. C., *The Naturalists. Pioneers of Natural History* (Hamish Hamilton, London, 1978).

Joyce, J., *The History of Passenger Transport in Britain* (Ian Allan, London,1967).

Lane, J., *A Social History of Medicine: Health, Healing, and Disease in England 1750–1950* (Routledge, London and New York, 2001).

Laudan, Rachel, *From Mineralogy to Geology: the Foundations of a Science, 1650–1830* (Chicago Univ. Press, 1987).

Leech, John, Satirical engraving 'Faraday giving his card to Father Thames; and we hope that the dirty fellow will consult the learned Professor', *Punch*, 21 July 1855, p. 27.

Locke, Richard A., 'Great astronomical discoveries lately made by Sir John Herschel . . . at the Cape of Good Hope' (1835), in Faith K. Pizor and T. Allan Comp, *The Man in the Moon. An Anthology of Antique Science Fiction and Fantasy* (Sidgwick and Jackson, London, 1971), pp. 190–216.

Lurie, Edward, *Louis Agassiz: A Life in Science* (Johns Hopkins Univ. Press, 1988).

Lyell, Katherine M. (sister-in-law of Charles Lyell) (ed.), *Life, Letters, and Journals of Charles Lyell, Bart*, 2 vols (John Murray, London, 1881).

Macalpine, Ida and Hunter, Richard, *George III and the Mad-Business* (Pimlico, London, 1993, 1995).

Macdonald, Lee T., *Kew Observatory and the Evolution of Victorian Science 1840–1910* (Pittsburgh Univ. Press, 2018).

Maddox, Brenda, *Reading the Rocks. How Victorian Geologists Discovered the Secret of Life* (Bloomsbury Press, London, 2017).

Mallet, Charles E., *A History of the University of Oxford*, vol. III, 'Modern Oxford' (Methuen, London, 1927; Barnes and Noble, New York, 1968).

McMillan, Dorothy (ed.), *Queen of Science. Personal Recollections of Mary Somerville* (Canongate Classics 102, Edinburgh, 2001). (Restores material from drafts of her autobiography which was not included in the original 1873 text.)

Michell, John, 'On the means of discovering the distance, magnitude, & c. . . . of the fixed stars, in consequence of the diminution of the velocity of their light', *Philosophical Transactions of the Royal Society* 74 (1784), pp. 35–57.

Miller, Hugh, *My Schools and Schoolmasters* (Edinburgh, 1854).

Morley, John, *Death, Heaven, and the Victorians* (Studio Vista, London, 1971).

Morrell, J. B., 'The legacy of William Smith: the case of John Phillips 1800–1874, in the 1820s', *Archives of Natural History* 16 (1989), pp. 319–35.

Morrell, J. B., 'John Phillips', *Dictionary of National Biography* (OUP, 2004).

Morrell, J. B. and Thackray, A., *Gentlemen of Science. Early Years of the British Association for the Advancement of Science* (OUP, 1981, 1982).

Morris, A. D., 'Gideon Algernon Mantell LLD, FRCS, FRS (1790–1852)', *Proceedings of the Royal Society of Medicine* 65 (1972), pp. 215–21.

Nasmyth, James and Carpenter, James, *The Moon: Considered as a Planet, a World, and a Satellite* (John Murray, London, 1874).

North, F. J., *Sir Charles Lyell: Interpreter of the Principles of Geology* (Cox and Wyman Ltd, London, 1965).

Penn, Granville, *A Comparative Estimate of the Mineral and Mosaical Geologies* (London, 1822; Supplement, 1823).

Porter, Roy, *The Making of Geology. Earth Science in Britain, 1660–1815* (CUP, 1977).

Prestwich, Joseph, 'Report on the exploration of Brixham Cave, conducted by a Committee of the Geological Society', *Philosophical Transactions of the Royal Society* 163, 2 (1874), pp. 471–572.

Margery Purver, *The Royal Society, Concept and Creation* (MIT Press, Cambridge, Mass., 1967).

Roberts, William (ed.), *Memoirs of the Life and Correspondence of Mrs. Hannah More*, 4 vols (London, 1834).

Rudwick, Martin J. S., *The Great Devonian Controversy: The Shaping of Scientific Knowledge among Gentlemanly Specialists* (Chicago Univ. Press, 1985).

Rudwick, Martin J. S., *Georges Cuvier, Fossil Bones, and Geological Catastrophes: New Translations and Interpretations of the Primary Texts* (Chicago Univ. Press, 1997).

Rudwick, Martin J. S., *Bursting the Limits of Time: The Reconstruction of Geohistory in the Age of Revolution* (Chicago Univ. Press, 2005).

Rupke, Nicholaas A., *The Great Chain of History. William Buckland and the English School of Geology* (Clarendon Press, Oxford, 1983).

Seaton, Sarah, *Childhood and Death in Victorian England* (Pen and Sword Books, Barnsley, UK, 2017).

Secord, J. A., *Controversy in Victorian Geology: The Cambrian–Silurian Dispute* (Princeton Univ. Press, 1986).

Sedgwick, Adam, 'Review' of *Vestiges of the Natural History of Creation*, *Edinburgh Review* 165 (July 1845), pp. 1–85.

Shapter, Thomas, *History of the Cholera in Exeter in 1832* (London, 1849).

Shortland, M. (ed.), *Hugh Miller's Memoir: From Stonemason to Geologist* (Edinburgh Univ. Press, 1995).

Somerville, Martha (ed.), *Personal Recollections from Early Life to Old Age, of Mary Somerville, with Selections from her Personal Correspondence, by her Daughter, Martha Somerville* (John Murray, London, 1873).

Sommer, Marianne, *Bones and Ochre. The Curious Afterlife of the Red Lady of Paviland* (Harvard Univ. Press, 2008).

Speakman, Colin, *Adam Sedgwick: Geologist and Dalesman, 1785-1873* (Broad Oak Press, Heathfield, East Sussex, 1982).

Sprat, Thomas, *The History of the Royal Society of London* (London, 1667; 2nd edn, 1702).

Thompson, Henry L., *Henry George Liddell D. D., Dean of Christ Church, Oxford: A Memoir* (John Murray, London, 1899).

Tickell, Crispin, *Mary Anning of Lyme Regis* (Philpot Museum, Lyme Regis, 1996).

Topham, J., 'Science and popular education in the 1830s. The role of the *Bridgewater Treatises*', *British Journal for the History of Science* 25 (1992), pp. 397–430.

Torrens, H. S., 'Mary Anning', *Dictionary of National Biography* (OUP, 2004).

Torrens, H. S., 'William Smith', *Dictionary of National Biography* (OUP, 2004).

Toulmin, Stephen and Goodfield, June, *The Discovery of Time* (1965; Pelican, 1967).

Tuckwell, William, *Reminiscences of Oxford* (Cassell, London, 1900).

Uglow, Jenny, *Hogarth. A Life and a World* (Faber and Faber, London, 1997).

Wendt, Herbert, *Before the Deluge. The Story of Palaeontology*, English translation by Richard and Clara Winston (Gollancz, London, 1968).

Whately, Richard, 'Elegy. Intended for Professor Buckland. December 1st, 1820', in Gordon, *The Life and Correspondence of William Buckland*, pp. 41–2. See Appendix for complete 'Elegy'.

Wilberforce, Samuel, 'On the Origin of Species, by means of Natural Selection; or the Preservation of Favoured Races in the Struggle for Life. By Charles Darwin, M, A., F. R. S., London, 1860', *Quarterly Review*, July 1860, pp. 226–64.

Woodham-Smith, Cecil, *Florence Nightingale, 1820-1910* (London, 1950).

Index

Index